P9-BTM-036

WORKED OVER

ALSO BY JAMIE K. McCALLUM:

Global Unions, Local Power:
The New Spirit of Transnational Labor Organizing

WORKED OVER

How Round-the-Clock Work Is Killing the American Dream

JAMIE K. McCALLUM

BASIC BOOKS
New York

Copyright © 2020 by Jamie K. McCallum

Cover design by Chin-Yee Lai
Cover image copyright © Michael Cogliantry / Getty Images
Cover copyright © 2020 by Hachette Book Group, Inc.

Hachette Book Group supports the right to free expression and the value of copyright.
The purpose of copyright is to encourage writers and artists to produce the creative works
that enrich our culture.

The scanning, uploading, and distribution of this book without permission is a theft
of the author's intellectual property. If you would like permission to use material from
the book (other than for review purposes), please contact permissions@hbgusa.com.
Thank you for your support of the author's rights.

Basic Books
Hachette Book Group
1290 Avenue of the Americas, New York, NY 10104
www.basicbooks.com

Printed in the United States of America

First Edition: September 2020

Published by Basic Books, an imprint of Perseus Books, LLC, a subsidiary of Hachette
Book Group, Inc. The Basic Books name and logo is a trademark of the Hachette
Book Group.

The Hachette Speakers Bureau provides a wide range of authors for speaking events.
To find out more, go to www.hachettespeakersbureau.com or call (866) 376-6591.

The publisher is not responsible for websites (or their content) that are not owned
by the publisher.

Print book interior design by Jeff Williams.
Library of Congress Cataloging-in-Publication Data

Names: McCallum, Jamie K., 1977– author.
Title: Worked over : how round-the-clock work is killing the American dream
    / Jamie K. McCallum.
Description: First edition. | New York : Basic Books, 2020. | Includes
    bibliographical references and index. |
Identifiers: LCCN 2020014358 | ISBN 9781541618343 (hardcover) | ISBN
    9781541618367 (ebook)
Subjects: LCSH: Hours of labor—United States. | Overtime—United States. |
    Wages—United States. | Work ethic—United States. | Work-life
    balance—United States. | Labor—United States.
Classification: LCC HD5124 .M355 2020 | DDC 331.25/70973—dc23

LC record available at https://lccn.loc.gov/2020014358

ISBNs: 978-1-5416-1834-3 (hardcover), 978-1-5416-1836-7 (ebook)

LSC-C

10 9 8 7 6 5 4 3 2 1

FOR ASA

The less you eat, drink and buy books; the less you go to the theatre, the dance hall, the public house; the less you think, love, theorize, sing, paint, fence, etc., the more you save—the greater becomes your treasure which neither moths nor rust will devour—your capital. The less you are, the less you express your own life, the more you have, i.e., the greater is your alienated life, the greater is the store of your estranged being.

—KARL MARX,
Economic and Philosophic Manuscripts of 1844

CONTENTS

ONE NATION UNDER WORK

THREE DAYS AFTER CHRISTMAS IN 1973 A GROUP OF WORKERS downed their tools and refused to work. They drew up a list of grievances and demands that they sent to management, and promptly went on strike. They'd been working sixteen-hour days, weeks without a day off, and they had finally reached their limit. The lead troublemaker was William Pogue, who was frustrated by the scheduling demands put upon him and his fellow workers. "We're just being driven to the wall!" he said. "No time for mental preparation . . . there's no way we can do a professional job!" He felt like "a one-armed paper hanger trying to get started in insufficient time!"[1]

Pogue's missive could easily describe a strike in some Rust Belt steel mill. After all, tens of thousands of those workers—frustrated by similar complaints about speedup, technological innovation, and unfair production demands—also struck during the seventies. But Pogue was orbiting the Earth. He and his two fellow astronauts were six weeks into what is to this day the longest and last manned mission aboard the Skylab, the first American space station. They made painstaking observations of the sun and Comet Kohoutek, performed extensive medical tests, took technical photographs of the Earth, and were on track to complete four dangerous space walks.

"We had been overscheduled," Colonel Pogue later wrote. "We were just hustling the whole day. The work could be tiresome and tedious, though the view was spectacular."[2]

None of the astronauts had been in space before, and with inadequate time to acclimate, Pogue became nauseous. The crew understood it to be just a passing sickness and decided not to report it to Mission Control. Unbeknownst to them, however, Houston was listening, spying on the astronauts' conversations, and would later castigate them for keeping secrets. Resentment built over the micromanagement, and their communication with Earth became increasingly hostile.

First Commander Jerry Carr, one of the three astronauts on board the space station, emphasized the unreasonable imposition of the Earth-bound bosses. "On the ground, I don't think we would be expected to work a sixteen-hour day for eighty-five days, and so I really don't see why we should even try to do it up here." The crew members gained a reputation for being notoriously irascible, even though their complaints echo those of many workers today. "We need more time to rest," Carr said. "We need a schedule that is not so packed. We don't want to exercise after a meal. We need to get things under control."[3]

Then he switched off radio communication. The crew rebelled with an unscheduled day off, stopping all craft maintenance, self-monitoring, and experiments. It was the first strike in space. Houston had a problem. With the flip of a switch, managers were cut off from the mission, and the workers were in charge, if only for one placid day. Given the nature of their relationship to the crew on Earth, which had no choice but to meet their demands, the astronauts enjoyed significant leverage, what sociologists call "structural power." Soon after their strike they negotiated a reduced workload, fairer schedules, and greater control over the planning of the mission. Houston gave them required tasks to perform, but the crew was able to plan how the work would be completed. Pogue, described by coworkers as "a down-to-earth kind of guy," later said that the final weeks of the mission were more enjoyable, allowing the crew time for "studying the Sun, the Earth below, and ourselves."[4]

Initial reports attributed the astronauts' insubordination to lethargy or depression. But Pogue corrected that interpretation. The flight had made him "much more inclined toward humanistic feeling toward other people, other crewmen," he told *Science News* in 1985. "I try to put myself into the human situation, instead of trying to operate like a machine." Upon their return to Earth six weeks later, the crew was met with a hero's welcome. But although no laws prohibit strikes in outer space, unlike on the ground in the United States, the three astronauts faced the ultimate discipline: NASA ensured they never left the stratosphere again.[5]

There's no evidence the Skylab strike had any lasting impact on interstellar labor relations, and it remains the only organized extraterrestrial work stoppage as far as we know. Can this vignette from over forty years ago tell us anything about our contemporary predicament? NASA astronauts, professional space travelers, are hardly representative of working America. They had, however, voiced a concern about long hours, surveillance, and bad schedules that still resonates decades later among all kinds of workers. Overwork is the new normal, and millions of Americans feel the time squeeze. Schoolteachers are increasingly moonlighting to make ends meet—and not just in the summer. The manufacturing renaissance over the last two decades, especially in the South, has put more people to work at longer hours in automobile factories, the industry most identified with heroically shortening the workweek through strikes and collective bargaining. Even those who work the fewest hours today have increased their time at work the most. Mandatory overtime is on the rise, especially among those workers who are exempt from overtime pay regulations. And then there are the corporate professionals and CEOs who often put in sixty- and seventy-hour weeks, topping the list of overworked Americans.

Continual reports of protracted stressful hours across the occupational spectrum suggest a provisional symmetry among the overworked, a unified mass yoked to a new reality of employment. Then again, not all overwork is created equal. Most professionals and managers, those who work the longest hours yet enjoy a greater degree of control over their time, live entirely different lives from those average workers forced into an endless grind. They typically guard their long hours, profitable as they are, and rely on others to do the dirty work around the clock.

Thus, focusing on overwork alone gives us only one part of the picture. In addition to long hours, workers suffer from irregular and unpredictable schedules that change at their employers' whims. And there's also the mass of the so-called involuntarily unemployed, constantly seeking, but not finding, enough work hours to survive. Consider the growing ranks of retail clerks, fast food workers, home health aides, and others who comprise the 80 percent of hourly workers whose jobs have atypical or variable schedules. Their hours are so frequently cut or extended that they cannot plan to live off one job but find it almost impossible to hold down two.[6]

Add to this list the gig economy serfs whose time is far more on-demand than the be-your-own-boss adage suggests. Nor should we forget that many Americans are working "encore careers" longer and longer into their twilight years, thanks to the indebtedness and lack of savings of many boomers. Combine those with long workweeks, those with erratic schedules, and those delivering your midnight app order, and you have almost two-thirds of the American workforce out of sync with what we think of as a "typical" workday.[7]

These three features—overwork, unstable schedules, and a lack of adequate hours—define the paradoxical time signature of the working life today, especially for low-wage workers. By considering these different dimensions together, we see a fundamentally divided labor force. Some are always on, others are scrambling to the next job, and still others are spending hours and hours just looking for more work, a job in and of itself. There was no simple across-the-board extension of work hours. Instead, the unequal redistribution of our labor time reflects deepening economic insecurity and social inequality.

This inequity was brought into sharp relief when the coronavirus pandemic hit the United States in the winter of 2020, just about the time this book went to press. Though my research was already completed by that time, the first few weeks of the crisis suggested that it was deepening preexisting inequalities in ways that mirrored the patterns I had observed. White-collar professionals, many of whom were able to transition to remote work, struggled to keep up with demanding jobs plus, in many cases, at least forty extra hours a week of childcare. Others endured similar conflicts while on the front lines of the public health disaster. Nurses were prohibited from taking vacations, doctors were beckoned from retirement, and EMTs were dragooned into 24/7 shifts. Grocery store clerks, warehouse and delivery workers, and low-wage security guards, none of whose jobs had provided them any cushion with which to weather hard times, kept working at great risk to their health. And yet, they were the lucky ones. Millions of their working-class peers watched their livelihoods evaporate overnight, with massive layoffs and record-setting unemployment claims that suggested the precarious nature of even full-time workers. They were dependent upon labor for their very survival.

As the country lurched toward a crisis set to rival the Great Depression, it became clear that the depth of the economic disaster was peculiarly American. Governments across the world acted to protect employment, paying salaries and wages to workers whose industries were shut down. But America's unemployment system required onerous compliance with a bureaucratic jungle, plus a long wait, to receive coverage. To make matters worse, most Americans who lost their jobs also lost their healthcare.

It was only through dozens of scattered strikes that those who still had jobs were able to exercise secure conditions that allowed them to work more safely and securely.

It didn't have to be this way.

•

AT THE HEART of this book is a deceptively simple question: Why do Americans lack so much control over the hours of their labor, and how can we reverse the trend?

I've chosen to focus on the temporal dimension of our work lives because it's a point of fundamental conflict in capitalist society. Whoever controls labor in any society also controls time. When we sleep, eat, raise children, spend time with our friends, bask in the sunshine, or take vacations is dictated by those who control our work. Overwork has ripple effects on family life and personal health in untold ways, fraying the intimate relationships and bonds that bind societies together.

These conflicts aren't easily resolved with typical solutions like higher wages, better safety conditions, or stronger labor law. They raise persistent questions that challenge the viability of capitalist society. If our time is so important to us, why is so much of it in the hands of an employer? Or, increasingly, a computer scheduling algorithm? Why is our work time so unevenly distributed? If we're unhappy with our working hours, why do we continue to perpetuate the cycle? Perhaps most crucially, do our varied experiences of work-time conflicts offer the potential for a universal struggle, a broad coalition against a common enemy? The most prophetic and seductive visions of a revolutionary movement have always included a unity of workers, a class cobbled together from the dispossessed and their would-be allies. If a shared experience of the nine-to-five was once the norm, our lives are increasingly governed by a new rhythm dictated wholly by employers. Can the unjust hours of toil unite us in a new mass movement to regain control over labor time?

Worked Over is my attempt to untangle these enigmas that have gnawed at me over the years.

The return of overwork is an unexpected development in American history. Though a more leisurely society was on the horizon for more than a century, we reversed course in the 1970s and slowly committed ourselves to long hours, even as they became increasingly unstable. From 1975 to 2016, the hours of all wage and salary workers increased by 13 percent, equivalent to about five extra weeks of work per year. This figure hides quite a bit of variation, as I examine in detail throughout this book, but it's a starting point for understanding an important historical change. This happened even as worker productivity increased dramatically during the same period, and as all our peer countries decreased their average work hours. Combine these trends with decades of flat or declining wages, and it becomes clear that workers are giving far more to the economy than they're getting in return.

I offer three general explanations for this historic shift. An economic explanation suggests that massive inequality, higher than that of any other country in the capitalist world, prohibited our wealth from translating into free time. A cultural explanation suggests that a new kind of work ethic that emphasizes "meaningfulness" has increased the subjective value we attach to work. (And if work is meaningful, isn't more of it better?) The third explanation points to American politics. In the past four decades both major parties have pursued agendas that have contributed to extending and worsening the hours of labor. The policies that created such poor labor conditions for American workers have been a shockingly clear example of bipartisanship at a time when political polarization grabs most of the headlines. Together these trends, all of which emerged against a backdrop of increasing inequality and insecurity, contribute not only to how we work, but also when, and why we do so damn much of it.

But any notion of overwork can't be measured in hours alone; it's a relative and subjective designation. This book examines how our work time has not only increased, but how it has been restructured and controlled. We experience changes in the nature of work not as macroeconomic forces, but as personal infringements on our dignity, liberty, and pursuit of happiness. Nearly everyone I interviewed *felt* overworked even if they wanted more hours. Many articulated the sense that their work lives were becoming more "intense." They meant that, first, the time they spend working—be it at long, irregular, or insufficient hours—makes them feel overly dependent on employers in their day-to-day lives or for their well-being. Second, timing matters too. A major source of stress was that work was too fast-paced, tied to tighter schedules, and reliant on technologies that ensure work creeps into nonwork time. Among high and low earners alike, there is a sense that we are more than ever under the influence of work, even when we're technically off the clock.

Professionals whose jobs demanded excessive hours, or who were lured to late nights by bonuses and gifts, expressed a deep frustration. "I feel tied to this company's success," said Olivia, who works in California's technology sector. "It's really exciting, but, yeah, a lot of us are driven by insecurity too. Like, if we're not at work, we'll miss out on an opportunity." Popular and anecdotal discussions of overwork tend to focus on white-collar, high-earning professionals like Olivia, even though similar schedules are present across many industries.

Overall, however, this book centers on those at the lower end of the pay scale, who report near-constant insecurity as well. As a class of servants—providing food, childcare, healthcare, and transportation—their work schedules are often determined by the long hours of professionals, the habits of consumers, or the demands of unregulated employers. Even if they work sporadically, or only at odd hours, they express their frustration in terms of overwork. They've gradually increased their hours over the decades and they're finally feeling it. "I work more than my dad did at the same job," said Amanda, a personal care attendant by day and travel agent by night in rural Vermont. "He built a life though, some stability—what do I have to show for all those hours?"

The American Dream offers what seems like a compelling promise—work hard, get ahead. By now a mountain of evidence refutes that simple formula. Amanda's plight is all too common, as many Americans work excessively and still fall behind. Or, despite their best efforts, they can't even find the work they need at regular hours and reasonable pay. What seems like a fair bargain is actually a raw deal. Thus, it is often said the American Dream is broken and must be repaired. But the death of the American Dream provides an opportunity not to breathe life into an old ideal, but to dream bigger. This book, therefore, offers a more radical proposal. We should redesign our economy so that trading most of our waking hours for money isn't the only pathway to a dignified life. Economic security, human satisfaction, and personal well-being should be rights, not the product of labor like other commodities. Winning such a radical new economic and political system will require the kinds of struggles that have occurred only intermittently throughout American history. And it won't be easy.[8]

Employers have long weaponized time through long hours, forced overtime, insufficient hours, or weekend work. Even daylight saving time was originally conceived to extract more labor as the seasons change. Of course, workers have always fought back. In the nineteenth and early twentieth centuries, work time was a hotly debated public issue. Workers fought for and won work time reductions, which slowly became generalized throughout society. But then they lost the fight for the thirty-hour week, undermining the momentum of a downward trend in work time. Today, many Americans work close to forty-seven hours per week yet earn far less than they did decades ago. Among full-time workers, nearly 40 percent report working fifty hours per week or more, and about 18 percent say they work sixty hours or more. This was not a change that we voted on, a public decision made for the good of the country—it happened bit by bit, behind our backs.[9]

The return of long hours in the United States is a daunting paradox for social scientists. Typically, the richer a country is, the less time its citizens spend working. But the United States is different. Though at midcentury Americans worked less than Europeans, the situation has dramatically changed. In 2018, we worked an average of 1,786 hours, far more than any peer nation. That's about six hours per week more than the French and eight hours per week, one full day, more than the Germans. We log slightly fewer hours than Turkish citizens, but more than the perceived workaholics in Japan, who even have a word, *karoshi*, that means "death by overwork." Among all peer nations, the United States has fewer paid holidays, and it is the only nation without a legal right to paid sick leave or vacation time, paid or not. It is also the only industrial nation without guaranteed maternity leave. More than one hundred countries have a legally mandated maximum length of the workweek— not the United States. Nevertheless, the next time you have a paid holiday or a rare respite from work, you should thank the nearest socialist. It was radicals within the union movement who brought you the weekend.[10]

An industrious spirit is typically considered to be a natural component of our cultural DNA, an inherited trait from ancestral Protestants. Perhaps, as the handmaiden of capitalism, the work ethic has built a sturdy foundation for our national character. But then why do we need constant reminders to work and produce? People are given different messages about why and how they should work all the time. Some are told to follow their passions, others to keep their heads down and follow orders. But the takeaway is always the same—work hard.

Yet everywhere you look there is anxiety that we aren't working hard enough, that our faith in work is not as strong as it should be. One national poll found that 72 percent of respondents said the

United States "isn't as great as it once was." The principal culprit was Americans' declining belief in the value of hard work. More people thought "our own lagging work ethic" was a larger threat to American greatness than "moral decay," the Islamic State, economic inequality, and competition with China. Widespread anxiety about a diminished work ethic is confounding when considered against the actual data on American labor time.[11]

The work world casts a long shadow over America, stretching far beyond the actual hours we spend on the job. To trace the drift toward a longer workday is to follow work's presence into cultural and political spheres, as the norms and values of the workplace have seeped into nonwork life. Our schools are job training programs. Digital technology allows work to invade our leisure. The gig economy proclaims its 24/7 work-anytime arrangements are liberating, while Silicon Valley tries to convince us that labor and play are interchangeable. The social safety net has nearly been replaced by the obligation to work for low wages. The promise that automation will replace the worst jobs, freeing up a bountiful leisure, never quite comes true. Doctors increasingly prescribe work for certain mental illnesses. Taxpayers in Nebraska fund a medium security prison called a Work Ethic Camp dedicated to promoting a pro-work ideology among those incarcerated there. Even in the fashion world, where blue-collar workwear has been getting lots of runway time recently, we flaunt our fealty to the working life. Moreover, at the same time the hours of labor grew longer, our beliefs about work transformed from something we do primarily as a sacrifice to something that fulfills the very essence of our identity. If status was once conferred upon those with a leisurely life, today nothing is more woke than work.

We need free time to exercise our freedoms in a democratic society as well as to ponder how we might change it. It was true for the Skylab astronauts, and it's true for all of us. The major difference, of course, is that none of us can flip a switch and demand immediate concessions. Time is the scarcest of resources, so it

makes sense that its distribution and control are inherently political questions without easy answers. Over the past four decades,
we have lost our power to demand much of anything at work.
Collective action takes time, and when workers have less of it,
they are less prepared to fight back. So while overwork has caused
social conflict in some spheres, it has muted conflict in others.

Usually, the diagnosis to overwork is an individualized solution, involving smarter time management, different professional
choices, or better balancing of family and work matters. But overwork is not a personal failing that can be resolved by lifestyle
changes. Reducing and improving the hours we work will require
a mass movement to turn back the power employers hold over
our lives and regain control over our time. Two flashpoints of
labor history, captured in photographs, reveal starkly different
stories of our country's struggle over labor time.

The first is from 1936 on May Day, the workers' holiday that is
hardly celebrated in the United States, the country of its origin.

A group of young women, dressed in nearly identical outfits,
proudly march behind a banner demanding a thirty-hour workweek. "Six-hour day! Eight hours pay! Keep depression away!"
read one leaflet from the time. In that era, winning a six-hour
workday and two-day weekend was the "paramount objective"
of the American labor movement. William Green, then president of the American Federation of Labor, surmised the fight for
the reduced workweek would inspire the rank and file to "make
effective new and widespread demand for goods and services."
He was correct.[12]

From 1933 to 1936 labor union membership tripled, going from
one million to just over three million members. The movement
won wage increases and vastly expanded welfare state provisions. Demands for shorter hours were also a bridge to win concessions from the state. In 1937 Alabama senator Hugo Black, a
former Klansman and future Supreme Court justice, sponsored
a bill to reduce the federal workweek to a maximum of thirty

Workers at a May Day Parade in 1936 demand a thirty-hour workweek.
SOURCE: *New York Daily News* Archive.

hours. And Green began threatening to enforce it with waves
of militant strikes. The legislation stalled after its passage in the
Senate, undermined by a competing bill, the National Industrial
Recovery Act, which guaranteed collective bargaining rights for
unions but only a tepid reduction in hours. The strikes never
materialized either, but the movement for shorter hours reso-
nated with larger ideas of the time.[13]

In a now-famous speech amid the Great Depression, "Economic Possibilities for Our Grandchildren," John Maynard
Keynes forecast that within the coming century, humanity would
grow the economy and create technological innovations in the
workplace that would make possible the fifteen-hour workweek.
For this he was not entirely sanguine, however, as it presented
a new conundrum: "How to occupy the leisure, which science
and compound interest will have won." Keynes's worries about

the coming leisure society reverberated throughout the century
as shorter hours ebbed toward a real possibility in American life.

In 1973 the US Department of the Interior released a white
paper that argued, "Leisure, thought by many to be the epitome
of paradise, might well become the most perplexing problem of
the future." After President Jimmy Carter briefly proposed a truncated four-day workweek in 1977, the *Washington Post* declared
that we were "within striking distance" of the leisure that had
seemed inevitable since midcentury. But history is cunning: half
a century later we've survived the looming threat of free time.
What defines most Americans today is not our bountiful leisure,
but a drudging commitment to work. Our contemporary predicament, which happened amid predictions of the opposite, is captured in the other snapshot.

In 2011 Walmart workers staging a one-day strike on Black
Friday demanded more hours and an end to short shifts. "I Want
to Work Full Time!" read one placard. "Stop Cutting Hours!"
said another. This moment is incongruous with the one above for
obvious reasons—the workers in the first photo demand a shorter
workweek in solidarity with the unemployed; in the second the
demonstrators demand more work time for themselves. Both
are the product of the same historical process, in which time is
wielded as a weapon that pits workers against one another. Today,
the Fair Labor Standards Act, the primary law dictating the minimum wage and overtime pay, offers only modest enforcement of
scheduling and work time regulations.

Today we work not only more hours, but worse and unstable
hours. More than a quarter of us do some work between 10:00 p.m.
and 6:00 a.m., with schedules that are unpredictable and constantly changing. The protest below is not about *wanting* more
work, as is often the case with the overworked professionals; it is
about *needing* more hours and a more reliable schedule. This high
level of underemployment is an important part of the story of

Walmart workers protest unstable scheduling and lobby for more hours on Black Friday. SOURCE: Associated Press.

labor time today. Although shorter hours were once a hallmark of social progress, today they signal a crisis for low-income workers and their families. Walmart workers don't just want more work; they want the work they need to survive in modern America, and low wages aren't the only challenge they face. Millions of Americans, including most of those who work at Walmart, wake up each morning not knowing when or if they will need to be at work, forced to cope with schedules that can change in an instant, even during shifts, making meeting the demands of school and childcare extraordinarily difficult. Less than a quarter of hourly workers have a regular standard shift, while 60 percent have a variable schedule. Staffing priorities at Walmart, as at most large retail firms, are designed by algorithms that determine the most cost-effective schedule. Which—I hate to break this news—is not the worker-friendly one. The combination of overwork, erratic schedules, and involuntary unemployment creates a

profound crisis of time. For this reason, labor movements for better hours aren't just fighting for leisure, free time, or relief from
overwork. Fundamentally, they are struggles for collective control over work time.[14]

The images are juxtaposed in another way too. In 1936 more
Americans worked for the big automakers than for any other
employer, and most were union members. Through militant
strikes, widespread organizing, and political victories, those unions
grew in number and power over the next two decades as workers
across the country won shorter hours, high wages, benefits, safety
standards, and a voice at work. But no surge in union membership followed the 2008 Great Recession as had happened after the
Depression. Today Walmart is the largest employer in the country,
dominating the labor market in a staggering nineteen states, and
exactly zero of those 1.5 million employees are union members.
Thanks to poverty wages, they simply can't afford to work less.

•

THE GREATNESS OF any society can be measured by how it treats
its workers. Ours steals their money. We take the massive wealth
that workers create and redistribute it upward to a tiny ruling
elite. American CEOs take home 312 times what their average
employees make. This elite plays a large role in a great legal theft,
helping elect policymakers who stand up for the big guy. A nine-
month investigation by *Politico* in 2018 found that employers
pocketed $15 billion that should have gone into workers' pay-
checks because of poor enforcement of minimum wage laws.[15]

It is also legal to steal their time. In 2014 the Supreme Court
unanimously ruled that workers at an Amazon warehouse did
not need to be paid for the mandatory security check, which
took upwards of a half hour at the end of every workday, adding
hours of unpaid time to their workweek. Time can be spent in a
way that satisfies us deeply or that makes us feel like we're being

robbed. And we are. Yet "time theft" is a crime that's uniformly alleged of workers, not bosses. One recent study found that employees "steal" 4.5 hours per week by falsely claiming they've worked when they were doing something else, such as talking with coworkers about their personal lives. All of this raises an obvious question: Why do bosses care so much about how work-ers spend their time? Because time isn't just money—it's power.[16]

While writing this book I spoke with workers, managers, policy-makers, union leaders, and technology experts—from Silicon Valley coders to Heartland autoworkers, from the retail sales floor to strip clubs, from scientists building robots to low-wage workers who are treated like them, as a passenger in the back of an Uber and a stowaway on a Google Bus.

Though their stories are their own, they're not just of their own era. I kept noticing the ways they intersected with the most pressing challenges American workers have been reckoning with for decades. In general, the crisis of time workers face today is the outcome of decades of free-market fundamentalism, sometimes called neoliberalism, the onset of which is often roughly dated to 1973, the year the Skylab workers struck. Neoliberalism's *raison d'être* was to squash ascendant worker power and redis-tribute their money and power toward the upper crust. It was a stunning success. As this book shows, neoliberalism has not only set back the fortunes of American workers, it has extended their hours and intensified their work.

The ability to overcome this crisis will depend upon an organi-zation of workers, one that recalls past traditions of labor militancy but is well suited for our contemporary moment. This prospect is dependent upon the realization of working-class consciousness, a phenomenon hampered by resurgent racism, xenophobia, and conservatism. Every now and then we see glimmers of that pos-sibility rekindling the radical spirit that inspired our forebears to fight for control over calendars and clocks. The movement for a fair workweek, led mostly by low-wage retail workers, has won significant legislative victories across the country, giving workers new rights to demand better schedules and more consistent hours. Meanwhile, tens of thousands of striking teachers—many struggling with poor pay, overwork, or the need for an extra job—have led inspiring movements to transform public education. Some workers have recently overturned decades of policy that require poor people to work for welfare, opening up the possibility of overhauling a highly punitive system. It's hopeful flickering lights like these that originally inspired me to write this book.

The first chapter outlines the central premise of the economic argument: that longer hours, unstable schedules, and economic inequality all tend to reinforce one another. Economic inequality, however, is the outcome of a power shift away from workers and toward employers, and the next three chapters offer a new account of how that shift was accomplished. Chapter 2 identifies the rise of managerial control over work time that transformed workplace dogma about productivity into a philosophy of life. This control manifests itself not just as longer hours but as speedup, a process recently amplified by digitalization, apps, and surveillance, which is the subject of Chapter 3, and by the widespread use of robots, which is illustrated in Chapter 4. Labor-saving automation has been conceived of typically as a means for managers to control work, not save time. That it occasionally did help reduce the workweek is an outcome of the ability of workers to exert control over machines, a power they sorely lack today.

Chapter 5 shifts the analysis toward culture. Here I make the argument that a new kind of work ethic has gained prominence since the 1970s, one that centers on meaningfulness and purpose as much as, if not more than, money. This new belief system, a cultural corollary to the rise of neoliberalism, acts as an ideological scaffolding for a more work-intensive economy. If people don't believe that work is inherently good for the soul, however, or are insufficiently motivated by economic necessity, American politicians force them to work anyway while hardly paying them at all. Thus, Chapter 6 examines the rise of workfare programs and other schemes that governments have found to enforce work by revoking access to necessary food or healthcare. Such programs are controversial, but they have nonetheless been the backbone of US welfare policy through many Democratic and Republican administrations. The chapter concludes on a high note, as a campaign has recently overturned such laws in New York City, which also marks another turning point in the book.

Scattered across these pages are stories of resistance to a work-intensive society that are every bit as political as union representation, worker safety, or fights to secure a higher minimum wage. In Chapter 7, this theme is central as readers meet a number of people fighting to control the temporal conditions under which they work. Some are desperately overworked, some gainfully underemployed, but all are leaders of new labor movements to democratize the ways we work. They hail from across the country but come bearing a singular message: greater worker power means better working hours. In the final chapter, I build on the data and stories collected throughout the book and outline a platform for a new shorter hours movement, which I believe is a moral referendum on the value of work. An important step to making work better is winning the ability to live well while doing less of it.

The voices in this book raise complex questions that force us to connect our individual experiences at work with the larger prospect of a better society. Why did the hours of labor decline for almost one hundred years, and then reverse course? Why is hard work the source of both so much misery and so much pride? Why is nonwork time—schooling, leisure, family life—increasingly designed to meet the needs of the workplace? Why, as a culture, do we seem to love work but hate workers? Perhaps most importantly, what can we do as a society to get control of our work time and democratize our workplaces in the process? In answering these questions, I uncovered seismic shifts over the past half century that have transformed our society and that help explain why we work the way we do. Decades of trickle-up in work hours, and a decline in our power over employers, mean that the only sane way forward is to regain control over our collective pacemakers. After all, time isn't just money *or* power—it's justice.

CHAPTER 1

THE HOURS OF INEQUALITY

IF YOU HAVE EVER STOPPED AT A DUNKIN' DONUTS IN NORTHERN New Jersey, before or after work, there's a chance that Maria Fernandes poured your coffee. She worked at three different Dunkin' locations, often back-to-back-to-back, and was described as a "model employee" by a company spokesperson. From 2:00 to 9:00 p.m. she worked the counter at a Dunkin' kiosk inside Newark's commuter rail station. She then headed to a second shop, open 24/7 in downtown Linden, where she worked until 6:00 a.m. If business was slow, she took a respite by settling into piles of doughnut containers to rest for a few minutes. On weekends she picked up a third shift beginning at 8:00 a.m. at a shop in Harrison, and always took on additional hours when asked. On average she worked about eighty-seven hours per week. Though she worked hard, New Jersey's minimum wage was not enough, and she often fell behind on the $550 rent for her basement apartment in Newark. Between shifts, Fernandes napped in her car, the engine running to keep her warm.

On Monday, August 25, 2014, Maria's shift ended at 6:00 a.m., and the next did not begin for two hours. Grainy security camera footage of a local Wawa convenience store shows her car pulling in and parking just after 6:47 in the morning.

"U can call if you like," she texted her boyfriend just as he got to work. After they chatted, Fernandes tilted back the driver's seat of her white Kia with the engine running, the windows shut, and the doors locked to catch up on sleep.

She never woke up.

A Wawa employee noticed her sleeping in the car and was shocked to find her there—eyes open, foaming at the mouth—when his shift ended hours later. Fumes poured from the car, reeking of gasoline. Fernandes was pronounced dead on site from a mixture of exhaustion and carbon monoxide inhalation. She was wearing, of course, her brown-and-white Dunkin' Donuts uniform.

Fernandes, a thirty-two-year-old immigrant from Portugal, quickly became the face of an endemic problem—overwork and poverty amid great wealth and prosperity. Her name appeared in the speeches of politicians for a time, and her plight made it into the mainstream media. There was even talk of a law in her name that would regulate work hours and schedule predictability. "The death of Maria Fernandes demands a call to action," a union leader wrote in an op-ed just after her death. But no action materialized. Still, the name of Maria Fernandes is revived episodically, when another person dies too early because he or she was working too late, too hard, or too often.

In May 2018 thirty-four-year-old Pablo Avendano was struck by an SUV and killed on his bicycle in Philadelphia while working for the Silicon Valley–funded food delivery app Caviar. Just days after his death, a banner was hoisted near the scene of the accident: "The Gig Economy Killed Pablo." Caviar, following the norm among Silicon Valley startups, classified Avendano as an independent contractor, making him ineligible for company healthcare and union protections, and rendering his family ineligible for any benefits upon his death. To collect money for his funeral expenses, friends launched a GoFundMe campaign, which claimed that he died "working a gig economy job that incentivizes riding a bike in dangerous and inclement weather." His best friend, George Ciccariello-Maher, penned a piece in *The Nation* that said Avendano had been riding through bad weather for hours the day he was hit. Where others see dangerous conditions, Caviar sees opportunity. The day before, the company texted its couriers an emoji-laden message that read, "When it rains the orders POUR on Caviar! . . . Go online ASAP to cash in!"

But few riders were really cashing in no matter how long or hard they worked or how quickly they got online. Couriers at Caviar made close to ten dollars per delivery until 2014, when the company switched to an algorithm that matched delivery demands with riders. As with other algorithm-based models, such as those adopted by Uber and Lyft, the software transfers power to those who design and own the technology. A 2018 study by JPMorgan Chase found that a flood of gig workers caused the wages earned by platform-based food deliverers to fall by more than 50 percent since 2013. Mirroring this larger trend, corporate profits at Caviar soared but wages per delivery declined, forcing many couriers to work longer hours, leaving them exhausted and overworked in dangerous conditions. As Avendano was the night he died.[1]

In *Working Ourselves to Death*, Diane M. Fassel argues that an increasing number of people are simply "addicted to incessant activity." Bryan Robinson, a psychotherapist and author of the book *Chained to the Desk*, compares "workaholism" to a disease like alcoholism. Other accounts blame our cultural endowment of American individualism, which manifests itself as a self-destructive need to get ahead. These explanations are common ones, but it is unhelpful to attribute a widespread social problem to a singular category—addict, workaholic—that raises far more questions than it answers. Workaholism can't explain why Fernandes and Avendano died.

Are we really just hardwired to work hard? Obviously not. Historical changes in the amount of time we work can easily dispel a psychological explanation. Fernandes didn't want to be

sleeping in her car any more than Avendano wanted to be weav-
ing through traffic for an app. Nor, it seems, are the vast majority
of workers giving their all out of an irrational commitment.

So what, then, are the social forces that have kept our work
lives stubbornly long and unpredictable? For a fuller explanation,
let's look at the structure of the economy and recent trends in
work time. In the decades leading up to the 1970s, most workers enjoyed a condition they would relish today—declining
hours and rising pay. But it didn't last. To find out what happened, we need a better understanding of the complex relationships between rising economic inequality, longer hours, and the
American class structure.

Work hours declined precipitously starting in the middle of
the nineteenth century. This data has led some to argue that
there's a built-in structural bias of capitalist economies to translate productivity gains into increased leisure. This is erroneous.
We can attribute the vast majority of that decrease in work hours
to trade union pressure and political interventions. It was striking
carpenters in Philadelphia in 1791 who inaugurated the movement to win the ten-hour day, a two-hour reduction. And about
one hundred years later, on May 1, 1886, thousands of strikers
in Chicago, eight of whom were later hanged, demanded "eight
hours for work, eight hours for rest, eight hours for what we will,"
the slogan of the struggle for the eight-hour day. These fights
for shorter hours culminated in two major pieces of legislation
toward the end of the sloping trend. The Wagner Act of 1935
gave unions the right to bargain collectively with their employer,
offering them a clearer avenue to negotiate over hours reductions. The Fair Labor Standards Act of 1938 attacked "starvation
wages and intolerable hours." It also outlawed child labor and set
the standard forty-hour workweek, mandating overtime pay to
de-incentivize employers to compel longer hours.[2]

Historian Benjamin Kline Hunnicutt shows that hours dropped so low that workers basically stopped fighting for further

reductions even as the context for doing so was perhaps better than ever. Instead, as leisure time grew, American families needed more money to take advantage of these opportunities and began advocating for higher pay more fervently than for fewer hours. Higher wages, in turn, made longer hours more desirable, and workers increasingly sought relatively lucrative overtime benefits to earn more. Still, high rates of unionization and relatively high wages ensured the downward trend in hours continued until about the mid-1970s.[3]

Social scientists disagree on how exactly to calculate the change in work time since then. The average workweek has remained relatively constant for the past few decades. But we've increased our hours dramatically by working more weeks per year. Juliet Schor ignited a debate about longer hours in her 1991 book *The Overworked American*. When she updated her book a decade later she found the trends had only accelerated. Using data collected by the Current Population Survey, she found that from 1973 to 2000 the average worker added 199 hours (about five weeks) to his or her annual schedule. The surge was staggering for some subgroups within that sample. For example, those in the middle of the income distribution saw an increase of 660 hours per year, a rise of more than 20 percent.[4]

Among Schor's main explanations was that as union strength waned and the state retreated from its commitment to shortening the hours of work, firms were able to restructure jobs as fundamentally longer-hour positions. Increasing employer power eroded a "market for shorter hours," a system in which individual workers were able to negotiate hours or trade hours for time off. Schor also found that workers adjusted their expectations as work time increased. On surveys, they reported satisfaction with their hours despite reporting a preference for shorter hours in previous years. She concluded that workers ended up "wanting what they get rather than getting what they want." Her research overturned the myths that working time today is a matter of individual preference for income over time and that personal choice plays a significant role in determining work time. To put it bluntly: employers decide, employees abide.[5]

Schor was criticized for overestimating the hours trend, and some critics argued that leisure had actually increased during the time period she studied. These scholars relied on time diaries in which survey participants recorded their daily activities in fifteen-minute increments. As such, bathroom breaks or time spent around the water cooler was not counted as "work time." By the mid-1990s, however, even these survey methods showed an increase in work hours. Still, some estimates today show only a modest increase in work time since the seventies. The difference is determined by the data that is used and the way the data is analyzed. When supervisory and managerial workers are excluded, or when women are excluded, the upward trend is less pronounced, because supervisory and managerial workers put in longer hours and men's share of annual hours worked has changed far less than women's share. Including all of the working-age population, not just those employed, creates a steeper increase.[6]

My calculations are based on data from the Economic Policy Institute, a nonpartisan think tank that conducts research and analysis to help inform policymakers. This data shows that the average worker put in 1,664 hours in 1975; that figure rose to 1,883 in 2016, a 13 percent increase equivalent to about five weeks. Though the workweek remained relatively stable over this time, this change reflects an increase in the number of weeks worked per year. Most of the change occurred from 1979 to 2007, during which time hours grew by about 11 percent, the equivalent of every worker putting in an extra 4.5 weeks. Hours declined rapidly in the wake of the Great Recession but fully recovered to their pre-recession high by 2016.[7]

One part of the story is that women have increased their work hours significantly while men's hours have fallen, a fluctuation that explains a good portion of the overall increase in work time.

Men still work the most, buoyed by their overrepresentation in careers in long-hour and high-wage legal, corporate, medical, and technology fields, while working women have substantially increased their hours in part-time jobs and in jobs with irregular schedules.[8]

Stories of women who are overworked, underemployed, or who have no control over their schedules dominate this book. But the increase in women's paid work alone isn't enough to explain the historic reversal of the trend toward shorter hours. After all, women entered the paid workforce in comparable ways in our peer countries, and they have actually decreased their hours in the past two decades in the United States.[9]

The overall trends are even more pronounced when we compare the United States to other countries. Typically, richer countries are more productive and work fewer hours. But the United States is different. Americans average 289 more working hours per year than comparisons with peer nations suggest is necessary to maintain our high level of productivity. Germans, for example, produce a comparable level of well-being in much less time. In 2018, the United States was only slightly more productive than industrious Germany, yet Americans worked 31 percent more hours, equivalent to more than two months of work. The gap between how much Americans actually work and how much our wealthy economy predicts we should work, has also widened. We're not *just* overworked. Our tendency to overwork has expanded year after year. And what do we have to show for all those extra hours? We have greater income inequality than any peer country.[10]

Rising hours are the result of, and contribute to, economic inequality. The skyrocketing profits generated by productive workers since the 1970s could have allowed us to work significantly fewer hours without a decline in our standard of living. But instead of being shared equitably, those profits were kept at the top by a small elite. About two-thirds of all income gains

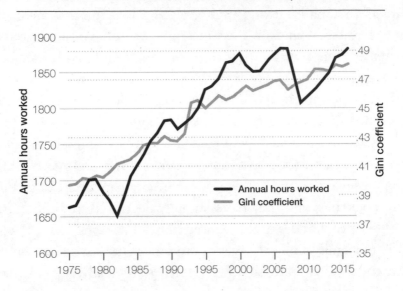

ANNUAL HOURS WORKED AND INEQUALITY, 1975–2016

SOURCES: Author's analysis of Gini coefficient measures from the US Census Bureau, Historical Income Table A-2. Author's analysis of annual hours worked measures from the Economic Policy Institute, State of Working America Data Library, based on data from the CPS ASEC, all wage and salary workers ages eighteen to sixty-four.

from 1973 to 2007 went directly to the top 1 percent of households. Analysis in 2019 by the policy expert Matt Bruenig shows that since 1989 the top 1 percent increased its total net worth by an incomprehensible $21 trillion. During the same period, the bottom half experienced a loss in net worth of $900 billion and now owns less than nothing, meaning more debt than assets. Simply put, most Americans today can't afford to work less.[11]

The graph above plots the classic measure of economic inequality, the Gini coefficient, alongside the number of annual hours worked. A Gini measure of zero expresses perfect equality, whereas a value of one signifies absolute inequality. Side by side it is easy to see a strong correlation between the two trends. As economic inequality increases since 1975, the amount of work we do each year does as well. Within the general trend, however, the two variables fluctuate together. The downward spike in 2007 shows the trends at the onset of the Great Recession, after which point both recover and rise again. It's important to remember that the drop in hours during that time doesn't signal a leisurely respite from hard work, but rather a quick slashing of work time by employers in the midst of the crisis.

Economic inequality helps maintain long and unpredictable hours because it creates precarious work, forcing people across the wage scale to put in more hours either because their wages are so low or because they're afraid the boss might see them leaving the office early. The relationship also exists from the other direction: long hours also drive income inequality because the pay that elites take home is so high at the top of the wage pyramid that it pulls the working rich away from everyone else.

In the past forty years CEO pay soared by an inconceivable 1,070 percent, and productivity increased by 70 percent, but hourly wages of average workers limped forward just 12 percent. From 2016 to 2017 average CEO pay rose to $18 million, making the CEO-to-worker pay ratio 312 to 1. Try to imagine someone working 312 times harder than someone else, or being 312 times more deserving, and the criminally disproportionate nature of our polarized economy becomes clearer. Anyone who tries to pin the blame on lazy workers will need to contend with this basic math.[12]

The graph below, produced by Thomas Piketty, Emmanuel Saez, Gabriel Zucman, and the *New York Times*, depicts the change in income between 1946 and 2014, illustrating the decades-long trend toward top-heavy rewards for the superrich. The light gray line, labeled "1980," shows the change in income from 1946 to 1980. Just a few decades ago, the incomes of the middle class and the poor were rising faster, in percentage terms, than the pay of the wealthiest Americans. The dark line charts the growth from 1980 to 2014, which is mostly flat until it jolts dramatically

THE INEQUALITY OF INCOME GROWTH

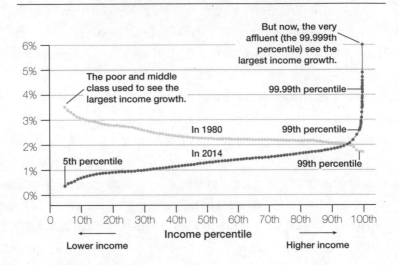

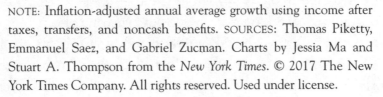

NOTE: Inflation-adjusted annual average growth using income after taxes, transfers, and noncash benefits. SOURCES: Thomas Piketty, Emmanuel Saez, and Gabriel Zucman. Charts by Jessia Ma and Stuart A. Thompson from the *New York Times*. © 2017 The New York Times Company. All rights reserved. Used under license.

upward at the end, illustrating the shocking gains that have recently gone to the richest Americans. Recently, only a sliver of the most affluent families have received such large sums. And as working families have been left behind, the main way they've tried to keep up is by increasing their work hours.

Most Americans lost their piece of the pie because they lost the power to take it. The destruction of labor unions is the crucial omission in most explanations of inequality and the return of protracted hours. When unions were strong, wages rose with productivity. Today, American workers are being denied the profits they are generating because they have no strong organization to demand their fair share. As a direct result, wages across the board have stagnated, social inequality has deepened, and

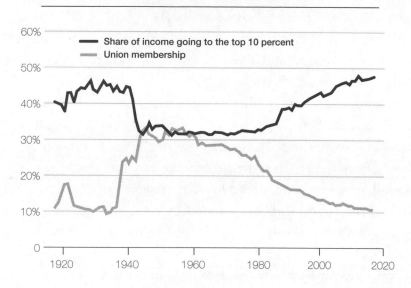

AS UNION MEMBERSHIP DECLINES,
INCOME INEQUALITY RISES

SOURCES: Data on union density follows the composite series found in *Historical Statistics of the United States*, updated to 2015 from unionstats .com. Income inequality (share of income to top 10 percent) data is from Thomas Piketty and Emmanuel Saez, "Income Inequality in the United States, 1913–1998," *Quarterly Journal of Economics* 118, no. 1 (2003), and updated data from the Top Income Database (updated June 2016), from the Economic Policy Institute.

intergenerational mobility—what we commonly think of as the American Dream—has been stunted.

The graph above helps us understand why. It illustrates the relationship between union power and inequality. As union organization spikes after the Great Depression, the share of income going to the top 10 percent nose-dives. Things flatten out for a few decades in the middle of the twentieth century, as the middle class blooms. Then, as attacks on labor become fiercer in the early 1970s, the rich once again regain power, and as a result they take more of the money that had been going to workers. This graph demonstrates a fundamental truism about American life today—class power, not "the market," is the primary factor determining what society looks like. When workers are in unions they have more power, make more money, and work fewer hours—and the rich get less. When workers lose their union power, it's the reverse.

Unions reduce inequality not only by raising the wages of the lowest-paid workers, but also by placing constraints at the top—by taxing the rich, fighting against absurd compensation packages at the peak of the income ladder, and decreasing the overall percentage of upper-level managers within firms. Yet their ability to do so is determined by the ability to help elect politicians sympathetic to labor's cause. And their influence in this regard has been deeply eroded. In the 2016 election, corporations outspent labor sixteen to one, according to the Center for Responsive Politics. It also found that whereas unions spend $45 million a year lobbying Washington, business elites spend $3 billion, more than sixty times as much. These numbers should make any notion of an equivalency between Big Labor, which really doesn't exist anymore, and Big Business, which has never been healthier, seem laughable.[13]

About one-third of US workers carried a union card at midcentury, and inequality decreased as unionization increased. During these prosperous (and anomalous) decades, unions helped keep the wages of ordinary workers high and also put a ceiling on what bosses took home. Moreover, high union membership helped elect politicians who favored, or at least dealt with, organized workers, providing broad support for unions. Republican Dwight Eisenhower's midcentury platform promised to increase unemployment benefits, create laws making it easier to join a union, and eliminate sex discrimination to ensure equal pay for equal work. As president, the five-star general addressed the American Federation of Labor, assuring the assembled crowd that "only a fool would try to deprive working men and women of the right to join the union of their choice."

Well, the number of fools grew and grew. And then it exploded in the 1970s. Although the weapons used to fight the union wars changed—companies stopped hiring armed thugs and relied more on lobbyists and lawyers—the answer to corporate woes was still union-busting. Nevertheless, throughout the midcentury, absolute union membership continued to rise even as union density, the proportion of worker members, declined.

Early in the neoliberal period, many workers still won shorter hours. In 1976, the United Automobile Workers won twelve new paid personal holidays, inspiring confidence in a new shorter hours movement. "The four-day week is inevitable," said UAW president Doug Fraser in 1978. "The only question is, How fast do we get there?" That was the question when, that same year, 700 unionists attended the first All Unions Committee to Shorten the Work Week conference in Detroit. "Across the country, in shop and union after union, a mighty demand for shorter hours is developing," said UAW Local 22 president Frank Runnels in his opening remarks.[14]

The conference brought together union members committed to reinvigorating labor's forgotten cause of less work for more money. They gathered to promote a legislative agenda for shorter hours across all industries, prohibit compulsory overtime, and persuade unions to bargain over hours during contract negotiations. These steps would ease unemployment by spreading more work around. "The forty-hour system has built a wall around our jobs . . . that wall has locked out ten million people," Runnels said. "It is time to tear that old wall down!" By today's standards, however, the wall wasn't impervious.

By that time many unions had secured every existing holiday as paid time off, and they were fervently creating more paid leave any way they could. The UAW more than doubled its number of paid personal holidays in its 1979 contract, taking them to twenty-six. Many other industrial workers won seven weeks of paid vacation for their members. The United Steelworkers of America even secured a thirteen-week sabbatical for high-seniority workers. Reporting on the conference, the *New York Times* argued that unions were committed to a "less-work ethic."

Subsequent attacks against unions, however, were major drivers of extended work hours. President Ronald Reagan's firing of 11,000 striking air traffic controllers in 1981, even after the union broke ranks with the wider labor movement to back his election campaign, was truly a turning point. The controllers' unmet demand for a four-day week helped push the stalemate toward a strike, even though federal workers didn't have the right to a work stoppage. Though the union was convinced it would win handily, Reagan held strong against the workers. Their mass firing, and even the arrest of some leaders, reverberated like a warning shot throughout the union movement. The following year, General Motors workers, who had been among the most successful at shortening hours, lost every paid personal holiday they had won over the previous few years. Throughout the eighties, with their bargaining power crippled, workers sacrificed time off in exchange for maintaining wages. Autoworkers at Chrysler, Ford, and GM lost two to three weeks of paid vacation. Rubber workers lost one week of time off, and the steelworkers' union even sacrificed its thirteen-week sabbatical program in certain places across the country.[15]

Nonetheless, American workers have continued to report increasing desire to join unions but have found far less success doing so. In 2019 public support for unions hit a fifty-year high, with a 64 percent approval rate. In other words, workers lost their voice at the same time a rising number of them said they wanted it. The same year, private sector union membership, which has historically had the largest impact on workers' livelihoods, clocked in at a dismal 6.4 percent, about the same level it was during the first year of the Great Depression. Unions not only promoted widespread pay equity; they also moderated the working day.[16]

As union strength has waned, the main mechanism that gave average workers shorter hours has ground to a halt. And as earnings have fallen, workers have made up the difference by working longer hours. Without a strong counterweight to business, workers have had to abandon their long-standing mission—less work for more pay—and instead accept the opposite. Today, wages are down and hours are up. Workers in countries with stronger unions tend to work fewer hours and enjoy longer paid vacations than those in countries where unions are weak. A recent study by Project: Time Off shows that Americans worked during more than 700 million of their earned vacation days in 2017 because they feared they'd be labeled lazy, grounds for replacement in the no-rest culture, earning us the moniker "no-vacation nation." These changes have thrown the working life for many Americans into a tumult.[17]

●

ON THE BACK of Amanda's ecru-colored Chevy is a bumper sticker that says, "The Labor Movement: The Folks Who Brought You the Weekend." When I point it out she feigns ignorance. "You mean like a two-day break? In a row?" she asks, sarcastically. "That'd be nice, but that's not really how we live."

Amanda is fair-skinned, with light hair and a welcoming smile. She wears small wire-rimmed glasses that sit loosely on her face and jostle around when she talks. Hers is a peripatetic life. In the time I've known her she has moved five times in five years—often dependent on the kindness of friends to keep her family from going homeless. It seems that just as often she and her family are offering the less fortunate around them a place to crash as well. A mutual acquaintance once described her as "the neighbor we need but don't deserve."

Years ago, when I was at her home, her son, Kaleb, was performing his "rain dance" in their living room, in the Lemon Fair Valley of Weybridge, Vermont, whirling his body from side to side, arms raised to the sky in exaggerated prayer.

"Boy never sees his dad except in bad weather," Amanda explained. "So he started doing this to get it to rain. It's not lookin' good today though," she said, half smiling, squinting into an eye-blue cloudless sky.

Kaleb's father, Tom Heustis, lives nearby, and is a dedicated part of Kaleb's life. But work as a manure spreader on local farms keeps him busy seven days a week. Except when it rains. The combines don't function well in inclement weather, but it does mean working double time when it relents. After all, as Amanda adds, "It's not like the cows stop producing."

It might seem like an ancient rhythm of work, in accordance with the dictates of nature and the elements. But Tom's predicament is all too modern. Low-income workers today are not trading lower wages for more free time. Those earning $25,000 a year spend only about twenty minutes less per day on paid work and childcare compared with those making $100,000. In other words, low-income families aren't in their economic predicament because they don't work hard. They simply earn less money while doing so. Low wages also mean that increasing work hours is a pathway to only marginally higher incomes. In mainstream economic theory, bad pay would discourage the poor from working, causing the hours of labor to drop. But it would also induce employers to raise wages to attract employees. The theory holds true in Europe to some extent, but Americans have consistently proved it wrong. The loss of workers' bargaining power has meant that despite bad working conditions and low compensation, US workers have had to accept long hours as a condition of making ends meet.[18]

"Every little bit counts," Amanda says. "We can't afford to stay home. Even when we're sick."

Despite this, or perhaps because of it, Amanda reluctantly became a leader to change the status quo. As a perpetually exhausted working mother, she thought people like her needed a break. As a healthcare aide, she *knew* they needed one, at least when they were sick. So she helped jump-start a movement to win paid sick days for all Vermonters, a movement that I enthusiastically joined. Amanda spent years of her scant "free time" going door to door, lingering into the small hours of the night in church basements talking with elected officials, speaking at local events, and attending endless meeting after endless meeting, her two kids running circles around the room or sleeping in the car.

During a press conference at the statehouse in Montpelier to advocate for a bill that would guarantee paid sick leave, Amanda testified, "The current system forces us to choose between going to work sick or losing our income or even our jobs."

Amanda's father was a home health aide too. But she makes far less than he did for the same work in the same region of the country. According to the Bureau of Labor Statistics, from 2006 through 2016, 2.8 million jobs were added in the healthcare sector, a rate seven times faster than the rest of the economy. Thanks to aging baby boomers, the demand for home health and personal care aides will continue to outpace the sector's explosive growth. Despite this high demand, average wages hover around $11.12 per hour, keeping caretakers tethered to the federal poverty line. To make extra money Amanda moonlights as an online travel agent, booking foreign trips for far richer clients, a luxury she herself will never afford. She describes this reality as "either really ironic or really screwed up, not sure which."[19]

Her paid work routine, which involves home visits to the elderly and indigent, racks up close to sixty hours per week. But the nature of her work requires that she be on call most nights, and her regular work schedule is often decided by the erratic lives of those she cares for, many of whom also have jobs with unpredictable time requirements or long hours. In her words, she's "always on." We typically associate this condition with those high-octane lawyers and traders and executives sleeping with cell phones under their pillows, never out of touch or offline. But it is worse for low-wage workers, whose lives are consistently disrupted for little reward.

"I spread myself so thin," she said. "I am hurting myself, I am hurting my family, I am a blight on the community. I do have to ask people to borrow money. . . . What I'm doing should be really rewarding, and it should be helping me thrive in my life. But I'm not."

"Precarity" is the condition of living in perpetual instability. The term is usually shorthand for the low wages, inequality, disappearing safety nets, and insecurity that so many experience when working in the parlous conditions of today's capitalist economy. Workers whose lives fit this description, a growing mass to be sure, have even been dubbed with their own portmanteau, the "precariat," a nod to Marx's proletariat. Although research has tended to focus on the economic dimension of precarity, the condition has also entailed an increased volatility in work hours and in the unpredictability of schedules, such that time should also be considered a fundamental dimension of precarious work.

Inequality has contributed to job polarization, which expands the number of workers who are competing for low-wage jobs, driving down wages, schedule predictability, and job security. Inequality has also created precarious jobs through what economists call "monopsony," the growth of the market power of bosses. Most people know that a monopoly is a market where there is just one seller. Because firms with monopoly power do not have to compete with other businesses for customers, they are able to set the price at which they sell their products. A monopsony, on the other hand, is a market where there is just one buyer. Firms with monopsony power are thus able to set the price at which they buy their inputs. In the case of labor markets, this means the wages they pay their workers. Monopsony power also allows employers to dictate the hours of labor, and bosses benefit from overworking employees, hiring more temporary workers, and having nonstandard work schedules because such policies reduce labor costs.

Precarity entails a paradox of time. While some are burdened by the time squeeze of excessive work, others spend their nonworking hours—which sounds a lot like leisure—searching for more work to cover their basic needs, commuting to and from work, juggling work schedules to maximize hours, or taking potentially lethal naps between shifts. Almost half of hourly workers who make less than $22,500 a year work either a night shift or an irregular shift, compared to less than a quarter of those who make $60,000 or more. Whereas exorbitant bonuses have greatly incentivized long hours at the top, excessive and irregular hours characterize life for those at the bottom.[20]

In the years since I've met Amanda, some things have changed. In 2017, the paid sick days legislation passed. It involved some compromises, but as a result of her efforts, nearly all Vermonters are now eligible for one week of paid sick leave per year. Her family is changing too. Newly a teenager, Kaleb has gone to work with Tom on farms. He spends most of his weekends and after-school time making money under the table, which he can use for himself or to chip in on family expenses. He still does his rain dance. But these days it's so that he himself can get a day off.

Amanda's family is indicative of many who, like her, work exceedingly hard and don't move ahead. She seems resigned to this fate. "That's probably never going to happen because I'm always going to be in the laborer role. I'll always be working for somebody else," she said. Is the situation less precarious for those a rung or two above her on the income ladder?

When Dairrai Doliber begins her morning as a high school social studies teacher, she's often exhausted from lack of sleep, especially if she was at her second job the night before. She stocks shelves at a local fashion retailer until 10:00 p.m., and skips dinner before crashing into bed. She's also working on her master's degree, which she hopes will increase her salary once she's done. At thirty-three, Dairrai, who lives outside Detroit, says she always thought she'd be better off, especially considering she has a solid job doing what she loves.

"I never thought I'd need two jobs to survive as a teacher," she says, adding "a *union* teacher."

Dairrai knows her situation is not unique. She teaches about American history, politics, and culture, and understands the recent changes that have created her situation, even if she thought she could beat the odds. "I thought I would be able to work my way out of the hole, but that's not really happening," she says. After school, Dairrai jumps in her car and drives to her second job, eating an off-hours meal in her car in the parking lot right before her shift starts. "I can't remember the last time I had a day off," she says.

Dairrai sometimes runs into her students and their parents when she's working the register. She's not embarrassed by her situation because she's only doing what's necessary to get by. But she feels at times that it might undermine her credibility as a teacher in the eyes of parents. "Parents want to talk about school when I'm at the other job, and it just gets awkward." Teachers are now about three times more likely than the average full-time US worker to hold down a part-time job, yet on average they earn about 20 percent less than other college graduates. Troubling as all this is, there's another dynamic at play. While Amanda and Dairrai are dealing with excessive hours, others are struggling for more.

Terrence Wiggins was working full time in the grocery department at Target when a scheduling conflict arose in his family. His sister had a newborn baby, which meant Terrence was left to care for his other nephew, who has cerebral palsy. Terrence now had to be at the bus stop to help his nephew get home from school, which meant the night shifts he was working weren't possible anymore. Target agreed to give him a day shift, but the store cut his total hours for the week to eight. In addition, he never knew which eight it was going to be, as his schedule was constantly being adjusted until just days before his shift, making the search for other jobs impossible. Target uses a high-tech scheduling algorithm to assign shifts to workers. The software accounts for myriad factors, including the weather, to determine the exact minimum number of hours that are necessary to meet projected sales goals. The result was that the store where Terrence worked was always filled with workers, most of whom were scheduled for short shifts or had their shifts extended or shortened with little to no notice.

Months later, Terrence got his hours back up to twenty, which was still only half of what he needed to earn. He took on a second job as a security guard at Ross, though almost immediately Target increased his hours to more than forty per week, so he quit the security gig.

In his second week back at Target full time, however, management sent him home early halfway through his shift. "I need all the hours I can get," he explains, "but I also need to be able to plan my life, to take care of my family. My work schedule made that impossible." Like many low-wage service sector workers with caregiving responsibilities, Terrence was forced out because of scheduling conflicts, and he eventually had to quit working at Target.

There are 6.4 million workers like Terrence in the United States. I met dozens of them while writing this book. They want full-time hours but are stuck in part-time jobs, often with schedules that are unpredictable or insufficient to provide a stable living. Involuntary part-time work declined after an all-time high during the 2008 crash, though economists have demonstrated it is still 40 percent higher than is normal for this point in the recovery. But even full-time workers aren't insulated from this unpredictability. Forty percent of hourly wage earners get one to two weeks' notice about their schedules and almost one-third get three days or fewer. Research by sociologists Daniel Schneider and Kristen Harknett has shown that this "temporal instability" is correlated with psychological distress, poor sleep quality, and unhappiness, even more so than low wages. Even a modest adjustment of scheduling stability has significant beneficial health outcomes for workers.[21]

Inequality and low wages are the wellspring of precarious life. People like Terrence live their lives by the hour, while those at the top can really plan a future. The stories above capture the precarity of life at one place in the labor market, a place where family and personal tragedies are too private or too commonplace to make headlines. In fact, when long hours are invoked in popular discourse, it is usually not the victims of the trend who get the spotlight, but the heroism of the rich who are supposedly doing all the work.

•

Martin Thompson likes to joke that he once considered moving into his office full time, but the inability to bathe regularly kept him from following through. "Besides, I'm not that young and dumb anymore," he explains. "Or at least not that young." At forty-four, Martin is less adventurous than he once imagined he would be. In his twenties, he was a familiar face on the Central American hitchhiking scene, and never wanted to settle down. Now, however, as a self-described "white-collar work addict," he's more or less wedded to his job. He's also a self-described "labor lawyer," but his practice mostly revolves around defending corporations from labor unions. "We work with employees, so that's what we call it," he told me. "Not everyone sees it that way, I guess." His income places him in the top 20 percent of earners in America, and he's able to support his young family of four. But there's another data point that signals his wealth, which he is not shy about sharing. "I work more than anyone else I know," he explains. "That's how it is today. We [high-income earners] work more. It makes a big difference."

In the past century the rich were largely defined by their plentiful leisure. Recall that "banker's hours" was once slang for the short workweek enjoyed by the top wage earners in society. Thorstein Veblen's *The Theory of the Leisure Class*, the classic examination of turn-of-the-century wealth, offered a vivid portrait of an upper crust committed to "conspicuous consumption," strategic buying practices to confer status and honor. But whereas idleness and leisure were once markers of having made it, today the rich acquire prestige through flaunting their extreme commitment to work. And they do have bragging rights. In absolute terms, the top 20 percent of income earners log more work hours per year than anyone else.

But flexing their commitment to work is highly performative, intended to justify undeserved wealth. When she got the job in 2012, Yahoo CEO Marissa Mayer announced that she would work through her maternity leave, sometimes putting in one-hundred-hour weeks. To make sure no one thought she was kidding, she built a nursery next to the office right after she ended the telecommuting option for Yahoo employees. Facebook COO Sheryl Sandberg, author of the corporate feminist manifesto *Lean In*, gloated about pumping breast milk while on conference calls and returning to work after the kids were tucked in to bed. Alphabet CFO Ruth Porat claimed she made client calls from the hospital delivery room bed, and it's often noted that she flips New York City real estate in her "spare time."

Does this incessant activity legitimate the existence of a ruling class? These days the working rich derive more of their income from wages, not capital. The top 1 percent in 1920 made 40 percent of its income from wages, but by 2000 that figure had doubled to 80 percent. Are the well-off really today's "working class?"[22]

Not quite. Economists Peter Kuhn and Fernando Lozano studied four decades' worth of work and leisure trends. They estimate that in 1979 the bottom 20 percent of earners were far more likely to put in more than fifty hours a week than the top 20 percent. But by 2006, the situation had basically reversed. It appears these trends have continued ever since, resulting in a leisure gap that mirrors the inequity between the top and bottom of the economic ladder.[23]

Kuhn and Lozano's explanation was simple. As a result of skyrocketing fortunes at the top tenth of the income spectrum, investing one's time in extra work generates an exceptional return. You look better to the boss when it's time to dole out bonuses, promotions, and better job offers because of a workplace culture that values loyalty and rewards long hours through performance-pay schemes. As Martin Thompson explains, "When the end of the year comes around, it pays to be the last guy at the office. Literally." Kuhn and Lozano showed that salaried men who logged fifty-five hours per week in the early 1980s earned 10.5 percent more than their equivalent working a standard workweek. Twenty years later that gap had more than doubled, to 24.5 percent. For the well-off, in other words, work time is more valuable.[24]

While it is undoubtedly the case that those at the poles of the income spectrum are working longer for different reasons, the rich are not completely sheltered from precarity either. Corporate downsizing since the Great Recession has emphasized the here-today-gone-tomorrow nature of even good jobs. The "long-hours premiums" described above rose alongside inequality of earnings *within* high-paying occupations. This inequality drives competition among employees who fear their own disposability during slumps as they see their peers moving ahead. This fear translates into working longer and longer. And of course, the higher the wage, the greater the opportunity cost of not working.[25]

When commentators write about today's working rich, they often use data on weekly hours and tend to write exclusively about

PERCENT CHANGE IN
ANNUAL HOURS OF EARNERS, BY WAGE QUINTILE

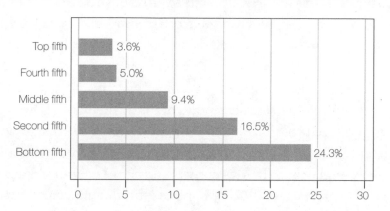

NOTE: "Earners" includes adults ages twenty-five to fifty-four who reported any wages or hours worked during the reporting year. SOURCE:
Economic Policy Institute.

men. It is true that high-earning men top the charts in terms of
long workweeks, and they are now the most likely to put in more
than fifty hours per week. But focusing on this statistic alone gives
a skewed perception of what's really going on.[26]

The graph above tells a different story. The largest shift in
recent history has been the increase in the annual hours worked
by low-wage workers, who are now working 24 percent more
than in 1979. Women are significantly overrepresented in this
category. They make up seven in ten workers at jobs that pay
under ten dollars per hour, where volatility in hours and earnings
is the most extreme. Meanwhile, the highest earners increased
their annual hours of work only 3.6 percent. Despite the popular
focus on hardworking male professionals, it is low-income workers who have increased their annual hours the most, and who are
leading the trend.[27]

Among the top fifth of earners, rising hourly wages account
for nearly all of the growth in annual earnings over the past

four decades. For the vast majority of low- and middle-income workers, however, annual earnings growth has been the result of working longer hours. This means the rich have pulled away from the rest because of much higher compensation, not more time at work. Even as average workers have dramatically increased their hours, they have actually fallen further behind. Between 1979 and 2014, incomes of the households in the top 20 percent rose by 95 percent. For households in the bottom quintile, who increased their work time the most, incomes only grew 26 percent. The most significant change for low-wage workers was that they increased their weeks worked per year, but for the rich it was hours in a week. What explains this difference?[28]

Martin has an answer: "We take vacations and they don't."

He has a point. Having the choice to take a vacation is determined by social class. Only one-third of low-wage private sector workers receive paid holidays or vacation, compared with almost everyone in the top 10 percent of wage earners. High-earning workers tend to work longer hours for defined periods of time. And they are far more likely to be allocated significant chunks of time off, even if they choose to forgo it or to write work emails from a deck chair on a cruise ship. They plan their schedules, their time off, and their family life. In other words, they're able to control when they work a lot and when they don't. This stands in stark contrast to those at the bottom, who are always on yet worse off. Hard work at long hours isn't a viable pathway to getting ahead for most workers today. Why not?[29]

Americans tend to link hard work and reward. A survey by the Pew Charitable Trusts found that 73 percent of Americans say working hard is vital to "getting ahead in life." Such belief is closely linked to income. Across the globe, high earners believe that hard work leads to success, and Americans believe it far more than any peer country. Seventy percent of low-earning Americans believe in the uplifting power of work too, more than do the rich in almost every country surveyed.[30]

CHANGES IN OCCUPATIONAL EMPLOYMENT SHARES AMONG WORKING-AGE ADULTS, 1970–2016

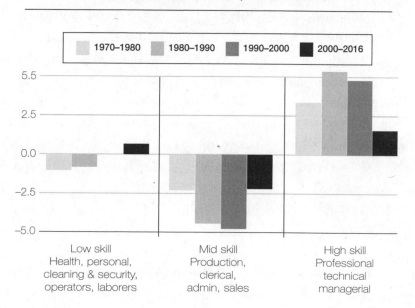

NOTES: Figure uses March Current Population Survey Annual Social and Economic Supplement data for earnings years 1963–2017. SOURCE: David Autor, "Work of the Past, Work of the Future," NBER (working paper no. 25588), February 2019.

But today hard work and upward mobility are further apart than ever. A good way to illustrate this bifurcation is to look at how American work time is divided across the economy.[31]

The figure above, by economist David Autor, depicts hours worked, not the number of jobs. In the early 1970s Americans worked roughly the same percentage of hours in each group: 31.4 percent of total hours were in low-skill occupations, 38.4 percent were middle-skill, and 30.2 percent were high-skill. Since then, the overall time spent working in middle-skill jobs fell precipitously, from 38.4 to 23.3 percent of hours. From 2000 to 2016 Americans have spent more aggregate time at low- and high-skill jobs. This polarization suggests that the middle class is joining the upper class, which, Autor claims, "is not something economists should worry about." By and large, however, as he notes, workers without a college degree don't enjoy that kind of upward mobility. Instead, as midlevel blue- and white-collar jobs have declined, non-college-educated workers are being pushed into generic low-wage work for which they're overqualified and underpaid. Getting a college degree is hardly the answer—by 2028 almost two-thirds of all jobs won't require one. Improving conditions for American workers in the immediate future requires making routine low-level jobs into better-paying jobs and decreasing our reliance on paid work in general.[32]

Middle- and low-income families like Amanda's, Dairrai's and Terrence's depend more on wages from work than any other source of income, whereas people like Martin Thompson benefit from activities that aren't direct outcomes of actual labor time, such as income from stocks, rents, pensions, and bonuses. The Great Recession increased the necessity of longer hours for those in the middle- and low-income segments of the labor market because it became the main way for them to regain their wealth and assets that were lost in the crash. By and large, however, the hours weren't available. This inflated the pool of the involuntarily unemployed, and the result was that workers fell further behind.

From the 1970s to 2000, a significant portion of inequality could be explained by what economists call a "labor-income" phenomenon, meaning that how much work you did mattered a great deal. Since 2000, however, the importance of "capital income" has become increasingly important to those at the very top. In other words, even as the rich are working more, their wages are often a complex mixture of earnings that are clearly not the result of more time. Differences in hours of work cannot explain why those in the top 1 percent have gotten so incredibly rich because there simply aren't enough hours in the day to account for their gains. For them, expecting to get ahead merely by going to work each morning might appear quaint, like collecting your morning milk from the door.[33]

Forty years ago, workers who put in fifty hours or more per week earned 15 percent less per hour than those working a normal nine-to-five job. Today, it's the reverse. Employees working fifty hours per week earn almost 10 percent more than those working a more traditional workweek, according to sociologists Youngjoo Cha, Kim Weeden, and Mauricio Bucca. The ability to get ahead by working long hours, however, is determined by class power. A study led by sociologists Annette Bernhardt and Ruth Milkman found that thousands of low-wage workers they surveyed worked more than forty hours in the previous week but were not paid the legal overtime rate for the extra time. This reality challenges our collective fantasy that hard work is still the gateway to the American Dream.[34]

Do the rich work hard? Sure, more than any other group they easily secure steady full-time jobs that pay handsomely. And they report higher work satisfaction than any group as well. If overwork was only a problem for the high-earning classes, confined to Wall Street trading floors or Silicon Valley campuses, it would hardly register as a social complaint. But when the rich are overworked, they drag the rest of society along with them, a snowball effect of weird and excessive work times. When people like Martin Thompson are threatening to occupy the office all night, who will deliver them food and care for their children?

The answer is people like Gina Sferra. Gina made good on the threat Martin balked at; she moved into her office about two years ago and has barely left since. Gina runs Tip Top Child Development Center, a 24/7 childcare facility in Las Vegas. The night I spoke with her there were approximately eighty sleeping children in the ten-thousand-square-foot space, getting picked up or dropped off all night and all morning. Casinos provide a steady stream of children whose parents work long and odd hours. But only half of her clients are employed by the casinos.

"It's not a casino problem," she explains. "This place exists because of the way people work, pure and simple. I'm in business because people are always working. Nonstop."

Parents often break down in tears of relief when they are told the facility will accept their child. She has flight attendants, lawyers, and nurses who drop their children off for days at a time when they're out of town for business or simply working long consecutive shifts. She points out that retail jobs, in particular, create havoc for childcare schedules, and thus parents in retail jobs account for much of her business.

The incredible success of her business model is tied to the fact that Gina has ingeniously tailored her career to the precarity of modern America. She has a lot of experience with balancing children and work. She got pregnant in high school, never married, and has a five-year-old foster son. Her twenty-two-year-old daughter, Alexis, is the assistant director of Tip Top, and also works for a local family caring for their child three days in a row while the parents work or catch up on sleep. Alexis insists that Gina take a break now and then, so they've worked out a compromise—Gina returns home for twenty-four hours per month; the rest of the time she's at the facility.

"We are a Band-Aid solution," Gina says. "I'm not sure it's healthy for people to have these kinds of chaotic lives." She considers that for a moment and adds, "Then again, look who's talking."

The differences in Martin's and Gina's lives are often theorized in class terms by social scientists. In the late 1970s, Barbara and John Ehrenreich coined the term "professional managerial class" to categorize the teachers, engineers, nurses, doctors, lawyers, managers, and technology workers who were making up a growing part of an increasingly white-collar economy. Their sociological analysis argued that such a class functioned as a buffer between the rabble in the factories and the elites who owned everything. Their initial analysis understood the PMC, as it is

commonly abbreviated, as a conservative force in society, hob-
bling the formation of a unified social class of the exploited by
dividing the factions that serve the ownership class.

They later revised their analysis, however, in response to
a growing progressive cohort within the PMC who understood their predicament and were actively struggling alongside
working-class people. Moreover, as a college education became
more common and no longer distinguished the working classes
from the middle, the PMC began to look much more like a demographic within the working class. "The center has not held," the
Ehrenreichs wrote, "and the PMC lies in ruins." Therein lies the
possibility for an alliance between downwardly mobile professionals and the rest of the working class, however schematic it
might be. Today, many professionals are overworked and worked
over too. They can see their prospects dwindling, soon to face
many of the same pressures of working-class Americans. In other
words, many professionals—people like me, and undoubtedly
like many of you, dear readers—occupy a contradictory and precarious social position. To argue that such a class alliance could
emerge, organized around the goal of decreasing labor time, is
not to ignore those contradictions, but to focus on them.

These contradictions were brought into sharp relief for me
personally when I was ordering coffee in California on a research
trip. The young woman at the register was visibly harried, to
the point where I had to ask her if she was okay. She nearly
broke down at the question, then immediately took advantage
of the situation. "I'd be a lot better if you'd give me a ride to my
next job," she said, pleading. "I start in fifteen minutes. I can't
be late." A few minutes later we were in my car headed for the
heart of Silicon Valley. Admittedly, I knew it would be a valuable anecdote. But I was surprised at the extent to which it fit
neatly into the narrative stream of this book.

Carmen had taken a job as a Starbucks barista only a few
months earlier to supplement her income as an adult caregiver

after her client decreased her hours. Then, after a few weeks, her client increased her hours again, and she was now struggling to make both shifts work. Because the money makes a difference. Her life is the essence of the precarity paradox. Juggling two jobs and sole responsibility for a young child, Carmen finds that her free time is nonexistent. She can make enough money to cover her expenses—if she gets the hours she needs at work, which too often does not happen. Yet the labor required to meet her basic needs incurs other expenses, like transportation and time away from her daughter.

As she's changing her clothes in the car to prepare for the next job, she mentions that her client's business offers its employees free transport to and from work.

"Google Bus?" I ask, and she nods her head. I was familiar with that system, which is why I was driving that day. I had barely pulled to a stop before she was out the door, briskly walking up the driveway toward her client's home.

Carmen's precarious work routine is like that of many others around the country, but it is especially prevalent in Silicon Valley. A Janus-faced economy driven by the likes of Apple, Google, and Facebook creates a "winner take most" system where superstar firms hoard their wealth, pushing others to work longer and harder. It's fertile ground for an at-will pool of laborers who suspend their lives for work where the hours are long, inconsistent, and often still not enough.

Inequality alone, however, can't fully explain recent trends toward long hours and inconsistent work arrangements. Economic inequality begets hours inequality, which in turn drives more economic inequality. But it's hardly an impersonal cycle. Most workers weren't set to work at a faster and faster clip by economics in the abstract, but by managers. The time we work, including the pace and intensity, is as much the product of labor relations as anything else. Thus, it's worth exploring how managers got so much control over our time in the first place.

CHAPTER 2

NICKEL AND TIMED

MANAGERIAL AUTHORITY IS THE FIRST LINE OF DEFENSE AGAINST popular control of labor time. Such authority rests, first and foremost, on the raw power to dominate the workplace. The political philosopher Elizabeth Anderson minces no words. Today's workplaces are "dictatorships" run by "private governments" that are unelected and unaccountable, she argues. Their power, however, rests not simply in their greater strength to dominate but in the consent of those governed. Achieving broad consent, what social scientists sometimes call "hegemony," is the background condition for the subordination of workers to overseers. It's what maintains the ability of managers to control the clocks, make the schedules, approve (or not) vacations, and determine the pace of work. That phenomenon, in turn, is what links our nonwork lives to the rhythm of labor. In other words, low-wage workers' schedules aren't exactly "unpredictable" today, but merely out of their control—volatile by design. To understand how this system flourished, we need to take a step back.

Benjamin Franklin, who authored the original to-do list, was among the early prominent Americans to equate time management with moral goodness. He popularized an economy of time for a burgeoning capitalist society well before the advent of industrial scientists. But it was Max Weber who gave Franklin's

cheery aphorisms real theoretical force. In Weber's most celebrated work, *The Protestant Ethic and the Spirit of Capitalism*,
Franklin is a chief protagonist, a personification of what Weber
saw as a new culture of restlessness, industriousness, and frugal-
ity. Inspired by Protestant devotion yet wholly secular, Franklin
represents a kind of missing link in a historical puzzle about the
rise of capitalist time. How did we go from being a society that
glorified hard work for God to one that viewed it as a social good
in and of itself? And how did we ever come to see long hours at
hard labor as a moral attribute?

Weber answers that question succinctly: rationality. He saw
Western society as the result of rational bureaucratic organization, systems of orderly rules and impersonal codes that are
divorced from religion and tradition. Timing, even more than
time, became an essential attribute of a society that had to coordinate political, economic, and social life on a mass scale. Time
brought people together. Wasting time, or not using it *wisely* to
maximize one's relative status or position, became a moral failing
that put you at odds with the synchronized world.

In a famous allegory, Weber tells the story of a group of precap-
italist farmers who tried to pay their field hands more to entice
greater efficiency during the harvest, a strategy that resulted in
the opposite effect. Workers reduced their rates, satisfied that
they could earn their old income in less time, and saw no reason
to want to earn more. Weber concluded, "A man does not by
nature wish to earn more and more money, but simply to live as
he is accustomed to live and to earn as much as is necessary for
that purpose."[1]

Capitalism, it seems, rid us of that "nature," and we would learn
to work hard whether our needs were met or not. What Weber
termed the "Protestant Ethic" was more than a commitment
to work; it was a self-discipline that manifested itself throughout our whole lives. He wrote, "Waste of time is thus the first
and in principle the deadliest of sins. . . . Loss of time through

sociability, idle talk, luxury, even more sleep than is necessary for health . . . is worthy of absolute moral condemnation."[2]

For Weber, Franklin's axioms explain more than just attributes of successful people; they contained truths even Franklin himself didn't appreciate. Time wasn't just money; it was the new common sense. Weber noted the application of this new logic in managerial practice. "Precision, speed, unambiguity, knowledge of files, continuity, discretion, unity, strict subordination, reduction of friction and of material, and personal costs," he wrote. "These are raised to the optimum point in the strictly bureaucratic administration."

Weber argued that early faithful Protestants believed they had no way of knowing if they were among the chosen or the damned because of the extensive ambiguity of the doctrine of predestination. They could have thrown up their hands, liberated by the knowledge that their fate was out of their control. Instead, they sought to bely their anxiety by living *as if they knew* they were among God's elect by committing themselves to ceaseless hard labor. Work thereby became understood as a pathway to a state of grace, an ethical good, as well as, conveniently, an absolute requirement for survival. "The Puritan wanted to work in a calling; we are forced to do so," Weber wrote. The affinity between the moral goodness of work and the necessity of labor under nascent capitalism seemed to require a new way to organize business.

To better understand the importance of managerial control over work time, consider another anecdote. From 1898 to 1901 a man called Schmidt loaded pig iron onto carts at Bethlehem Steel on the banks of the Lehigh River. Enticed by rising wages that reached $1.85 per day, and by not a little bit of prodding, Schmidt increased his daily load from 12 to 47.5 tons, setting a new standard for his coworkers. Schmidt was short, stout, and dim-witted, and was chosen to prove a point—if he could do it, so could any man.

But Schmidt wasn't any man, in fact. Before him, ten "large, powerful Hungarians" had been put to the same test and failed. Schmidt would jog miles to and from work each day, and as a result of his lack of social life and his thrift, he had saved up enough money to buy a small piece of property on the south side of Bethlehem. He had been handpicked because of a combination of his impressive physique and less impressive intellect—not exactly a random selection.

We know all this because of the diary kept by Frederick Winslow Taylor, the pioneering industrial scientist who transformed Schmidt from a lowly molder into America's most famous Stakhanovite. In heavily accented Pennsylvania Dutch, Schmidt tells Taylor he is a "high-priced man," willing to do just about anything for a few extra cents.

TAYLOR: Well, if you are a high-priced man, you will load that pig iron on that car to-morrow for $1.85. Now do wake up and answer my question. Tell me whether you are a high-priced man or not.

SCHMIDT: Vell—did I got $1.85 for loading dot pig iron on dot car to-morrow?

TAYLOR: Yes, of course you do, and you get $1.85 for loading a pile like that every day right through the year. That is what a high-priced man does, and you know it just as well as I do.

SCHMIDT: Vell, dot's all right. I could load dot pig iron on the car to-morrow for $1.85, and I get it every day, don't I?

TAYLOR: Certainly you do—certainly you do.

SCHMIDT: Vell, den, I vas a high-priced man.

"A penny looks about the size of a cart-wheel to him," one of his coworkers said of him. But Schmidt's story is more than a simple tale of motivation and financial incentives. Taylor understood, perhaps more than anyone else in his day, that when you control labor you also control time.

Industry owners were searching for a cure for lagging productivity as a result of rampant shirking, absenteeism, slowdowns, and on-the-job drunkenness. Taylor positioned himself as the man for the job. He thought that an unmotivated workforce with high levels of independence on the job was the death knell of productivity. After decades of hopping from plant to plant—presaging the consultancy industry that followed in his wake—Taylor collected his principles of measurement and control into a coherent organizational form that substituted "science for the individual judgement of the workman." "Any improvement the workman makes upon the orders given to him is fatal to success," he wrote.

After the pig iron experiments in Bethlehem, he tackled shoveling routines, vastly increasing the amount of coal that average workers were able to move in a given amount of time. These studies earned the interest of managers who were excited about ways to extract profit without the dirty deeds of class warfare—just tweak the labor process. And to mollify the resistance to these changes they offered a few cents more per hour, which was easily worth the price of labor peace.

Managers also allowed Taylor to develop time and motion studies. Conducted by foremen with stopwatches and slide rules, these studies measured in exacting detail the bodily movements of workers and timed them to determine the quickest route to the finished product. Once a study was complete, jobs were broken down and performed as routine tasks. Every motion a worker undertook was assigned a monetary value. The movements of bodies, according to Taylor, had a measurable price, a calculable risk, a known cost-benefit trade-off. If work had any meaning at all, there was a growing consensus that it was only expressed in dollars and cents.

For a man who professed the objective rationality of a stop-watch, Taylor's work was notoriously unscientific. His colleagues at times even admitted what his enemies had claimed all along: Taylor made stuff up. His numbers were falsified, his successes were exaggerated, his methods were biased. For a decade after his work at Bethlehem Steel, Taylor's science was still just a col-lection of semi-regularized experiments and recommendations. But an unlikely champion elevated his profile and gave meaning to the madness. It was the public advocate Louis Brandeis, not yet Supreme Court Justice Brandeis, who coined the phrase "sci-entific management." He beta tested the phrase with two other management experts, Henry L. Gantt and Frank B. Gilbreth, both of whom agreed it was far superior to Taylor's "process man-agement," "task management," or "shop management." Taylor took the name for the title of a monograph he published a year later, *The Principles of Scientific Management*, which endured for half a century as the top-selling book on business.

But Brandeis's coinage bestowed upon Taylor something far greater—the power of an enlightened truth teller, the ultimate objective party. Taylor was then able to carve out a place for him-self as a social and economic necessity by comparing his science to the work of folks like Schmidt. "The science of handling pig iron is so great and amounts to so much that it is impossible for the man who is best suited to this type of work to understand the principles of this science," Taylor wrote. "Or even to work in accordance with these principles, without the aid of a man better educated than he is."[3]

To equate scientific management to time and motion study would miss what was most historic about Taylor's contribution to the modern world. Taylor always professed his desire for a "mental revolution." What distinguished scientific management from other forms of work organization—and, presumably, other kinds of science—was not its lack of objectivity or inexactitude but the power it bestowed upon managers to exercise their will. Once it had been firmly established that managers simply knew more about the labor process, their knowledge gleaned from some kind of "study" unknown to the common line workers, who could argue with them?

After all, Taylor was better educated than the average Schmidt. The son of prominent Philadelphia Quakers whose roots reached back to a Mayflower passenger, Edward Winslow, he was often regarded as a renegade for thumbing his nose at law school and an offer to study at Harvard. Nevertheless, he launched his career on the basis of his privileged social lineage and enjoyed effortless promotions to managerial positions through his time at local manufacturing plants during the 1870s and 1880s. Taylor's goal was to make money at the expense of workers, which raises a question about why he won the favor of Brandeis, dubbed "the people's attorney," an outspoken proponent of unions whose later nomination to the Supreme Court was hotly opposed on the basis of his alleged sympathies with socialists. Brandeis saw in Taylor the power to harness industrial production to the betterment of the social condition. Rising corporate profits also meant rising taxable income and, potentially, a rising standard of living for everyone—better living through industrial capitalism. "Efficiency is the hope of democracy," Brandeis said. "How else can we hope to attain the new social ideals?"

Taylorism was widely adopted by American businesses and had impacts far beyond efficiency gains. After the International Harvester Corporation oriented its factories to Taylorism, its education programs for new immigrants changed with it. One of its early brochures directed at Polish immigrant workers, once known for their on-the-job radicalism, included the following sentences to help them learn English:

I hear the whistle.

I must hurry.

I hear the five-minute whistle.

It is time to go into the shop.

I change my clothes and get ready to work.

I work until the whistle blows to quit.

I leave my place nice and clean.

"Educational materials" thus became tools of indoctrination.

Throughout the first half of the twentieth century Taylorism gained a steady flow of admirers and practitioners across the world. Even Vladimir Lenin, hardly a capitalist stooge, thought Taylor's rationalistic approach might serve as a model for the kinds of disciplined workers whose true productive capacity could be harnessed to the socialist movement. Despite calling Taylorism "the refined brutality of bourgeois exploitation," Lenin noted,

> The task that the Soviet government must set the people in all its scope is—learn to work. . . . The Soviet Republic must at all costs adopt all that is valuable in the achievements of science and technology in this field. The possibility of building socialism depends exactly upon our success in combining the Soviet power and the Soviet organization of administration with the up-to-date achievements of capitalism.[4]

Yet Taylor was caricatured as much as he was revered. Ordinary workers hated him. For decades they protested his science and other modes of "time discipline." This on-and-off class war was partially resolved by striking a bargain—higher wages would offset the inhumane working conditions. Under pressure from a growing labor movement to reduce work time, Henry Ford introduced the five-dollar day, a wage so high that line workers made enough to buy the Ford they assembled, should they choose to do so.

To attract workers, other employers followed suit. (Compare this situation to today, when Walmart employees—sorry, *associates*—make so little money that the only place they can afford to shop is Walmart.)

A revolution in the global labor process was set in motion by fudged books and a story about a guy named Schmidt who could load pig iron like you wouldn't believe. Nevertheless, Taylor was fired by Bethlehem Steel, his most prominent client, after the company paid him vast sums of money without receiving a noticeable uptick in profit margins. Yet even afterward, Taylor was never in want of work. Though his science was a failure in some ways, it exceeded expectations in others. As a way to transfer knowledge from workers to managers, Taylorism was undeniably revolutionary. As detailed measurements of time became a more important element in the production process, managerial skill began to erode as well. A stopwatch is hardly a whip, but a timekeeper is hardly a manager.

Nonetheless, Taylor is credited with birthing modern management, though he probably did not experience it that way. The portrait painted by his biographer, Robert Kanigel, is of someone so driven by the secular rhythms of the present moment that he couldn't possibly fathom the future. In that sense Taylor was strangely out of sync with the momentum of Taylorism, which was forward-looking and progressive, the frontier of industrial capitalism. After reading of poor Schmidt, Samuel Gompers, the cigar maker at the helm of the American Federation of Labor, found scientific management novel "only in its cold-bloodedness," enough to make "every man a cog or a nut or a pin in a big machine." The popular charge that Taylor viewed workers as spare parts, mere adjuncts to machines, was true. And it provoked a reaction to what was often called "the one best way."[5]

There was, of course, another way. While Taylor was busy trying to stop time, or at least recapture it in the name of efficiency,

the Gilbreths were setting people in motion. In 1911, after giving birth to her fifth child, Frank Jr., Lillian Gilbreth was in
the throes of some postpartum editing of her husband's manu-
script, *Motion Study*, Frank Gilbreth's reprise to Taylor's magnum
opus. Frank and Lillian Gilbreth were early backers of Taylor,
though they would come to build careers as both a friendly
adjunct to his science and then as opponents. Whereas Taylor
had Taylorism, the Gilbreths had "therbligs," an anagram they
named after themselves, which dissected human motions at work
into discrete movements. The Gilbreths agreed with Taylor that
subjecting the labor process to scientific scrutiny and, inevita-
bly, routinization would have wondrous impacts on profitability.
Their method differed, however.

The Gilbreths filmed people at work or staged the scenes,
critiqued the tape, and instructed workers on how it could be
done faster and better. Their silent films are mesmerizingly banal,
like reality TV, and yet it is impossible to look away, like reality
TV. Frank set up a hand-cranked 35mm camera and put a running micronometer in every frame to record the time. They captured people laying bricks, packing boxes of soap bars, putting
lids on canning jars, stamping requisitions, and much more. The
Gilbreths would then instruct workers to perform the tasks differ-
ently. Bricks would be repositioned, soap boxes and jars would be
arranged more conveniently, and a foot pedal would be added to
the stamping machine to free up an extra hand. Frank later affixed
tiny light bulbs to workers' fingers to capture their hand motions
in long-exposure photographs he called chronocyclegraphs.

The "Gilbreth method" was presented as the apogee of technological and corporeal functionality, prompting a kind of *aha!*
moment for the viewer. To some degree, the Gilbreths' work pre-
saged what we call ergonomics.

The Gilbreths knew a lot about how to manage complex tasks
efficiently. As a kind of social experiment, they decided to have
twelve children to prove to the world that . . . what, exactly? It's

Frank Gilbreth tied luminescent bulbs to workers' fingers to capture their hand motions in images he called chronocyclegraphs. SOURCE: Frank Gilbreth.

still not clear. At any rate, two of their children chronicled the madcap adventures of a family of fourteen with two working parents in the slapstick dramedy *Cheaper by the Dozen*. In the book and film adaptation, Lillian's roles as a scientist, author, and social reformer are largely ignored, as is often the case with her role in the managerial revolution when historians have occasioned to write it. (To some extent, the sequel, *Belles on Their Toes*, corrects the record.) For the most part she's the multitasking mom making it look easy, nursing a child on each breast.

The Gilbreths, or Lillian at least, developed a distaste for the vitriol Taylor spewed at average workers. Taylor was a privileged elitist who fudged his own research in search of a fortune at the expense of those who worked harder and understood far more. This led Lillian to an epiphany.

In 1912 the family relocated to Providence, Rhode Island, so that Lillian could begin her formal study of psychology at Brown University. She completed her doctoral dissertation, *The Psychology of Management*, two years later. Her work put motion study in its place, developing a far more holistic view of management. Lillian focused on worker welfare. She asserted a management style that required restful breaks, improved lighting, better safety standards, higher wages, ergonomic furniture, plus skills development and job training. "The emphasis in successful management lies on the *man* not the *work*," she wrote.[6]

Her husband agreed, and the two developed a consulting business, Gilbreth Inc., that signed contracts with both bosses and labor unions to promote efficiency gains and higher wages, thus moving them out from under Taylor's shadow—scientific management with a human face. The Gilbreths avoided many of the criticisms leveled at Taylor exactly because of their humanist and quasi-sympathetic appeal to the plight of average workers. They saw themselves helping to maximize worker potential and productivity, not profits, though of course it was a lucky fact of the matter that the two were linked.

In search of a catchphrase to embody their emphasis on the intrinsic rewards of work, the Gilbreths invented a new measurement of time called "happiness minutes." The term referred to the greater degree of joy workers would have at their jobs once fatigue and stress were reduced to a minimum, and the enthusiasm workers felt as they contemplated efficiency challenges in their own lives. In essence, happiness minutes were a dividend of productivity, to be saved or spent as one preferred. Happiness minutes were especially applicable to the home economy, where time saved on housework could be more easily converted into leisure than in the factory.

Frank's untimely death in 1919, however, put Lillian's career, her family's prosperity, and her already-scarce free time in jeopardy. After floundering for some years, she eventually decided to focus her industrial psychology on the sphere of life she knew the least: the kitchen. For all her accomplishments—her work with special needs workers, the pioneering science, a slew of honorifics—Lillian never learned to cook and never did dishes. But why should that stop her? Taylor never worked a lathe either.

Her biographer, Jane Lancaster, notes in *Making Time* that Lillian created a niche for herself, forging a new career by marketing her verified expertise on management with her presumed knowledge of homemaking, plus her public persona as the sole leader of a wacky family. Lillian took scientific management into the home, becoming internationally recognized as a designer—pioneering the kitchen island, for example, and a remarkable number of other time-saving innovations for someone so poorly acquainted with housework. She sought to make women the masters of their domains.

In 1926 Lillian began motion study experiments on a variety of household tasks, including making a bed, washing dishes, baking, setting the table, and more. She also taught women how to conduct their own motion experiments in their homes. The commercial outcome of these experiments was the Kitchen Efficient, as she called it, which could help a homemaker (she preferred this term to housewife) reduce the walking associated with a traditional poorly designed kitchen.

According to the *New York Herald Tribune*, this revolutionary design "cut almost in half the number of motions required in preparing any given dish, and reduced to one sixth the amount of walking required." When a strawberry shortcake was prepared in a traditional kitchen and then the new Gilbreth kitchen, the number of kitchen operations was reduced from ninety-seven to sixty-four, and the number of physical footfalls dropped from 281 to 41. She gave her daughter Ernestine the drawings of a prototype for a wedding present.[7]

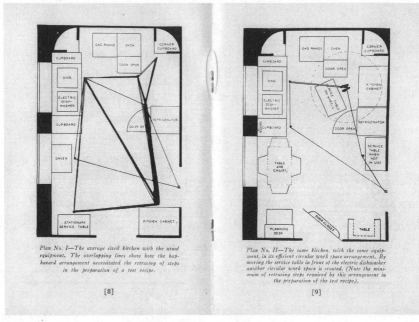

Plan No. I—*The average sized kitchen with the usual equipment. The overlapping lines show how the haphazard arrangement necessitated the retracing of steps in the preparation of a test recipe.*

[8]

Plan No. II—*The same kitchen, with the same equipment, in its efficient circular work space arrangement. By moving the service table in front of the electric dishwasher another circular work space is created. (Note the minimum of retracing steps required by this arrangement in the preparation of the test recipe).*

[9]

"Before" (left) and "after" (right) diagrams of Gilbreth's kitchen plan in the *New York Herald Tribune*, 1930. SOURCE: Reprinted with the permission of Purdue University Libraries.

Unveiled at the 1929 Women's Exposition, the Gilbreth kitchen corresponded to a time of intense marketing toward housewives. Adjustable-height countertops helped women hack their own kitchens, creating a space where housewives could tailor their space to their needs. New appliances were appearing in middle-class homes, and Lillian's purported expertise on these matters helped her translate her wide-ranging experience into a stable career.

Her efforts to streamline the home eventually wound their way back to the world of work, this time on the retail sales floor and the undomesticated world of the corporate office. As a contractor for Macy's, Gilbreth redesigned the sales stations in a way that reduced the time it took retail workers to reach their peak efficiency from four months to two days. Then, at the 1933 Century of Progress Exhibition in Chicago, IBM unveiled the Gilbreth Management Desk, promoted as the "business headquarters of the household manager." Harry Braverman, a Marxist historian who popularized debates about Taylorism, notes that others also saw the office as ripe for Taylorist study. He quotes a 1960 office guide that timed common tasks. Opening and closing a side desk drawer took 0.015 minutes, but closing the center drawer took a whole 0.027 minutes, about half as long as it took to execute that classic office maneuver, the "move in chair to adjoining desk or file," which clocked in at 0.05 minutes.[8]

What separated Gilbreth from Taylor, however, was not the industrial setting or the disposition toward workers. The main point of Taylor's scientific study, in breaking down production into its constituent parts, was to rob craftsmen of their time-honed skills and to teach those skills to employers. Over time, once the workers' knowledge of the production process and their skill levels were sufficiently debased, they were less effective at demanding the process be altered in any way. Deskilling undercut the traditional power of the workman. By contrast, Lillian Gilbreth sought to teach women new skills, a leitmotif of Progressive Era femininity, for which she's often been praised. But what if domestic routinization is just a corollary to deskilling? After all, the result is the same: peak efficiency. Whatever her Progressive bona fides, Lillian provided, even if only inadvertently, a model of Taylorism that anticipated a postindustrial society and thrived as a way of life outside the workplace.

•

TOWARD THE END of the nineteenth century, a creeping *fin de siècle* consciousness seemed to suggest that industrial workplaces were simply destroying people physically and debasing them emotionally. Fatigue and exhaustion had become major concerns for medicine, national security, and economic prosperity. It was in this context that an Australian polymath named Elton Mayo became the patron saint of workplace happiness. Today, modern administration bears his distinctive imprint.

In 1927 Mayo helped establish the interdisciplinary Fatigue Laboratory at Harvard, complete with temperature-controlled rooms, to study the malaise and exhaustion of the working masses, including their mental and emotional health, nutrition, blood, urine, and muscle physiology. Records indicate he left few details out of his exhaustive investigation into the effects of work on the human body. "Body and ears normal," he noted, adding, "underwear is clean and sufficient." He thought the stress of working under industrial capitalism would be revealed as psychosomatic trauma in the human body, as cellular breakdown or mental anomie.[9]

Yet there was clearly another motive for Mayo's clinical practice. Referencing the "pessimistic reveries to work," he wanted to "remove the fatigue and the irrationality which manifest themselves in the phenomena of social unrest." In other words, it wasn't just the work that led people to exhaustion, but their ceaseless struggle for reform. "It is at once evident that the general theories of Socialism, Guild Socialism, Anarchism and the like are very largely the phantasy constructions of the neurotic," he wrote. Mayo sought to understand the degradation wrought at the emotional, mental, and physiological levels, hoping to turn discontent into company loyalty.[10]

The genius of Mayo's insight was to focus on exactly the thing Taylor ignored: the emotional well-being of people at work. Predicated on the logic that happy workers don't rebel, Mayo's science was useful as an explanation of worker dissatisfaction but also as an antidote to the rattling resistance to capitalism that, he felt, was always a tremor or two away from breaking through the surface of mainstream society.

In Cicero, Illinois, he embarked on what would become his landmark study at Western Electric's Hawthorne Works Plant, a telephone production corporation that at its peak employed forty-five thousand people. Mayo had a professional record marked by failed attempts at advanced degrees. But it was not his scientific credentials that excited his champions; it was his zealous insistence that noneconomic incentives held the key to improving a company's bottom line. Workers could be motivated by something else besides money; they just didn't know it yet.

At Hawthorne, Mayo's focus shifted decisively from the body to the emotional realm. In one well-documented experiment, Mayo and his team found that productivity increased with both less *and* more natural light. Rather than take this to mean that the results were contradictory, he explained the overall effect as a result of the increased happiness of workers that came from being placed in small groups that could more closely relate to one another. In response, Mayo changed the length of break times, staggered schedules, and offered midmorning meals. Mayo's ultimate conclusion was that efficiency gains were contingent upon an informal happiness among members of a work group. As their ties to one another deepened, their commitment to work increased, and they were, in turn, more productive.

Mayo then personally oversaw the program to train hundreds of Hawthorne's supervisors as amateur therapists, which included workshops about strategic questioning, active listening, and other skill sets that should have been conducted by those with advanced psychology degrees. Whereas Taylor wanted workers to do their jobs no matter what, Mayo insisted they enjoy them too.

Today's managers haven't abandoned the older methods of extracting greater productivity, but there has been a marked shift away from the factory demagogue and toward industrial psychology. Modern-day scientific management is premised on the need to control workers' bodies and dispositions even when they're not actually at work. One approach has been to introduce games and play as motivational tools, evinced by the explosive growth of a billion-dollar fun-at-work industry. Through the use of measurement, observation, and a little friendly competition, gamification aims to blur the distinctions between fun and functional by redirecting the creative juices squeezed out through casual play into a marketable product. All time becomes productive, work becomes leisure, and play becomes a routine obligation.

There's no doubt that most drudgery would be more defensible if there were a cooperative element and a ludic sensibility built in. Some Progressive Era reformers saw drudgery as work's saving grace. As historian Daniel Rodgers notes, they thought "routine emancipated the worker by wearing deep and comfortable tracks in the nervous system that set his mind free for thought." A healthy dose of workplace boredom, in other words, allows for occasional moments of mental escape that help us survive the long workday. But gamifying work is different. It transfers skills that workers learn during a playful exercise into a profit-seeking enterprise, and the rules of the games can also reinforce codes of conduct on the job.[11]

The current managerial obsession with gamification is often heralded as an innovative weapon to deal with the modern malaise that has befallen so many workers, exhausted by not only the work but also by what feels like a never-ending quest to derive meaning from meaningless tasks. But it isn't as new or revolutionary as it seems. With great élan, the Soviet Union encouraged "socialist competition" as an alternative to the monetary rewards on offer in capitalist societies. One common example was to have two teams build a bridge. Whichever group reached the midpoint fastest was awarded the Order of the Red Banner of Labor badge. Trotsky, who did not share Lenin's zeal for Taylorism, referred to such tactics as "backwards capitalism . . . under the whip of a bureaucracy."[12]

American managers have also long encouraged the use of "funsultants" to enhance morale at work. Such ideas were at the heart of Mike Judge's instant cult sensation *Office Space*, in which three unwitting heroes, who desperately hate their white-collar jobs, partake in a massive act of corporate sabotage. A prime target of the film is the forced fun of Hawaiian Shirt Fridays; in another thread, a character is asked to wear "flair" on her uniform to reflect her personal commitment to her low-wage waitressing job. In the documentary *Live Nude Girls Unite!*, dancers at the Lusty Lady peep show in San Francisco reported that management insisted during union negotiations on having their jobs classified as "fun," which workers successfully rebuked.

Today the practice of gamifying work has gained momentum through the use of new technologies. Uber and Lyft give "badges" to those who accrue the most miles or even have the best conversations. Target (a.k.a. Walmart for liberals) uses the Checkout Game, which scores the speed and precision of low-wage checkout clerks. Color-coded screens display the productivity rates of employees in real time and in public as they scan and bag items. Workers, therefore, can monitor themselves and their coworkers without a manager even being present. Cold Stone Creamery trains its army of mall-based ice cream servers through a video game called Scoop It Up, which workers are encouraged to play in their nonwork time. The game compares the size of scoops that players offer to customers to the company's predetermined optimal size, and then calculates how much the company wastes by overzealous scoopers. The training game became so popular that it is now marketed for general use.[13]

Additionally, hundreds of apps offer employers the ability to gamify work while surveilling productivity. Challenge Timer uses the Pomodoro Method to break down complex jobs into smaller, more manageable bits. Pomodoro's namesake is the tomato-shaped timer that Francesco Cirillo first used in the 1980s to structure time in twenty-five-minute increments to help make tasks more manageable and goals more attainable. Beeminder helps you meet productivity goals you set for yourself by lightening your wallet if you don't. You sign up for the app with a credit card, and if your goals go unmet for the day it deducts five dollars from your account. Lest you think I am too cynical for these tricks to be of any personal value, research for this book interested me enough in time use that I also began using a gamified time management app. If this book comes out on time, I will have the Forest app at least partially to thank. Forest allows you to set a time limit that restricts use of your phone while it grows a virtual tree. Accrue enough points from focused time, as I did, and the app partners with a nonprofit that will plant a real living tree on an African farmer's land. Somewhere in Kenya there's a small forest that my hard work grew.

The titillating prospect of an über-productive workforce, one motivated internally and receptive to external nudges, is seductive to anyone looking to turn a profit. Industrial science had a profound impact on the way managers thought, and their ideas reverberated throughout the century as Americans shifted from a manufacturing to a service economy. They gave rise to the human relations movement and should be considered the forebears of those tireless (and tiresome) gurus like Peter Drucker and Tom Peters, who spread the gospel of worker management with a cheery disposition and countless volumes of organizational psychology.

What began as a philosophy of work has evolved into a way of life. Some might suggest our growing fascination with productivity is just a rational response to mortality—as soon as you're born you start dying. Alternately, efficiency is intuitively appealing. It's just doing what you already do, but faster. But it would be wrong to think our growing time-consciousness is just good sense.

Clocks were first introduced into British industry in the sixteenth century as a way to regularize the working day. The history of early industrialism is peppered with fierce and sometimes deadly battles between workers and factory owners for control of the clocks. Over centuries, according to historian E. P. Thompson, workers became habituated to working according to clock time, dulling, though never fully ending, struggles to control time measurement devices in the workplace. The result of these battles is what he called time-discipline, the subjective orientation of working people to the boss's clock. Our ancestors hated clocks. So where does our modern obsession come from?

Taylor's stopwatch has become our collective pacemaker. Does that make us more like Taylor or Schmidt? Whereas Taylor and his contemporaries forced efficiency on a resistant labor force, our strict adherence to efficiency and productivity demands now functions like an internal mantra: get things done.

In fact, *Getting Things Done* is the title of the bible of contemporary productivity guru David Allen. Saying all those words takes time, however, so he has rebranded it simply as GTD. GTD is a mixture of individual responsibility, self-help, and corporate-friendly messaging. The point is to transfer the responsibility for an inefficient life onto the individual and away from any mediating social problems. "Time is not the problem" for the overworked and stressed out, Allen says; the problem is that "you need psychic bandwidth." Allen stresses adherence to a hierarchical system of personal time management ("do it, delegate it, defer it") that is accomplished through a paper-based to-do list system, eschewing technology tools unless they are "GTD-enabled" (i.e., designed and sold by David Allen).

Personal productivity apps and time management advice books promise individuals a greater degree of control in an increasingly haphazard society. Globalization created a spatial problem. It demanded that workers be footloose and uprooted, willing to move for jobs and chase opportunities or lose out in perpetual competition with someone far away who was willing and able to work for less. In similar fashion, the disruptions caused by precarious employment mean that we must be available at any time, on offer to anyone, competing against our own life commitments. In that environment, time management might provide us with a measurable distinction from others, especially if we are among the growing number of task rabbits, freelancers, and gig workers who, after all, only have ourselves to blame if we are not ready for the next "opportunity."

There are literally thousands of apps in the productivity category available through Apple. Some call this Digital Taylorism. It's more like productivity porn, because it doesn't just offer tools, but also a fantasy world in which the self is completely quantifiable, docile, and controlled. Apps like Self-Control block your access to certain websites you might deem distracting— like Pornhub. Others, like Rescue Time, operate behind your back, tracking your online activity to let you know, for example, exactly how much time you wasted on Pornhub. Todoist helps you track your entire day as if you're moving down a to-do list. You can cross off "watch porn" and feel like you're getting somewhere. The point is that porn isn't the problem, but rather the time we spend indulging in it.

Yet the most time-conscious among us have become nonbelievers. The more time they managed, the less of it they actually had. Take Merlin Mann, the productivity evangelist who created Inbox Zero, the solution du jour to endless email, the major time-suck of white-collar workers everywhere. In response to the growing number of expensive "personal digital assistants" that were cashing in on the time management craze, Mann invented what he called the hipster PDA, a series of blank note cards and a pen held together by a binder clip. The joke wasn't that funny, but people took it seriously, especially thousands of GTD devotees. Mann spun this popularity into his next big thing. Inbox Zero blew up after his influential Google Tech Talk, as it promised to be a bizarre mix of Zen Buddhism and pragmatism. He seemed to say, "empty inbox, happy life," anticipating the obsessive-compulsive joy sparked by Marie Kondo's home-tidying wisdom.

Mann's philosophy was captivating because it caught hold of a problem that had yet to be named. The promise of the 1990s was that email would make communication quicker, cheaper, and easier, freeing up time for something else. Instead, it seems to have exemplified Zeno's paradox: If you approach a finite point halfway each time, it will take an infinite number of halves to get there. Every email demands a reply, and every reply produces another email, requiring yet another reply. The more we delete, the more emails pile up. In her 1983 book, *More Work for Mother*, historian Rose Cowan argued that the much-anticipated leisure for housewives after the widespread introduction of new home technology never materialized. Instead, standards of hygiene and cleanliness only rose. Now that vacuums made everything cleaner, we expected homes to be spotless. Our appetite for starchy white shirts and unscuffed jeans grew as washing technology improved. The notion of "labor-saving technology," in other words, was simply a lie. In *Counterproductive*, the Intel-based technology writer Melissa Gregg offers a scathing indictment of the "attention economy." Time management schemes, she argues, are what we have instead of predictable schedules, a fair workweek, and adequate family and medical leave policies. It is the inevitable result of having to do more with less, the governing logic of precarity.[14]

The appeal of time management software is not just to save time or increase efficiency, as one might suppose. Rather, it represents the apogee of a new cultural logic with particular material underpinnings. Gregg's theory points to productivity as a demonstration of one's awareness of the dictates of twenty-first-century rationality. Wasting time is not only wasteful; it is the essence of bad character. Time management literature first appeared in the 1950s but went through a boom during the 1970s, just as the first wave of corporate downsizing took off. Against the backdrop of layoffs and increasing competition for scarce jobs, a growing discourse put pressure on workers to prove themselves valuable to employers who were on the offensive after a few decades of forced compromise with unions and the middle class. In this environment, mastery over the ability to use time wisely came to be seen as an important job qualification, a means to distinguish oneself as worthy in a sea of qualified candidates cautiously navigating the fog of economic uncertainty.

This new corporate morality carries important implications for how workers view not only themselves but one another. The emphasis on individual productivity prioritizes the "competitive office worker, whose individual feats increasingly come at the expense of workers . . . obliterating recognition of collegial interdependence in contemporary workplaces," Gregg writes.[15]

Technology is often portrayed as the ultimate devil on our shoulder as we try to focus on work. But productivity apps, digital extensions of our time-consciousness, can put us back to work as much as take us away from it. Time management, as it is currently practiced, is less about striking a balance between work and leisure as it is about the transformation of our subjective disposition toward life in general. Consider this launch of Microsoft's new computer and tablet line, which appeals to our desire to master time through technology's ability to help us move "fluidly between our work and personal lives":

> We believe Microsoft can uniquely help you manage this digital lifestyle by delivering technology that empowers you rather than overwhelms. We are centering on our area of strength and passion to empower a *new era of personal productivity* in every aspect of your lives. Not just at work, but also in how you live, learn, and play. We will help you make the most of your time, with experiences that help you across your whole life and across all of your devices.[16]

Productivity apps, or what Gregg calls "techno-mediated efficiency infrastructure," "fuel a lifestyle that does not differentiate among work, home, and leisure." Where, in the discourse of productivity, is the place for the limits of work, the boundaries of the workplace, the ends of the working day? Indeed, one central demand of management theory is that work, in some form, is performed all the time. That way we can find time for the most fulfilling and rewarding careers or the most productive performance during rest periods.

Yet time is not just managed, but consumed. The sociologist Lisa Wade offers up the example of luxury tea. "It takes a full day to hand-roll 17 ounces of our Jasmine Dragon Pearl Green Tea," the product's advertisement reads. "But in just three minutes you can watch these aromatic pearls unfurl gracefully into one of the world's most soothing and delicious teas." In other words, the consumption of others' toil—"A whole day of their labor for just three minutes of curly goodness," as Wade puts it—enhances the product. Rather than celebrating efficiency, here we are fetishizing the pleasure we get from a product predicated on the daylong slog of women in China. Social class has always been delineated by whether or not you sell your labor or purchase that of others. Attaching status and, literally, good taste to the consumption of others' time highlights the extraordinary nature of labor time as both an economic good and a cultural status symbol. In other words, the idea of time management assumes our time is up for grabs. It's yours so long as you use it right, but it belongs to someone else—bosses, consumers—if you're inefficient.[17]

Taylor and those he inspired were successful not just because of their forceful brutality, but also because of their rationality. They tapped into an existing common sense that was foundational to capitalism from the very beginning and is still with us today. Parents and their children, pushed by relentless busyness, increasingly resort to workforce planning apps like Slack— its slogan is "Where Work Happens"—to schedule their private lives. Of course, it makes sense to make the most of our days, but saving money for our bosses isn't the same thing as enjoying the time we have to the fullest. Corporate co-optation tends to erode the actual benefits of time management. Moreover, management control didn't mean just more work, but faster work. Speedup compounds the paradox of long hours. The normalization of time management as a way of life has hidden the human taskmasters and whip crackers of the past. They're still with us, though, partly because some new technologies are giving them a second life.[18]

CHAPTER 3

THE ELECTRONIC WHIP

TAYLOR AND THE OTHER MANAGEMENT GURUS WERE TRUE REVO-lutionaries. They transformed the way production is performed and services are provided, changes that affected the ways we live our day-to-day lives. Their science became the new metronome of American capitalism. Through the deft control of labor, they delivered management the upper hand, transforming the factory into a fiefdom. Today's workplaces bear their unmistakable imprimatur.

But what Taylor and others started, modern productivity experts have intensified. Look at the work sites of the country's largest employers, and it's clear that when work time is weaponized effectively today, it's not only measured but mastered and monitored too. We must know *how* people fill their hours, and at what speed, not only that they do, in fact, fill them. Taylor and his contemporaries sought to uphold a bureaucratic rationality, with workers and bosses fulfilling their respective roles. Today a temporal rationality rules, as the role of time in the exploitation process has become more central to management than ever. The result has been not just longer hours but speedup, tighter deadlines, more technical control over schedules, and a surveillance and policing system to make sure every second of work is accounted for. For the most part, there's no bawling foreman timing workers' every move or specialist to advise managers on efficient motion. But that's not to say that similar processes aren't at work. Many of them have been amplified by new technologies.

In 2010 Amazon announced it was coming to Lehigh Valley, Pennsylvania, in a series of billboards that lined local highways. I grew up there, and most people I knew received this news as necessary relief. There were five job seekers for every open position, and as the official unemployment rate gained on 10 percent, the oft-heralded recovery from the Great Recession felt nonexistent to most locals. Several old friends and family members received postcards in the mail recruiting for Amazon's new fulfillment center in Breinigsville, not far from my hometown of Bethlehem.

Amazon's Lehigh Valley fulfillment center is located just a short drive from where Frederick Taylor first pushed Schmidt to load forty-seven tons of pig iron onto a cart at Bethlehem Steel more than a century ago. Since then the United States has passed myriad labor laws that are supposed to protect workers from undue pressure, dangers, stress, and theft. Their time, however, is still largely unprotected by federal statute. Scientific management is no more scientific than it ever was; it has merely been moved into the digital realm. Imagine today's Taylorist factory worker, the ghost of Schmidt, hard at work at an Amazon warehouse. She's not loading pig iron but moving packages. And rather than being timed, she's racing against herself. Her name is Nichole Calhoun.

At first Nichole was excited about the prospect of working for Amazon. Work was hard to come by and she was frustrated by the moralizing platitudes of local career counselors promising jobs if only she "mastered the art of 'personal branding' to stand out among the competition." At the time, she knew Amazon only as an online bookseller, and when she went to hand in her résumé she imagined the local office might look something like a dazzling library. But after a drug test and a background check she landed a gig on the night shift making $12.75 an hour.

"They never looked at my résumé. It was too easy," she wrote later, though her opinion soon changed when she started working. Amazon made $34 billion that year. Instead of a glorified bookstore, she found the paradigmatic warehouse we are familiar with from news reports. Amazon's Lehigh Valley facility covers more than six hundred thousand square feet, with floors on each end the size of football fields.

When orders came in, Nichole's handheld scanner began a countdown clock as she followed the instructions to find the item, scan it, and place it in the correct bin. The scanner also gave her a "pick path" to follow to the next item. All night long. She walked up to fifteen miles a night through the endless rows of shelves, scanning thousands of bar codes. "Everything had a bar code—even me," she told me. A white badge that hung around her neck tracked her location, and the scanner in her hand monitored her productivity. "The scanner was your master," she said.

She wasn't alone in the cavernous place. She worked alongside moonlighting teachers, debt-laden students, parents who split their childcare shifts, skilled laborers, veterans, migrants, and others who sometimes drove many hours to and from the facility. "We had plenty of time to get to know each other," she said, facetiously referencing the work schedule. As a result of mandatory overtime, she often worked fifty-five- to sixty-hour weeks and was routinely roused early from the break rooms and told to get back to work by security guards. During peak season around the winter holidays, schedules were altered frequently to meet productivity goals and sick leave was eliminated. Yet despite needing all hands on deck, firings were common, a churn-and-burn mentality that was made possible by a slack labor market. The challenges of excessive hours were compounded by the lack of job security, as the company sent notoriously mixed messages about their employment future after the Christmas rush died down. It was common, Nichole told me, that when pickers passed each other in the shelving units, racing against their individualized countdown clocks, they would raise their scanners to their heads and pretend to pull a trigger.

By Amazon's standards, however, Nichole was the ideal worker. She easily surpassed the required 125 picks per hour. As one of the facility's most productive pickers, she quickly rose through the ranks to become an ambassador, a title that came with more money and the responsibility to train other pickers. At pick school, as it was called, she followed the company script, but also took the opportunity to caution against overwork, burnout, and fatigue. Though she was hired by a temp agency, the promise of full-time work for Amazon was always dangled in front of her, and kept her motivated and working harder.

But she was let go after Christmas anyway, and then rehired late the next summer. In the meantime, the local newspaper, the *Morning Call*, had run an exposé on the Breinigsville facility, for which Nichole had been a major source. It was the first close encounter with Amazon the public had ever read, and it quickly became a global news story. What she had seen on the inside was suddenly in the public domain.

Temperatures were frequently over 100 degrees inside, and it was not uncommon to see workers carried out in stretchers or wheelchairs from dehydration or heat stroke. On a single day in June, fifteen workers collapsed on the job as temperatures reached above 110 degrees. After management installed fans, one worker was quoted as saying it was like "working in a convection oven while blow-drying your hair." In response, Amazon arranged to have paramedics parked in ambulances outside the site to treat those who suffered from the heat and pace of work. Nichole said it got so hot on the upper floors that she sometimes had trouble reading the bin numbers correctly. "It made me crazy. I literally couldn't see straight."

If it wasn't the heat, it was the ever-increasing pace of work. Many hired at the facility weren't even employed by Amazon. They were brought in by a temp agency, ISS, a global security firm with which Amazon contracted to handle its warehouse employment. The temp agency's job, however, was more than subcontracting. "They were the ones always cracking the whip," Nichole said.

The *Morning Call* quoted Stephen Dallal, a Kutztown resident who had responded to an advertisement to work in a "fun, fast-paced atmosphere." Dallal was fired after six months for failing to meet productivity targets. "It just got harder and harder," he said. "It started with 75 pieces an hour. Then 100 pieces an hour. Then 125 pieces an hour. They just got faster and faster and faster."

Nichole stayed at Amazon for another peak season. Things did not improve markedly. She began talking about a union in hushed tones in the break room, but the only responses were scrawled on the bathroom walls, because she said people were scared to speak for fear the company was listening. Management began flooding the work site with temps. Nichole started being short-shifted, sent home in the middle of the day, and she wasn't getting enough hours to make a living. "First I'm worked to death; then I'm practically starving for work. This is what they did to us," she said. "And the whole time they're watching us. . . . It was the cruelest, most sadistic workplace I've ever seen."

Nichole was creeped out by the surveillance technology she and the others labored under. But it was the all-too-banal problems of poverty and bad luck that eventually did her in. Her apartment was broken into. Her car was towed for a parking violation from the Amazon lot while she was at work. And without enough money from inconsistent shifts, she was forced to leave and look for work elsewhere. To get the Amazon job she had signed a non-compete contract, a legal document that forbade her from working with Amazon's direct competitors for a specific amount of time. "But Amazon competes with everyone," she told me, clearly exasperated to this day as she relives the memories. She couldn't find any work, so she maxed out her credit cards on food and other essentials and moved west, tramping around People's Park in Berkeley, California, and eventually landing in Seattle.

Fast-forward a few years and she was flying a sign, street slang for panhandling: "I was an order picker at Amazon.com. Earned degrees. Been published. Now I'm homeless, writing, and doing this. Anything helps." In all, she spent six years homeless, sleeping on the streets, in shelters, and occasionally on a friend's couch. She said people she met panhandling were often surprised by her story. She rebuked them first on the street, and later in the *Guardian*. "My homelessness isn't a mystery," she wrote. "I simply could not afford to keep a roof over my head. . . . I've met other intelligent hard-working homeless people."

By the time I spoke with her, things had improved. She was managing to avoid some of the worst flak that came from being an enemy of Amazon and had finally gotten a roof over her head. But it hadn't been easy. "I did American Studies on the ground for six years," she said, referring to the ethnographic data she collected on those with whom she lived and lived off of when she was panhandling. Now she does paid work for a group that helps manage a tent city for the homeless, an encampment practically in the shadow of Amazon's new West Coast headquarters. "I found more respect on the streets flying signs than I ever did working for Amazon," she said. "Every time I see that place I'm reminded of how awful it was."

Nichole's story would be gut-wrenching if it was just one person's saga. But years after Nichole and others blew the whistle on Amazon's Lehigh Valley facility by speaking to the *Morning Call*, court cases began to paint a broader picture of the company, giving her story a universal quality. When a worker in Baltimore sued the company, Amazon defended itself with evidence that the worker had committed an offense it listed as "productivity_trend." In many cases, workers were automatically fired, without managers actually speaking to them, when the company's monitoring system found that they had dipped below productivity benchmarks. In that one facility in Baltimore, three hundred workers had been let go in one year, a decrease from previous years, the company said. In another case, hundreds of East African migrants at an Amazon facility in Minnesota protested the lack of time to pray during their shifts. Their protests resulted in a shocking reversal of company policy for Amazon that allowed them extra time to meet the requirements of their Muslim faith. But others weren't so lucky. A group of workers in Nevada lost a Supreme Court case that ruled they did not have to be paid for the lengthy mandatory security screenings at the end of each shift, which sometimes took up to half an hour, before they were allowed to leave the warehouse.[1]

AMAZON PATENT: ULTRASONIC BRACELET AND RECEIVER FOR DETECTING POSITION IN 2D PLANE

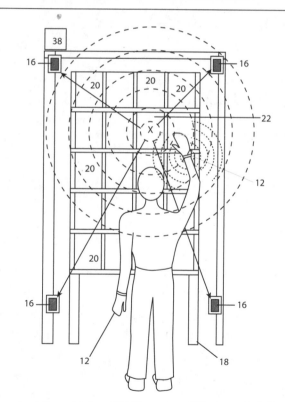

SOURCE: Jonathan Evan Cohn, US Patent and Trademark Office, 2016. Ultrasonic bracelet and receiver for detecting position in 2d plane. US patent pub, US 009881276B2.

After Nichole left Amazon, the company patented a device to further direct pickers' time and motion. An image of the bracelet from its patent application is above. It counts your footfalls, maps your route through the miles of shelving, and times your bathroom breaks. It alerts you every nine seconds with "haptic feedback," an "ultrasonic sound pulse" that senses the location of your hands in relation to an item on a shelf, electronically guiding them toward the object. Then it's a race against a countdown clock to find a specific item, scan its bar code, and place it in a bin, before moving on to the next item. If it's an enhanced environment, the picker barely walks at all, standing on a foam pad for comfort, as Kiva robots, communicating autonomously with the wrist device, deliver her shelves one at a time so she can find specific items and send them along.

•

WHILE NICHOLE FACED sweltering heat on the top floors at the Amazon center in Pennsylvania, Isabel Barrera was sweating out her shift in the basement of a laundromat in California. Deep underneath Mickey Mouse's House and Roger Rabbit's Car Toon Spin, buried below throngs of jubilant park visitors, a massive industrial laundry rumbles on 24/7 in Anaheim, California. Isabel worked the day shift. Years earlier she had fled violence in El Salvador and made her way to the United States. Eventually, she landed here, cleaning linens at Disneyland. She loaded bedsheets, cloth napkins, comforters, and clothes into giant washers and dryers. Luxury accommodations like those at Disneyland offer what hotel industry designers call a heavenly bed, an overstuffed mattress with weighted blankets and a pile of fancy pillows, for the ultimate relaxation after a long day on vacation. But in the bowels of the place, the work was hellish—excessively hot, incessantly noisy, and dangerous.

Isabel was in a union that made some of the worst aspects tolerable. She made good wages and enjoyed generous healthcare benefits. After the union contract expired in 2008, Disneyland made some changes to how it measured worker productivity. Workers used to count on paper the number of linens they washed per shift, but the company had recently instituted an automated counting system that also acted as a productivity tracker.

One day workers arrived to find giant screens affixed around the workplace, with their names color-coded like traffic lights blinking off and on. As they worked, those who were keeping up with the predetermined productivity goals saw their names flash in green. But when they slowed down or dipped too far below Disney's efficiency standards, their names flashed in yellow or red. Managers could monitor the screens above ground and adjust their productivity targets based on average performance. Later, the laundry machines were programmed to flash colors as well, to further identify which workers at which machines were speeding up or falling behind. Workers were routinely disciplined for failing to keep pace with the speedup. They called it the electronic whip.

Managers could crack the whip without even being in the room by making miniscule adjustments to productivity goals from an upstairs control room, monitoring the behavior and performance of individuals and the group. It was not long before workers began cracking it too. They began racing against one another to meet the new productivity goals. Sometimes, they accused one another of slowing the whole shift down, sowing dissension among their ranks. Workers feared that using the bathroom would lose them precious minutes, and the break room went empty because they were scared of management reprisals. Injuries increased as they strained to keep up the quicker pace, while morale plummeted.

Isabel hated the electronic whip. And it wasn't long before she found others who hated it too. It's a small world, after all. So she organized her shift to beat the whip. If one or two workers fell behind, they had a problem. But if they all worked at a reasonable pace, management had a problem. Isabel encouraged her coworkers to work at their own paces, ignoring the colored lights. Eventually, management was forced to loosen its grip on time, restoring a more regular pace with fewer midshift changes. Collectively, they slowed down the pace of the workday to decrease accidents and injuries, and to exert control. Disney eventually capitulated a bit and agreed not to use what it saw as decreased productivity as a reason to discipline workers. The electronic whip, however, remained. Today such a whip is everywhere. Yet the Isabels of the world aren't always there to push back.

Beatriz Casasola-Topete, the union organizer who helped Isabel and her coworkers fight the whip, has also seen these types of technologies used in hotels. Receptionists are monitored by electronic services that time their calls and their interactions with guests. The stated goal, Beatriz explains, is efficient customer service. Housekeepers at major hotels—Beatriz has seen it firsthand in Hawaii, though the practice is widespread—are often monitored via phones or tablets they are given to track which rooms have been cleaned. Cleaners used to perform that work the best way they knew how, and documented it and communicated it among one another. Now, management can see which rooms are being cleaned in real time, and an algorithm dispatches workers all over the hotels. "It's often not very logical," says Beatriz. "At least not from a worker's point of view."

But there is a logic to it, of course. HotSOS and Rex Room Expeditor, two major services in the electronic hotel management industry, both promise to save hoteliers millions by streamlining services. Over her twenty years as a union organizer, Beatriz has noticed a clear trend that hotels expect to provide better service and more amenities, with fewer employees, in less time. "Someone's always cracking the whip," she says. "They act like it's a computer program. You think computers just program themselves?"

These two anecdotes underscore how the timing of tasks and calculating of small periods of time are crucial to the business model of large corporations. As they've modernized and grown, so have the requirements of exactitude. The effects on workers are obvious—stress, poor health, exhaustion, work-family conflicts, not to mention the claustrophobic feeling of being constantly surveilled.

It has always been easy for major employers to treat working-class people as parts of a machine. But white-collar professionals are a different story. The kind of management protocol adequate to a professional environment requires more data, because workers are performing fewer routine tasks. Their actions are harder to guide and, most crucially, harder to predict. And that's where an even more advanced form of scientific management becomes useful. Nichole and Isabel were disciplined to varying degrees by new modes of control. Their white-collar counterparts might be facing a new kind of capitalism. To see how American managers are gaining a greater edge over professionals, we turn first to America's pastime.

Michael Lewis's 2003 best seller, Moneyball, recounts how the general manager of the Oakland A's, Billy Beane, revolutionized how teams look for new athletes. Baseball has always been defined by its split personality—an obsession with inane statistics and a feel-for-the-game romanticism. Rather than rely on the gumption of old-fashioned scouts, Beane turned to a Harvard-trained statistician to find the empirical standouts in the field of new recruits. Who were the kids, in other words, who were scientifically predicted to be rising stars? The Yankees ultimately won more games that season—though Oakland racked up 103 wins, the longest winning streak in American League history—but the success of the 2002 A's ignited a revolution. Since then, teams have increasingly relied on complex predictive algorithms to assess talent.

Baseball is big business. But it's hard to completely remove the romance of a day at the ballpark. The Field of Dreams will not be 3D printed! The office, on the other hand, is easier to imagine as a vapid social experiment in numbers. Enter Humanyze, a Boston-based technology firm that applies what it refers to as Moneyball principles for the workplace. Humanyze employs detailed statistical models to measure workplace success. CEO and MIT scientist Ben Waber created a credit-card-sized "sociometric" badge that employees wear around their necks, which records all interpersonal interactions through an embedded microphone. How often do you talk to members of another gender? Does your voice convey confidence or anxiety? Are you waiting your turn to speak or constantly interrupting others? Humanyze can hear it all. Bluetooth capability and infrared sensors can locate you in physical space, and an accelerometer records when you move. The badges can even detect the degree to which you empathize with others. The hundreds of data points the badges collect each minute are merged with dates and times from emails and calendars to paint a full picture of how, where, and with whom workers spend their workdays.

The curious twist is that Humanyze doesn't exactly record conversations. "It's not the content of communication that matters," according to Waber, "it's the structure." Humanyze badges do not reveal what is said, but rather create a spatial and cognitive map of when and how employees interact in order to "optimize performance." When I spoke with him, Waber offered the example of one of his clients, a "major US bank" that realized performance among its various call center locations was very uneven. What could explain the variation and how could the bank make the less productive call centers be more like their more productive peers? Call centers are an important case study because every second is spoken for—success means getting on and off calls fast. Moreover, they were early experiments in how to offshore service industry work, so figuring out ways to make them even more profitable is in line with basic economic history. Using Humanyze technology to measure internal communication patterns, it became clear that the most productive teams had an unusual advantage—they talked a lot to one another during breaks.

The takeaway was that strong social ties that formed during nonwork hours improved productivity. By implementing a new break schedule at the underperforming call centers, the bank saw a 23 percent increase in productivity and a 28 percent increase in employee retention rates. For such a new technology this is a very old insight, calling to mind Elton Mayo's Hawthorne Effect findings on workplace break rooms, discussed in the previous chapter. The point of all this, however, is not simply more productive banks, which ranks possibly last on the list of ways to make the world a better place. Humanyze represents the future of "people analytics." People analytics describes the use of data about human behavior and characteristics to make business decisions. This helps companies make smarter decisions than they would if they relied on the experience of seasoned managers, anecdotes, or corporate aversion to risk. As a revised version of scientific management, people analytics uses data the way Taylor used time.

If Humanyze is *Moneyball* for management, Teramind is *Black Mirror* for business. For the uninitiated, *Black Mirror* is the dystopian TV drama that is premised on depicting a near-future society rent apart by the unintended consequences of new technology. Threats to privacy is a recurrent theme. Teramind is a tool to surveil employees that remotely accesses a person's private webcam and takes photos of him or her every ten minutes.

Combining that data with keystroke counts, number of emails sent, app use, screenshots, social media content, productivity measures, and time use, it can develop a productivity picture of every employee, complete with photographic evidence. This is especially important when hiring freelancers, who aren't in the office and aren't in tune with "company culture." Over time, Teramind constructs an ideal-typical employee—let's call him Schmidt—that can, in theory, be used as a standard to which all real employees must compare. And Teramind can, of course, let you know if Schmidt could work just a little harder.

Teramind's ability to offer live streaming video surveillance distinguishes it from a tight field of competitors, but it is not alone in its quest to wiretap the workplace. There's also Activtrak, Avaza, Vericlock, Boomr, Hubstaff, TSheets, Staffcop, Time Doctor, Desk Time Pro, Track View, Interguard, and, yes, even one called Wiretap. These services are marketed as part of a larger strategy to lower costs by decentralizing operations and relying on independent contractors, specifically because they can lower the associated risks by providing long-distance surveillance. Moreover, as they create minute-by-minute records of on-the-clock activities, this new level of granularity allows managers to decide what counts as payable work time, and to exclude "unproductive" periods like bathroom breaks. One 2017 study on time-tracking programs discovered the default setting on many of the software systems automatically reduced employees' reported time by factoring in breaks, whether workers took them or not.[2]

"No more checking in or circling back. Just moving forward," promises Hubstaff, which monitors employee productivity via random screenshots. Veriato, which dutifully guards your company secrets against internal threats, bills itself as "Security's Achilles' Heel." Interguard, which serves the same function—apparently a company's own employees pose the largest threat to its secrecy—warns, "Your biggest asset is also your biggest liability." Preempt can give your employees "conditional access anywhere," a strange mix of elite gatekeeping and democracy.

Those for whom "big data" is a new way of doing business are often attracted to its democratic promise. "No longer is the alpha male or the senior leader or the loudest person in the room making the decisions," said Daryl Morey, general manager of the Houston Rockets. "Let the data decide," he told me. Morey is the Billy Beane of basketball, and his laid-back demeanor belies his passionate embrace of this new science of sports management. "You have to optimize your championship probability." To that end, those in the NBA who have embraced Moreyball, as it has come to be known, have customized technology to collect the most precise biometric data—heart rate, pulse, skin temperature, perspiration levels, and more. As for on-court changes, high-percentage dunk shots are still desirable, but there has been a movement toward eschewing once-reliable midrange shots in favor of once-reviled distant three-pointers, because simple math dictates that four successful three-pointers are better than five successful two-pointers. If that makes the game look worse, well, stat heads like Morey don't care.

Yet to many players, the data-driven game is about more than maximizing shooting percentages. The players' union has challenged the wide use of the data collected through wearables because it could help coaches or management discriminate against players if their fitness is found to be lacking. There are professional basketball leagues around the world that display a player's heart rate on the jumbotron when he is shooting free throws. But the players' union here is much stronger and has largely resisted the unregulated use of biometric data.[3]

Of course, most workers don't have the bargaining power of professional athletes. And sensitive healthcare data might be even more damaging in the hands of managers in other industries.

Randy Howell has been a pediatric nurse at the University of California San Francisco Medical Center for eleven years. As a caregiver, he comforts young patients and their parents when they are sick and vulnerable. In 2018, when rumors finally got back to him that management was electronically surveilling nurses at the hospital, his union, the California Nurses Association, confronted management point blank. "We said, 'Are you doing this?' and they said, 'No.'"

But almost a year later he found out they were. Nurses in various clinics and hospitals throughout the University of California health network were being made to wear a two-inch square badge, a "Real Time Locating System," that tracked their movements throughout the hospital. The badges are made by Midmark and are specially designed to track and time healthcare professionals as they "interact" with badges on patients and devices attached to patients' beds. The badges are designed to recognize the type of employee in a given room—nurse, doctor, technician—and automatically alert other kinds of workers, in the event of an emergency, for example. For that reason management markets the system as a communication device among coworkers. Considering the nurses initially didn't even know they were being tracked, it's no surprise they didn't see it that way. "As soon as we found out, we put out a cease-and-desist order to UCSF," Randy said. "But it's hard to stop something when it's already happening. We might be too late." There are clear benefits to using AI in healthcare, especially when it offers workers the ability to spend a higher percentage of their time with patients. Caregivers themselves, not managers, are best positioned to figure out how to implement that technology.

•

WHAT DO AN Amazon warehouse in Breinigsville, a Disneyland laundromat in Anaheim, and a hospital in San Francisco have in common? Workers have always been monitored, but at a time when employers already have a great deal of power over employees, concern over new workplace surveillance methods shouldn't be brushed off as mere paranoia. What exactly will our bosses do with all that data? And how did they get to own it in the first place?

Shoshana Zuboff conceived of "surveillance capitalism" a few years ago to help answer those questions. Surveillance capitalism is more than spyware technology, platforms, or management algorithms, even though it requires these to realize its full potential. Technology facilitates surveillance capitalism, just as it does all social behavior and economic activity. "If technology is bone and muscle," she writes, "surveillance capitalism is the soft tissue that binds the elements and directs them into action."[4]

Surveillance capitalism emerges when major technology firms monetize the huge untapped surplus of user data generated by online activity. It was invented as a solution to the crisis after the dot-com bubble burst, which threatened the big tech firms. Google combined its sizable, though to that point unused, cache of data logs and computing power to create ad revenue that was bolstered by the company's ability to predict a click-through rate. The success of this strategy encouraged Google to seek out new ways to extract even more data, including data that users wanted to be kept private, prompting a patent application for "Generating User Information for Use in Targeted Advertising." It wasn't until Google went public in 2004 that its sheer size and power became popularly known—its revenue had increased 3,590 percent since 2001. It had a new business model, and search capability was only a tiny part of it.

Online activity offers the ability to convert raw and relatively meaningless "data exhaust" into what Zuboff calls "behavioral surplus," a vast reservoir of usable information about our activity. It's the source code of our preferences, aspirations, fears, sexual kinks, personal secrets, geographic location, and, of course, work lives. Yet for most of Internet history, that data was useless to capitalism because no one knew quite what to do with it. Though it was there for the taking, no one knew it was worth grabbing.

Zuboff understands this wide extension of digitized data collection to be crucial to this new species of power.

> Extension wants your bloodstream and your bed, your breakfast conversation, your commute, your run, your refrigerator, your parking space, your living room, your pancreas. . . . Surveillance capital wants more than your body's coordinates in time and space. Now it violates the inner sanctum, as machines and their

algorithms decide the meaning of your sighs, blinks, and utter-
ances; the pattern of your breathing and the movements of your
eyes; the clench of your jaw muscles; the hitch in your voice; and
the exclamation points in a Facebook post once offered in inno-
cence and hope.[5]

The sheer ubiquity of digital life has slowly made a lay understanding of surveillance capitalism the new common sense,
and we grudgingly acknowledge our complicity in a Faustian
bargain—the exchange of unfettered communication and data
for our private information. But we know far less about how data
mining operates in workplaces.

The forces of surveillance capitalism have been intensified
through their extension into the workplace. The paradigmatic
example is that of Uber drivers. Driving people around the city
is important. But the labor these "rideshare" drivers perform is
less valuable than the information they generate while driving—
information Uber collects, analyzes, packages, and sells in its bid
to become a global transportation logistics platform. What this
means is that drivers are far from being compensated according
to the real value they generate for Uber. It is often stated that
data is the new gold. But unlike gold, data isn't merely mined;
it is produced. Generating data requires labor, yet it is not even
recognizable as work. As a by-product of work, it is produced
simultaneously as the drivers' stated mission and is, therefore,
unacknowledged as work specifically because it takes no extra
time. The more Uber drivers drive, the more data and information they generate, the better the company is able to extract
it and profit from it. If data is the new gold, the likes of Uber,
Google, and Facebook are its new thieves.[6]

Watching what workers do as a way of governing the workplace
is one thing. But anticipating what they will do even before they
do it—and acting accordingly—is another. A new suite of AI
tools combs through employees' social media use, phone records,

and personal data in order to predict which employees are most likely to quit. Google especially has been lauded for dealing with turnover issues through AI. The company's former head of "people operations," Laszlo Bock, told *Harvard Business Review* that predictive analytics allows Google to "get inside people's heads even before they know they might leave." This is important because, as the management consulting company McKinsey explains, it would be foolish to waste expensive pay increases or bonuses on those "who would have stayed put anyway."[7]

A stated promise of an AI-enhanced workplace is that it's fairer. Humans have biases, but computers are brutally honest, meritocratic, and blind to the things mere mortals get hung up on, like race, gender, and sexual preferences. But let's remember that technology's a social mirror, not a better lens. A mountain of academic research shows that humans program their biases right into their AI, algorithms, and platforms. The popular myth that "data doesn't lie" persists, and is often used for cover by bosses when they face protest. But in private, they seem to understand the dangers. According to a survey by Accenture, two-thirds of business leaders said they are "not very confident" that they are using new sources of workplace data in a "highly responsible way." And less than a third of employees say they have consented to employer use of workplace data, while more than half of employers say they do not even seek consent.

This lack of consent has occasionally prompted blowback. The transition to surveillance capitalism didn't draw blood, but it took hold of our bodies in other ways. And although most of us hardly knew it was happening before it was ubiquitous, it has not gone uncontested.

"For many of us, that kind of surveillance was the straw that broke the camel's back," said Jay O'Neal. Jay teaches eighth grade history in Kanawha County, West Virginia. He's referring to a fitness tracking app called Go365 that was the beginning of the end for what teachers at his school were willing to take. Year after year, Jay and his coworkers attended public hearings where representatives of the Public Employees Insurance Agency told those assembled that their healthcare plans would get more expensive and less effective. In the winter of 2018 Jay learned the insurers had a new idea—workers would have to sign up for an app that counted their steps. The program coaxed—some might say coerced—employees into using an app that monitored their bodies, using a point system to incentivize exercise, sobriety, diet, and more. (If the app listed "rest" as an important component, the West Virginia teachers didn't see it.) A Fitbit counted their daily footfalls and was able to cross-analyze those numbers with other data, such as weight and heart rate. Those who reached the set goal qualified for an Amazon gift card. Teachers who failed to accumulate three thousand points by the end of the school year would be billed twenty-five dollars per month until they reached their quota, and they would incur higher deductibles on their health insurance.

"We have a very unhealthy state," Jay said, but he noted that most teachers felt neither their employer nor their insurers had their well-being in mind when they came up with this plan. "All it really did was piss us off." Teachers faced onerous deductibles and coinsurance for everything from prescription drugs to childbirth. In that context, forced use of a "wellness" app was hardly going to go over well.

Apps like Go365 exploded after 2010, when the Affordable Care Act incentivized partnerships between large employers and wellness corporations to identify health risks associated with rising healthcare costs. Such apps might save companies money by shifting the costs of care onto sicker workers, but they don't improve health.

The official teachers' union didn't raise much of a fuss. But for the rank and file—who hadn't seen a raise in more than a decade, who worked summer jobs or moonlighted during the school year, who lived paycheck to paycheck—having their bodies surveilled and monitored during work time and free time was too much. It was an unusual start to a nationwide strike wave. Go365 was just one more indignity that turned the rumblings of anger and frustration over unaffordable healthcare costs into a mass movement that roiled West Virginia, quickly becoming a statewide general strike. After rural Mingo County teachers led the way, reports trickled in from across the state. Donning the red bandannas that were worn by armed coal miners in the 1921 Battle of Blair Mountain against a company militia, teachers drew on their history as a militant union state. But in the end, their victories relied on their present-day allies, not fallen martyrs. Bus drivers refused to transport kids to school, and parents rose to the teachers' defense. Within a short amount of time, every single school in the state was closed. After nine days, teachers returned to work with a significant raise.

•

THE US OFFICE of Technology Assessment first sounded the alarm on electronic workplace surveillance in 1987, a decade before the Internet became commonplace. The report considered that the simultaneous fall in unionization rates and the advances in workplace surveillance technologies could lead to "unfair or abusive monitoring." The report states, "The uses of technology discussed so far are controversial because they point out a basic tension between an employer's right to control or manage the work process and an employee's right to autonomy, dignity, and privacy."[8]

This report makes clear that workplace surveillance is facilitated not by technology, but by a weak and disorganized working class. Surveillance capitalism makes it easier to strip people of healthcare, but it was happening long before Fitbits. It also suggests that strengthening unions would be a good way to fight back. Militant strikers in West Virginia won a weeks-long battle for near-universal healthcare in 1946. The benefits had all been gutted in subsequent decades—not by technologists and their fancy algorithms, but by an alliance of politicians and employers.

Resistance to surveillance capitalism is only one way in which all of this monitoring might be counterproductive from the firm's point of view. A large 2015 study by MIT found that workers are more productive when bosses allow them the option to work outside the office unsupervised. The findings were even more significant when workers were also given control over their own time, with more latitude about when to log in to work and how often to report their activities to their direct supervisor.[9]

Karl Marx wrote in his 1844 *Manuscripts*, "In the end, an inhuman power rules over everything." It is tempting to see surveillance capitalism as merely an inhuman force, partly because it is inhumane, and partly because we fetishize technology. But that's not quite right. Managerial control over workers is a human power that has been greatly enhanced by the technological advances discussed here. Those technologies have, in some cases, even erased the physical managers altogether, reinforcing a perspective that sees workplace hierarchies and status inequality as natural, the way things are and the way they've always been.

But in the examples above, there's not an inhuman force presiding over workers. In fact, there are two discernible regimes of control. On the one hand, managers push the working class harder and faster. On the other, white-collar professionals are manipulated, from a distance, through their personal data. These different forms of control are attempts to organize workers in a way appropriate to their class character.

It will be up to a conscious labor movement to make connections between these forms, which undoubtedly have similar goals, and this chapter offers some hints of that. Isabel fought the electronic whip in the Disneyland laundromat with a union. Randy Howell and Jay O'Neal fought wearable tracking devices with a union, and even the NBA players mobilized their collective power as workers. Nichole Calhoun tried to do the same at her fulfillment center in Pennsylvania, and it's possible that unions at Amazon aren't as doomed as the company would like us to believe. Tech workers at all the major firms have turned toward union campaigns to raise these kinds of grievances. When I spoke to a member of the Tech Workers Collective, a labor organizing group within the tech industry, she told me, "Of course we want Google to be better. We spend a lot of time here after all. And that's no accident either."

I asked Beatriz, the union organizer who helped Isabel and her coworkers fight the electronic whip, if she thought there was any shot of beating the whip for good, and she was quiet for a pensive moment. "It's not about stopping the train," she said, "but more like, How do we drive it?" That is exactly the right question to ask of all technological developments, because control over technology is a social struggle as much as a technical problem. And it is always possible that that struggle will end in a way that enables ordinary workers to harness its power to a movement for justice. Nowhere is that possibility imagined more than in the realm of labor-saving robotics. The stated promise of workplace technology has usually been that it saves us time and can deliver us from a life of toil. It still could, and the next chapter examines the hopes, fears, and potential of realizing that dream.

CHAPTER 4

TIME MACHINES

BY NOW EVERYONE HAS BEEN APPROPRIATELY WARNED: THE robots are coming. Modern-day Paul Reveres have been alerting anyone within earshot. Algorithmic management, surveillance, and digital Taylorism are still part of the world in which most of us work, but vast advances in robotics are potentially rendering that system obsolete. We are told free time, lots of it, is close at hand—ready or not.

The stated promise of automation is that our future portends less work and more free time, or at least more creative labor alongside robot colleagues, because robots can do some of the work humans can do. Realizing this potential—as changes in the material conditions of our lives—is a utopian aspiration, and one we must work toward. Too often, however, that promise has been broken by a system that doesn't allow the benefits of widespread automation to be shared equitably. The result is not more free time, but worsening inequality, and more jobs that make humans feel like robots.

This tension between the utopian and dystopian potential of automation is the subject of a shocking amount of popular concern. The pages of newspapers and magazines are filled with paranoid articles about a robot apocalypse, and robots are appearing on talk shows and late-night television. Computer science is among the fastest growing majors on college campuses. Roboticists are often heralded as having a special relationship with the future of our economy, as if it depends solely on available technology. Although some of this concern is obvious hyperbole, at some point all this palaver congealed into an actual discourse. Some might even call it a theory. This theory holds that current levels of technological unemployment—our displacement by machine technology—are evidence of a revolution that could usher in the advent of a society that requires far less human labor.

Oxford University scientists Carl Frey and Michael Osborne calculated that 47 percent of American workers are vulnerable to automation in the next two decades because of the rise of big data and more advanced algorithms that have the potential to replace human decision-making processes. Another headline-grabbing account, by rock star economists Daron Acemoglu of MIT and Pascual Restrepo of Boston University, was widely said to herald the coming robot apocalypse, even though the authors predict only a small negative impact on jobs.[1]

Indeed, a growing cohort of techno-enthusiasts have looked over the horizon and seen a parade of veritable renaissance robots. Robots of the past were mostly constrained to replacing manual labor jobs with repetitive motion tasks that are relatively easy to automate. And humans were particularly skilled at coming up with other jobs to do that robots couldn't touch. But thanks to vast improvements in artificial intelligence, machine learning, and cloud computing, today's machines already have the capacity to do far more human labor that involves high-level cognition and judgment. There are functioning robot journalists and fiction writers, robot chefs, robot secretaries, robot lawyers, robot doctors, and robots that can overcome the challenges of last-mile delivery, bringing packages from warehouses to your front door. They can compose symphonies, and the advance orders are already in for highly anticipated robot sex partners. And even though bots can't vote, they still have a hand in determining the electoral process.[2]

The point, made time and again, is that this time is different. In the words of Erik Brynjolfsson and Andrew McAfee, the MIT scientists perhaps most identified with this discourse, we are currently "at an inflection point—a bend in the curve where many technologies that used to be found only in science fiction are becoming everyday reality." And Moore's Law, which predicts a doubling of computing speed every two years, will only push us past the inflection point, right?

Moore's Law is a market principle, not an inevitability. And the rate of increase in computing speed has been slowing considerably since the law was first proposed by Gordon Moore, the cofounder of Fairchild Semiconductor and CEO of Intel, in 1965. A study by a team of economists from Stanford and MIT found that the number of researchers needed to achieve Moore's Law is eighteen times greater today than in the early 1970s. For all the popular fascination with the looming threat of a robot takeover, rates of automation and productivity seem to have slowed compared to previous periods. The Economic Policy Institute argues the "zombie robot argument lurches on" despite there being "no evidence that automation leads to joblessness or inequality." So why is there so much robot chatter now?[3]

At the end of 2019, as the economy hovered around full employment, overwork and involuntary unemployment were major news stories, and productivity growth was slow. These were all indicators that a robot takeover was not imminent, and that projections to the contrary were overblown. Moreover, for more than a century the percentage of Americans in the workforce has steadily grown. But there's good reason—three of them, actually—why robots grab headlines today, even if they aren't poised to destroy work.

First, as long and irregular hours became a static feature of our contemporary work lives, robots emerged as a potential way to ease the burden. Technologists and Silicon Valley investors have stoked complaints about overwork as a rationale for robots. Even the AFL-CIO, often considered the enemy of labor-saving technology, sees advances in automation as a means to reduce the workweek while spreading excessive work around so that everyone will have a fairer and more reasonable amount.

Second, robots are getting cheaper. In decades past the cost of labor-saving technology was a major impediment to its implementation. As the graph below illustrates, humans are becoming costlier relative to their technological counterparts.

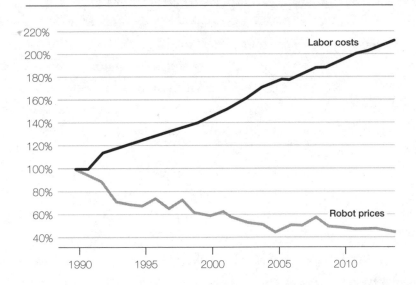

INDEX OF AVERAGE ROBOT PRICES AND LABOR COMPENSATION IN US MANUFACTURING

NOTE: From 1990 to 2015 the real (adjusted for inflation) cost of labor steadily increased. The real cost of labor in 2015 was more than double that of 1990. Meanwhile, the real average robot price has decreased about half since 1990. SOURCE: McKinsey Global Institute analysis of data from Economist Intelligence Unit, IMB, Institut für Arbeitsmarkt und Berufsforschung, International Robot Federation, and US Social Security data. Reproduced with permission.

A 2015 Reuters study claimed that the cost of repetitive-task robots was about one-tenth as much as it was in 2005. Although human labor is still cheaper than comparable automated systems, workers' comparative advantage has a breaking point.[4]

Third, popular culture has promoted the automation discourse in the past few years. The most prominent recent example was the long-shot bid for the 2020 US presidency by Andrew Yang, robot fearmongerer extraordinaire and Obama's former "ambassador of entrepreneurship." Yang's one-trick policy solution was to dole out a monthly $1,000 stipend to everyone over eighteen, a program he first outlined in his polemic *The War on Normal People*. "All you need is self-driving cars to destabilize society," he said. "That one innovation will be enough to create riots in the street. And we're about to do the same to retail workers, call center workers, fast-food workers, insurance companies, accounting firms." This messaging taps into a definite fear of falling common among America's working class, but that fear is not so simple. Americans are actually in favor of automation if it can erase the dirtiest, worst-paying, least meaningful jobs. Recent history, however, reminds us that the jobs most popularly associated with being killed by automation provided a stable living for mid-century families.[5]

The graph below shows a historic shift that occurred in three waves. From 1939 to 1970, the United States employed more people in manufacturing while output increased. This postwar economy and emergent middle-class society is often attributed to the good union jobs in US manufacturing, leading to consistent calls from the Left to "bring back manufacturing." Nostalgia for industry is misplaced, however—it's the strong unions that made those jobs profitable that we should return to.[6]

Beginning in 1970, output increased dramatically even though the United States employed nearly the same number of people. This period is associated with neoliberal restructuring and the rise of the service economy. Around 2000 things changed again, as US output nose-dived after the Great Recession and then recovered. Today we see a slight overall uptick in output produced by even fewer workers. Although it is commonly known that fewer people are employed in manufacturing, we often mistakenly assume that this means Americans produce less, which isn't true. The United States once employed more people to produce less, and now the opposite holds true. This extraordinary change is commonly attributed to the use of automation technology, a management scheme that substitutes labor-saving machines for workers.

EMPLOYMENT AND MANUFACTURING OUTPUT, 1939–2018

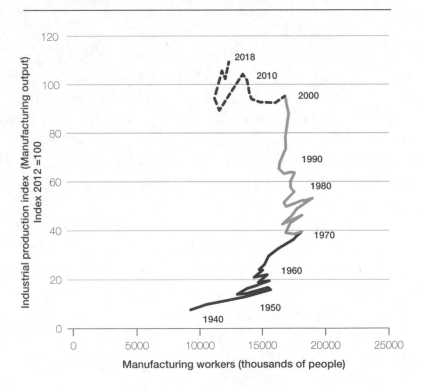

SOURCES: All Employees, Manufacturing, from US Bureau of Labor Statistics, retrieved from Federal Reserve Bank of St. Louis (FRED); Industrial Production Index, from Board of Governors of the Federal Reserve System, retrieved from FRED.

The predictions of the automation discourse *might* come true eventually. We can't know for sure what the future holds, but we can certainly compare our time with the past. As robots arrived in midcentury factories, Americans became worried, engendering widespread "automation hysteria." In 1949 United Automobile Workers president Walter Reuther received a strange letter from a mathematician named Norbert Wiener, the father of cybernetics, the science of communications and automatic control systems in both machines and living things. Wiener represents a kind of real-life Dr. Frankenstein, horrified by his own life-threatening creation, which escaped his control. He briefly described a specific servomechanism he had devised but refused to share with industry because he feared it would "undoubtedly lead to the factory without employees," predicting that "a critical situation is bound to arise under any conditions in ten to twenty years." Wiener continued:

I do not wish to contribute in any way to selling labor down the river, and I am quite aware that any labor, which is in competition with slave labor, whether the slaves are human or mechanical, must accept the conditions of work of slave labor. For me merely to remain aloof is to make sure that the development of these ideas will go into other hands which will probably be much less friendly to organized labor . . .

Under these circumstances, I should probably have to try to find some industrial group with as liberal and honest a labor policy as possible and put my ideas in their hands. I must confess, however, that I know of no group which has at the same time a sufficient honesty of purpose to be entrusted with these developments, and a sufficiently firm economic and social position to be able to hold these results substantially in their own hands.

He then suggested Reuther might "steal a march upon the existing industrial corporations in this matter" because, he added with alarming urgency, "these ideas are very much in the air."[7]

Reuther never challenged capital's control of technology as Wiener urged because he believed that fighting to harness the benefits of automation was a better strategy than fighting against it. But his union didn't lie down either. The UAW struck for almost the whole month of May that year, an action remembered as a "defense against being exhausted by overwork." GM's plan to raise its employees' wages involved having Congress legislate a forty-five-hour workweek to replace the traditional forty-hour week. But the UAW fought back. At the union's convention, Reuther, who mostly opposed shorter hours, opined from the podium, "We insist that reductions in the unit cost of production must be made possible by improved technology and production processes . . . and not by placing an unfair workload on workers."[8]

The next year the UAW signed its landmark contract with GM, the so-called Treaty of Detroit, which guaranteed a "cooperative attitude" on the introduction of labor-saving technology. In practice, this meant that wages were tethered to productivity increases but that workers lost much of their power to negotiate where, when, and how technology was used. Still, as wages in the auto industry continued to rise and hours declined—less work for more money—autoworkers were the envy of most other industrial producers.

Against that backdrop and with an expanding welfare state that ensured that workers displaced by technological advances found similarly paying employment elsewhere, it wasn't joblessness that concerned Americans then, but idleness. "Mankind's major struggle will be against boredom," explained an article in *Parade* in 1959, "with the suicide rate zooming as people lose the race." In 1964 the science fiction writer Isaac Asimov penned an op-ed in the *New York Times* titled "Visit to the World's Fair of 2014," in which he expressed his concern that mass automation would transform future generations into an idle race of "machine tenders."[9] A decade later the Department of the Interior drafted its Nationwide Outdoor Recreation Plan. It declared, "Leisure, thought by many to be the epitome of paradise, may well become the most perplexing problem of the future." The prospect of a world without work—or at least much less of it—was in the air.

The fear of idleness became a real crisis of joblessness, however, as the heart of the industrial economy saw significant hours increases and unemployment. In the late seventies, workers began vehemently denouncing unemployment associated with factory robots. In 1957, three autoworkers produced thirty-six vehicles per hour, but by 1977 that had increased to fifty-four. During the same time period, the transportation equipment industry increased its output by 93 percent while employment only grew 16 percent (a decline of 244,000 employees), and the primary metals industries shed 218,000 jobs. In testimony before the Senate, UAW Local 22 president Frank Runnels showed that from 1955 to 1976, a 3 percent increase in industrial manufacturing jobs produced a 125 percent increase in output. These basic facts suggest that incremental shifts in efficiency were able to erase a shocking number of jobs. But evidence for the effects of automation doesn't mean automation is the cause of those effects. It's likely that the impacts of higher productivity and output in basic industries are caused by a multitude of factors, not just, and perhaps not principally, automation.[10]

Longer hours play a role too. Runnels understood this, testifying that industrial workers have it good "if they are willing to work seventy to eighty hours a week working for substandard wages in a nonunion shop." Unions lobbied for federal legislation to shorten the workweek to save jobs, but instead the opposite happened. Part of the way the US economy produced more with the same number of people was by extending hours, enforcing overtime, and busting unions. By the year 2000 manufacturing workers were putting in two more weeks per year than they were in 1975. As more women entered the workforce during this time, married couples increased their combined paid hours at work by almost 20 percent, a change that mostly showed up in the service economy. Still, those left behind in the factories today work longer and faster than their parents or grandparents, producing more by working harder.[11]

Indeed, this time *is* different, but not for the reasons the automation discourse suggests. The main difference has to do with our contemporary economy, not the kinds of robots we have. The churning nature of automation is a steady feature of capitalist history. A significant number of jobs we did half a century ago no longer exist, and there's reason to expect that trend to continue without wiping out employment altogether. Automation contributed to the decline of the workweek for most of the twentieth century because it led to rising productivity, a change often embraced by many industrial workers whose jobs were dirty and dangerous, and whose unions were strong enough to exercise some control over the profits they generated. Up until the 1970s, new technologies that helped workers produce more translated into higher pay, but also the chance to trade some wage gains for leisure, even as their standard of living continued to rise. According to economists Deborah Sunter and Rene Morissette, "It was in employers' interest to accommodate worker and union demands for more free time."[12]

Today, however, the mere specter of automation is often a convenient scapegoat for keeping wages low, hours long and unpredictable, and management control high. In a *Washington Post* article headlined "Minimum-Wage Offensive Could Speed Arrival of Robot-Powered Restaurants," Lydia DePillis reiterates a tale meant to chasten would-be unionists fighting for fair wages. Others cynically referred to the Fight for $15 campaigns as the Robot Employment Act. The message is clear: *Raise your wage too high and the robots will be clocking in tomorrow instead of you.* This could, of course, be an argument in favor of higher wages, not against them, so long as there's a process to ensure that workers kicked off the burger assembly line can share the benefits of their jobs disappearing. Most of us can agree that a world with a less labor-intensive fast food industry seems idyllic, not to mention more appetizing. Should we welcome Flippy, the world's first "autonomous robotic kitchen assistant" from CaliBurger, or keep wages and benefits so low that it is cheaper to treat humans like machines? The answer is obvious even if the consequences aren't—bring on the burger bots but only under terms favorable to displaced workers.[13]

Those favorable terms are hard to come by, which is why the fearmongering has been so effective. Neoliberalism imposes fetters on the potential gains from labor-saving technology because they always accrue to a ruling elite, the owners of robots, or those close to them in the social hierarchy. It's not surprising that workers are scared of automation. Recent surveys by the Pew Research Center show that American workers are more afraid of being replaced by robots than by immigrants, are hesitant to apply for jobs in which applicants are sorted by algorithms, and strongly believe automation will drive down wages. As so many workers complain of being treated like robots, it's reasonable to believe they'll be easily replaced by them. Yet it's not new immigrants or advanced robots we should fear, but the same old strategies bosses have always used to keep workers in line.[14]

In contrast to the automation of sixty years ago, automation is happening today against a backdrop of precarious work, low wages, declining unionization, long hours, and a shrinking welfare state. This time we fear not idleness but destitution, for without a strong workers' movement the loss of a job means the loss of a livelihood. When workers were displaced from midcentury factories, they were largely able to find similarly paying work elsewhere. Not so today, as there's some evidence that automation actually contributes to the growth of low-wage jobs. This happens through what's known as Moravec's paradox, the finding that robots tend to be good at difficult tasks but comparably bad at things humans find easy. The result is that we increasingly automate tasks that involve high-level cognition or complex data processing, but after years and years of trying we still can't build a robot that can fold laundry.

There's also evidence of upskilling, of course, as automation has created jobs in which humans interact with computers in complex ways, forcing them to develop new skills for which they can demand a higher wage. The more educated workers are, the more likely they are to believe that technology has increased their opportunities or made their job more interesting or even lucrative. Blue-collar workers with less education, however, tend to fear robots far more. These findings suggest that less economic security correlates to a higher fear of robots and workplace automation. As debates about automation have gone mainstream, bosses have been let off the hook because robots themselves take the blame. And as sophisticated as bots have become, they still can't speak for themselves. But there's no shortage of those willing to be their enthusiastic advocates.[15]

•

HIREBOTICS COFOUNDERS Matt Bush and Rob Goldiez set out to solve a perplexing problem they'd seen in their twenty years of manufacturing across the country—people don't want to work in factories anymore. Ending up on the assembly line, once a paradigmatic pathway to the American Dream, has, according to them, become the antithesis of success. They claim that young people see these jobs as boring, meaningless, old-fashioned, and unsafe, inadvertently reviving a critique that was popular among student leftists in the sixties. "We're trying to change that perception," Bush said. To do that, he and Goldiez looked past the traditional strategies to attract workers—higher wages, better safety conditions, stronger unions, shorter hours—to a different idea. "We wanted to make it just as easy to hire a robot as it is to hire a person," said Bush, adding, "and just as easy to fire one too."

That's what's most fascinating about Hirebotics, the leading robot rental service in the country. Yes, Bush and Goldiez have managed to fill employment gaps when firms needed them filled. And they've pioneered a way to profit for the full time their robots are working by billing not by the hour but by the second. They've even decreased the sunk costs associated with expensive automation projects, thereby spurring the wider use of industrial robots where they were previously out of reach for smaller and midsize firms.

But their biggest selling point is not that they're quick or cheap, but that they're easy. They have reimagined robots as if they were human workers, except that their ideal of a human worker is one who is treated like a robot. "The main difference is that our workers have electrons instead of neurons," Bush said, as if our interview was a *Shark Tank* pitch. Their actual sales pitch is a cost-benefit analysis between hiring a "traditional employee," represented as unproductive, unreliable, expensive, and inconsistent, or hiring one of their robots, which monitor their own productivity, work eighty-hour weeks, and never go on strike.

By combining capitalist common sense with a simple value proposition—our robots are better than your humans—Bush and Goldiez have tripled their client base since 2018. It also helps that their price point is right. Their robots cost about seventeen dollars an hour, which is competitive with mean wages in industrial manufacturing, according to the Bureau of Labor Statistics. It wasn't long ago that industrial robots were largely mammoth creatures performing mechanized tasks in confined spaces. But as bots have become more complementary to human-oriented tasks, they've been, well, humanized. Hirebotics appreciates that blurring of the human/machine dichotomy. So does Amazon.

When I visited the Amazon robotics factory outside Boston, I was told that ramping up tens of thousands of Kiva robots wasn't going to displace jobs, but simply help Amazon meet its growing demand for faster delivery. Indeed, its fleet of warehouse workers grew 50 percent in 2017. One day the skies will be filled with buzzing delivery drones, a technologist I met with said, but that won't come at the expense of warehouse or mail room jobs, at least not at Amazon. Yet Amazon and other online retailers have displaced many more workers in brick-and-mortar retail than they have created, and because labor is the most costly aspect of business in warehouse work, it makes sense that Amazon's own staff will eventually be made redundant. Ultimately, however, the fear of joblessness distracts us from a potentially worse alternative: that humans will end up doing robots' jobs.[16]

Mechanical Turk, or MTurk for short, is Amazon's on-demand labor brokerage platform, where workers can sign up to get paid to perform short tasks, called HITS, that are posted by job sellers called Requesters. It has become common for researchers to use the site to administer surveys, transcribe interviews, and train AI systems. Kristy Milland has earned the dubious distinction of becoming one of the world's most well-known Mechanical Turkers, with a hard-earned story that resonates across the online "clickworker" community, the newish designation for those whose labor takes the form of short tasks like tagging, categorizing, transcribing, or annotating web-based content.

Need computer-based work done quickly and cheaply? Want to circumvent decent labor standards? Amazon Mechanical Turk is your one-stop shop. Tag these images (body, head, car, building, door, etc.) for one cent a tag, complete this survey for twenty cents a page, identify colors or images on the screen to help computers learn the difference between a cat and lemur. A 2018 study found that although workers in the United States earn fifty to eighty cents of every dollar of value they generate, Turkers make about twenty cents, with the remaining eighty going directly to the platform.[17]

The name Mechanical Turk is taken from an eighteenth-century machine called the Turk, which was exhibited throughout Europe as an autonomous chess-playing apparatus. It was actually an elaborately constructed box that housed a human player who famously defeated opponents across the world, including Benjamin Franklin and Napoleon Bonaparte. Amazon has its own version of the hoax, coyly maintaining the illusion that the platform, not workers, is performing all the work. Sometimes Turkers don't know the details of the job they're selecting until they've received their directions, and often the entity selling the labor is obscured as well.

That was the case when Milland conducted target practice for military drones, a job she suspects was posted by the Department of Defense. She described to me one such HIT:

> The video was black and sepia, and it was shot from the air so that you would see somebody from, like, above and behind. And they were typically in a dirt area, which matters when you think about the outcome of it in the end. They were often walking away from a vehicle, and so the training was, let's say, five video stills. I had to identify where the person was in image one, and then where the person was in image five. And then after a while they would just show you shot one and say, Where will they be in five frames? We were training drones to know, in this amount of time, where the person would be. It was an algorithm training for drones. And the only reason to know that is to shoot a projectile at them, because you would shoot it at frame one, but it needs to hit them at frame five.

Milland has identified images of Islamic State soldiers holding baskets of decapitated human heads and drawn little boxes around the bodies of children in illegal pornography. She has coded violent animal abuse and identified child predators for police authorities. If you've never seen these things during your morning online scroll, you have people like Kristy Milland to thank, workers who scrub the toxic images off the public Internet.

If you've ever had your expense report done on time via an online service, that's her too. Expensify advertises itself as an AI-powered tool for submitting expense reports. "Our patented OCR technology automatically reads and codes the receipt details for you, then adds the receipt to an expense report that can be automatically submitted, approved, and even reimbursed," its site says. "We do all that," says Milland, with a hint of indignation. "Receipts would come to us and we would transcribe it. It went to us for years until one of the MTurk activists outed them on Twitter. We're actually physically doing the work, we're the ones putting it [the receipt] through."

This work, which has been called ghost work or fauxtomation, reifies technology and obscures the human labor being performed. As Milland sees it, that's the main selling point of MTurk. "Amazon attempts to make us invisible, hiding us as if we're an algorithm," she says. "A lot of AI is just stuff on MTurk or other sites where we're doing the work as a human. But companies tell clients they use AI." The workers' invisibility is guaranteed not only through the anonymity of the platform or company advertisements, but also through the independent contractor status of the Turkers themselves. They have no rights as workers, no voice as workers, no identity as workers. "Talk to Amazon warehouse workers, Amazon Mechanical Turk workers, Amazon janitors—all of these people who have organized, they always say the same thing: 'We are not robots,'" says Milland. "What we have in common is that we're all made to feel like robots at one time or another. That and the fact that we're all independent contractors."

For Milland the work has been hardly invisible—it shows up on her body. She began working in 2010 when her husband was laid off from his factory job. It started as a side hustle to make extra cash but soon bloomed into a near-24/7 job. She would sleep on the floor of her home office so she could be alerted by a computer noise when certain well-paying HITS became available. After almost a decade on the platform, she has the battle scars of vet-eran industrial workers. She developed carpal tunnel syndrome, tennis elbow, and a ganglion cyst on her wrist. She tore her tra-pezius muscle from her shoulder blade as a result of repetitive motion and now suffers pain in her cervical spine from so much time spent sitting and clicking. She gained more than one hun-dred pounds, which caused heart problems, and she has experi-enced PTSD-like symptoms from the content moderation work.

The intensity and degradation of the work encouraged her to improve platform labor. Occasionally, workers can invert the invisibility foisted on them by labor law and company culture—as Milland did by founding Turker Nation, a forum of online workers who fight back against exploitation in the digital realm and offer assistance to other Turkers by pointing them toward high-paying HITS. "The invisibility is a weapon," says Milland, "because the second we terminate it, the second we become visi-ble, the system seems to upend."

Turker Nation uses social media shaming to call attention to particularly exploitative job sellers. The best example might be the letter-writing campaign Dear Jeff Bezos, launched via Dynamo, a website created by sympathetic academics to help coordinate actions by Turkers. Timed around Christmas of 2014, the campaign urged Turkers to write Amazon's CEO directly with their grievances, but especially to call attention to their rights as workers. The campaign (really more of a PR stunt) had three core demands: Turkers are human beings, not algorithms, and should be marketed accordingly; Turkers should not be sold as cheap labor, but instead as skilled, flexible labor that needs to be respected; Turkers need to have a method of representing them-selves to Requesters and the world via Amazon. No one, least of all Milland, thinks that a barrage of Christmas cards will turn Bezos into a compassionate capitalist. But a clickwork coopera-tive, or worker-owned platform, might be widely beneficial, even if all it did was push Amazon to reform its practices. "We'll never change Amazon without pressuring them through competition, and a co-op could do that," says Milland.

Clickworkers would benefit from a cooperative structure, but also from simple workplace regulations, exactly the kinds of things that robot enthusiasts often oppose. As much as workers tend to fear robots, sometimes for the wrong reasons, roboticists and employers are often irrationally afraid of regulation. "Manufacturing should be as efficient and effective as possible," Hirebotics's Matt Bush told me, as sure as if it were catechism. "There's no reason to hold back progress." Nothing is more reactionary than flaunting the idea of industrial progress without a proposal to share the gains with the vast majority of people. Ultimately, we need a vision not just for the future of work, but for the future of workers.

In talking to labor leaders, I uncovered a surprising number of ways in which today's unions have instituted policies to govern the use of workplace technology. The fights aren't as connected to public debates about long hours as they were in the middle of the twentieth century, but unions are slowly facing the challenge and potential that robotization poses this time around. Janitorial and hospitality workers' unions in some major cities have provisions in their contract that curtail management's absolute right to replace workers with robots. Such protections against displacement are becoming common where low-level service workers are unionized. The Las Vegas Culinary Union, which claims that its most recent contract has "groundbreaking" protections for workers, gives them a high degree of control over how technology affects their jobs. That's good news, given the fact that Sin City now employs robot bartenders, touchpad ordering restaurant systems, and even robots on its stripper poles.[18]

Another particularly enlightened job-saving agreement came about between Kaiser Permanente and SEIU, whose chart room workers were at risk of losing their jobs when the company moved to electronic medical records in 1997. A major problem with paper charts is illegible doctor handwriting, which leads to prescription delays, inaccurate test analyses, and thus wrong-headed diagnoses and aftercare. They are also occasionally lost or misplaced. The union-management collaboration on electronic medical records meant that sensible automation entered the workplace with relative ease, without job loss, and with benefits for patients. Kaiser followed an agreement that management and union coalition leaders created to govern "the effects of the technological change on the workforce," which included new contract language on job and wage security, the creation of new jobs in the bargaining unit, and a fund to address training needs. Additionally, Kaiser addressed job security concerns by preparing displaced workers for new positions within the company. The partnership was established unevenly across the country, making it easy to compare places where it was especially strong because it was in those places where the technological advances were the smoothest.[19]

In addition to giving workers the power to control the kinds of technology used in the workplace, there are other ways to check the power employers exert through tech. For example, we could tax robots, an idea endorsed by Bill Gates, himself a kind of robot in desperate need of taxing.

History shows that workers benefit from technology the most when they have power to determine how and when it's used. Only a fraction of the American workforce even has a union. But if workers had more control and fewer risks to their livelihood to fear, they could embrace the gains associated with automation in the interest of bringing about a less work-intensive, more robot-dense employment landscape. And that big "if" brings us to the policy solution du jour: universal basic income, or UBI.

Now that wages are decoupled from productivity, the next logical step might just be to decouple income from work. It seems simple enough, which is partly why it's so seductive, championed superficially by a politically ambiguous group of adherents.

Charles Murray, the right-wing author of *The Bell Curve*, thinks it's a vehicle to abolish federal welfare programs, including poverty relief, Pell Grants, Head Start, school lunch, and more. Silicon Valley titans like Elon Musk and Mark Zuckerberg, and futurists like Martin Ford, think it will be necessary to provide a cushion of consumption dollars to save capitalism when technological unemployment threatens the stability of the free market. They're motivated more by fear of major firms' declining profitability than by concerns about the livelihoods of those without jobs.

For the most part, however, the socialist left was the wellspring of UBI. Martin Luther King Jr. advocated it, many feminists prefer it to the old call of "wages for housework," and a growing cohort of young radicals see it as a path to "fully automated luxury communism." Hard work has its apostles but also its apostates. A new brand of technophilic Marxists, called accelerationists, casts workers as active campaigners for "full automation" to "abolish work." To them, full automation must be accompanied by a robust basic income, not to stave off capitalism's collapse but to speed it up. A UBI was endorsed by the Black Lives Matter movement as part of its reparations platform. To further distinguish the left view from its more recent right-wing appropriation, some have proposed a UBI-plus, a supplement to existing welfare state provisions, not a stand-alone policy.[20]

Basic income is a fine idea, and a robot tax could raise some of the money to pay for it, allowing workers to live off the dividends of machine-made profit. It's faulty logic, however, to link basic income to technological unemployment. Automation only helped us free up time when unions were stronger. Otherwise, it drove labor out of the equation, replacing it with docile, efficient, voiceless automata. As the sociologist Judy Wajcman writes, the technological determinists "shy away from addressing the extent to which the pursuit of profit, rather than progress, shapes the development of digital technologies on an ongoing basis, and the ways in which these very same technologies are facilitating not less work but more worse jobs."[21]

The fierce debates about a basic income policy are often framed as a for-or-against dichotomy. In most cases, however, the varied versions are all seen as means to an end, a libertarian free-market paradise on the right or the capitalist road to communism on the left. These arguments are mistaken. Basic income could be the outcome of a struggle for more time, but it won't be the pathway to it. Current experiments with basic income see it as an antidote to the historic weakness of labor power, a kind of consolation prize that will support us once all those jobs are gone, or even something that can stimulate work effort. But we won't get something as good as basic income without first getting far more control over time and technology. That should be our priority. Automation can only move us closer to diminishing toil if there is far greater society-wide control of technology and time.

The AFL-CIO has grown more interested in automation to produce a thirty-two-hour workweek. In 2018 Richard Trumka, the federation's president, responded to questions about how prepared union members are for a robot takeover. He redirected the question toward politics and employer strategy, not technology, insisting that "a generation of bad policy choices have created an economy where many new industries have grown up with no unions at all." He clarified that labor is in no way opposed to tech, offering the example that modern autoworkers are embracing exoskeleton technology. Based on the conviction that "automation should mean even greater prosperity for us to share in," he said labor "can demand a world where the gains from technology translate into better pay and working conditions for everyone, where being more productive means we can work less and live more, where artificial intelligence allows us to have better, safer, and more interesting jobs."[22] Trumka's optimism is heartening, a good reminder that robots are the product of human hands, and can be likewise controlled by their creators.

While writing this book I met with a handful of roboticists, but none who understood this fundamental truism quite like Dr. D. One day in May I found myself out in a University of Nebraska–owned soybean field flying robots with Carrick Detweiler. We were joined by Jacob Hogberg, an electrical engineer, and Adam Plowcha, a veteran navy helicopter pilot who was now a graduate research assistant for Detweiler—Dr. D, as Plowcha called him. As a young leader in field robotics, Detweiler cofounded the university's Nebraska Intelligent MoBile Unmanned Systems Lab to undertake his research, combining effective robotics with government and scientific exploration. A legal roadblock appeared immediately in the form of a state law that required some kinds of drone operators to have a private pilot's license. So Detweiler promptly learned to fly a Cessna, which is what resourceful geniuses do. He has so far failed, however, in his mission to convince his wife that they need to *own* a Cessna. "She thinks we need a college fund," he says, pointing toward a child's car seat.

Since leaving MIT as a graduate student, Detweiler has built robots for land, sea, and air that the Department of Defense uses for . . . well, he doesn't quite know, because it's, you know, the Department of Defense. On this day, the robot took off when Plowcha started its whirring engine, and it hovered for a few seconds before flying to a pre-programmed location across the field. Then it gingerly descended, landing in the soft soil, as its 3D-printed bit drilled into the ground with such precision it barely made a sound. Once the hole was the appropriate depth, the robot deposited a trackable sensor, then flew back and landed in front of us.

This particular robot allows government workers access to dense forests and mountainous terrain that they wouldn't otherwise have. Detweiler's other robots have flown over lakes to test water samples for scientific evaluation and around the periphery of forest fires to drop golf-ball-size explosives that help contain the fires' spread. His research has focused on expanding the reach of human workers by allowing deep exploration where manned missions are either too expensive, time-consuming, or dangerous.

At one point one of the drones failed to launch. After a rather lengthy investigation as to why, it turned out that two wires had simply become disconnected. "Robotics is the science of cables and connectors," Detweiler said. His point was not just about robots; it relates to automation and jobs. Robots are merely built devices, under human control, despite popular Frankenstein-esque fantasies of them outpacing their human creators. Likewise, robots don't replace workers—employers do. And they don't have to.

"The only real issue is whether robots take our jobs or help us do them better," Detweiler said, succinctly summarizing much of the automation debate. In other words, the real question is whether we, as a society, see robots replacing or augmenting human labor. When most people think of automation, they assume it means that machines are replacing human workers, and that's one definition. Robots can also assist human workers, making them more productive, or replace only certain tasks. The difference is between a robot that can completely replace me as a college professor and one that can only grade papers, thereby freeing up my time to do something else, or simply decreasing my overall labor time by a significant amount. I'll admit there are days when I think a robot could do my job. In fact, there are many days when I wish it would.

"The only thing we have to fear," Detweiler said, "is letting the power to make that decision slip away from us."

Detweiler is correct—almost. It's not the *only* thing to fear in this debate. There's another fear, more an existential threat, that has gained greater purchase as robots have occupied more of the news recently. What if automation takes our jobs and, with them, a major source of meaning in our lives? There has been a turn toward valuing work not only for its monetary rewards, which have been significantly eroded, but for its power to enhance our individual sense of self. In other words, even if we could afford to live without work, via a basic income or by some other means, would our time be less rich with a lack of purpose? The threat of a robot takeover raises questions that cut to the core of our humanness. But why are our jobs such a source of identity to begin with? I turn to this question next, and examine the ways that a shift in how we think about work affects the amount of time we spend doing it.

CHAPTER 5

MORE THAN MONEY

CHANGES IN AMERICAN CAPITALISM—HISTORIC INEQUALITY, the rollback of worker power, technological revolutions—have led to the paradox of long hours, underemployment, and volatile schedules. These changes pushed low-income workers into jobs that they've been powerless to shape. And no matter how long or hard they work they aren't getting ahead, and still live in fear of being displaced by migrants, machines, or management's latest trick.

Some of those same factors have pulled middle- and upper-class workers toward longer hours as well. But we need a fuller accounting for the work time of those who, by dint of their status and occupation, are lucky to have more discretion at work and control over their time, yet still work more than anyone else. Salaried professionals aren't necessarily earning more money as they stay at work long after their bosses have gone home. To better understand this phenomenon, we need to look inside the cultures of today's workplaces, particularly at a new gospel of work arguing that our time is enriched through hard work even if our paychecks aren't.

The concept of meaningful work has served as a kind of cultural scaffolding, what social scientists call a superstructure, for the building of a long-hours economy. It's not that beliefs about meaningfulness have forced us to work longer. Rather, those beliefs prompt us to look for individual value in a job rather than to transform our economy so that it works for everyone. Because of this popular ideology, the demands of the modern workplace seem like less of an imposition and more of a pathway to fulfillment.

This cultural shift is the outcome of roiling discontent within two different kinds of workplaces since the seventies—the white-collar woes and the blue-collar blues. For a while it seemed these complaints reflected not only the exploitative nature of work, but also the prophetic demands of the New Left. Campus activists, feminists, and even young technologists sought to rescue work from its alienating quality—or to abolish it altogether. The new "politics of identity" also encouraged young workers to look inside themselves and to seek out career opportunities that reflected an inner authenticity.

Then an expanding class of managers and supervisors stepped in. They intercepted these new demands for meaningful jobs and repackaged them as a new ideology of work. The result was the popular discourse on meaningful work we have today, where finding personal worth and fulfillment in one's job has become, in a sense, part of the job itself. This managerial revolution was successful because it seemed to deliver something we already desired. Today, however, the promise of meaningful work rests on the victories of neoliberal capitalism, not as an alternative to the deadening reality of lifelong labor.

The result of this change wasn't actually more good jobs, but an increased emphasis on the noneconomic benefits of hard work. The significance of these events is rarely appreciated, because we typically think of the notion of meaningful work as an individual preference rather than a society-wide shift. But part of the story of rising hours in America, especially among higher earners, is this: as work became a larger source of individual meaning, more of it became better.

At first blush, the concept of meaningful work seems to resolve a fundamental problem, a synecdoche for all of work's exploitative and alienating qualities. It indulges our interests, helps complete our identity, hones our skills through practice, and contributes to a better society. Whereas we loathe dedicating hours to pointless tasks that don't enrich our sense of self, even if they earn us money, meaningful work offers a viable alternative. Our jobs can reflect our values and improve our sense of self-worth by offering a positive account of who we are to others. In that sense, we rely on work to serve an individual and social function far beyond its economic rewards.

To comprehend this phenomenon one must begin with the corporate ecosystem nestled in the foothills of the Santa Cruz Mountains, the global center of high tech and social media, headquarters to a few dozen Fortune 1000 companies and an untold number of startups. Silicon Valley is not just a place that makes apps. It's a philosophy, a dreamscape, a *realm*. All that and a TV show to boot.

The scions of tech launched a revolt against the relentless conformity of cubicle life, a movement to overcome the anomie plaguing so many offices across the country—the white-collar woes. Jobs were boring, hours were long, life was short, and a critical mass of young computer geeks thought there was a better way. Offices—once full of lofty hopes about a more sociable future of work, the refuge of those spared the indignity of factory labor—had become partitioned wastelands of broken promises and dreams deferred. Indeed, by the late 1970s they had begun to feel much like factories themselves.

Detroit once meant cars, but the mention of Silicon Valley doesn't just conjure up tech. It's where the counterculture went to cash in. Plugging seamlessly into the relaxed, creative, liberal spirit that was then thought of as the definitive California culture, tech pioneers sought to transform the office into a petri dish that could spawn a cooler kind of capitalism. Today's tech companies inherited the managerial principles of such early Silicon Valley entrepreneurs as Robert Noyce, who founded Fairchild Semiconductor in the late 1950s as a "community," not a corporation. The passion Noyce brought to the workplace was accompanied by an equal vitriol for ordinary workers, much like at a major corporation, a tradition nobly carried forth by the doyens of the industry like Steve Jobs, Marc Andreessen, and Elon Musk.

By the early nineties, this ethos had become mainstream with the success of the computer and Internet companies that came to embody the New Economy. Although it is difficult to draw across-the-board conclusions about working conditions in Silicon Valley, of this there can be no doubt: Silicon Valley has played, and continues to play, a major role in fomenting the idea that we not only can but *should* derive a sense of meaningfulness from our work.

Silicon Valley was built by the ardent couriers of this new Zeitgeist, who proselytized that hard work and long hours were their own reward. In fact, work wasn't even work. In a 2009 interview Mark Zuckerberg explained Facebook's mission as such: "We don't build services to make money; we make money to build better services." In other words, Facebook, valued at $350 billion, sees itself as a nonprofit, using its resources for charitable ends. And it's not alone. "Your work is going to fill a large part of your life," Steve Jobs told the 2005 graduating class at Stanford, "and the only way to do great work is to love what you do." Did he really think no one would remember that his love affair with work was only possible because Apple products are assembled in Chinese sweatshops? The point isn't to highlight hypocrisy, but rather to understand the way the discourse around meaningful work is used as subterfuge, a mask for profit-making.[1]

I encountered this phenomenon firsthand a few years ago as an interloper in one of tech's most private spaces: I was kicked off a Google Bus for talking about John Maynard Keynes. I was leaving the Google campus in Mountain View after a day of interviews when the bus pulled up to ferry employees back to San Francisco's Mission District. Most of the big tech companies have buses like this, but they are routinely referred to as Google Buses, in the same way that all tissues are Kleenex. Google Buses have come to represent everything the world outside Silicon Valley hates about the tech takeover of northern California: though they are company-specific private coaches strictly for tech employees, they use public bus stops and clutter the narrow streets of the most desirable neighborhoods as they make their way to deliver Googleites to and from work. The buses are regularly stopped by street protests, graffitied, and vandalized.

I hopped on board, moved decisively, kept my head down, and took my seat. It was a great opportunity for research—a captive audience of subjects for the hour-long ride home, with the added allure of behind-enemy-lines reportage. It was dark inside, the shades having been drawn to prevent glare on ever-open laptop screens. No one spoke. Once the bus pulled into the carpool lane, I introduced myself to a group of people working at a fold-out table. Noting that the sun was setting after a long day at the Googleplex, I wondered if any of them thought that the company's well-known celebration of meaningful work was in tension with the excessive hours expected of employees.

"We work this way because we *want* to, not because we *have* to," someone said, sensing judgment on my part. I nodded assent and then mentioned that John Maynard Keynes once predicted technology and efficiency would deliver mankind from arduous work lives. Did they think Google might one day fulfill that promise?

"If so, we would be the last people to make use of it," he said.

Apparently, I needed a softer touch. I noticed one of them had a sticker of Scripture on his laptop that read, "Ezekiel 33:31." But before I could ask him about it, someone suggested that I might be a spy from a startup. "What are you even doing on this bus?" another asked. "It's private property." At first, I thought he was joking, but it soon became clear that a casual conversation about working hours was not in the cards. I endured the rest of the ride in tense silence until the bus pulled over and I was asked to leave. Someone even snapped a photo and threatened to call the police. So ended my first lecture on Keynesianism in Silicon Valley as well as my first, and only, ride on the Google Bus.

I had brought up Keynes because his was among the clearest early voices to speak of the potential repercussions, positive and negative, of economic abundance. In his famous 1930 address, "Economic Possibilities for Our Grandchildren," he forecast that within the coming century humanity would expand the world economy exponentially and create technological innovations in the workplace that would deliver a fifteen-hour workweek. But Keynes himself was not entirely optimistic. A truncated work-week might present a new conundrum: what would workers do with their excess leisure? For those buried in their laptops on the Google Bus, he needn't have worried.

People generally like working at Google. Despite long hours and chronic gender discrimination, which has inspired protests in the past few years, employees rank Google near the top of "great workplaces" in the annual ratings done by Glassdoor, the website where workers anonymously assess their employers. Surely this has something to do with the exalted position of Google in the cultural labor food chain. To be a roadie for the Stones is probably horrible work much of the time, but you're still a roadie for the Stones. The same status is attached to other tech companies too.

The doors to Facebook's front office are labeled "Sun Microsystems," a Silicon Valley sales giant that gradually drifted toward obscurity until Oracle, a database management company, acquired it in 2009. Facebook headquarters are located in the old Sun Microsystems building, and though Facebook overhauled most vestiges of the old company, the doors were kept on their hinges as enduring motivation for employees. As Lindsay, my personal

Facebook tour guide, told me, "Mark [Zuckerberg] thought it would be a good idea to leave these doors on here as a reminder of what happens when you don't work hard enough."

"What happens?" I ask.

"You die," Lindsay stated flatly. "Your competitors kill you."

"Who are Facebook's competitors?"

"We don't have any competitors," she said. "But you never know."

It is hard to argue with uncertainty in these uncertain times, but data suggests that young coders and engineers at Facebook, or virtually anyone for that matter, are not lacking motivation. As Lindsay explained, the old doors are kitschy; no one at Facebook needs external motivation. "We are here for us," she said, gesturing toward the patio full of employees eating lunch. "Not for the company. For the work."

Facebook popularized the all-inclusive workplace, a new twist on the paternalistic corporation of my grandfather's era. The company offers complimentary laundry services, three square meals a day, a hair salon, free transportation to and from work, and a sabbatical program called Recharge. Recharge encourages workers to take time off to recover from a hectic work schedule so that they can prepare to go back to work. "It's like your phone," one employee told me. "It dies a lot from overuse, so you have to recharge it. So you can kill it again."

These perks were hardly enough to win company loyalty. I wrongly assumed that Facebook was a tech worker's dream job. But few people stick around very long. Lindsay, who had just passed the three-year mark, described herself as a "fossil." It turns out many people were looking to meet others with whom they could launch a startup and try to out-Zuckerberg Zuckerberg.

"People in the Valley want to do something big," she said. "That's why people come here. It's more than money." When we were nearly done with the tour Lindsay mentioned a local bar, the Rosewood, a renowned magnet for tech workers where I was likely to meet others to interview and could "take in the scenery," as she put it.

The horseshoe-shaped entrance to the Rosewood Hotel and Bar is lined with Teslas and zero-emission motorcycles. In addition to its underfunded schools and hospitals, California is in the middle of a drought, but here is an oasis of excess. You can hear the wind brush through the palm fronds and high heels clacking on the cobblestone walkway. The interior of the Rosewood, a cross between a tawdry Ibiza club and a Vermont ski lodge, provides the perfect alchemy for tonight's unofficial theme: it's cougar night in Silicon Valley. Thursday nights developed a certain reputation after *Vanity Fair* profiled a duo of professional matchmakers who specialize in connecting older women with rich young tech bros. They're outnumbered, however, by those who just want to mingle after work. Or, as is often the case, to continue working while mingling. The bar is situated amid the money fueling the tech boom, and people say that deals get brokered in its cavernous interior.

"Those guys made Skype a thing," someone near me says. Apparently, that's how you strike up a conversation here, a place that simultaneously resembles a feudal estate and a capitalist paradise. His name is Nikil, and he's right: The venture capitalists at Andreessen Horowitz placed an early bet on Skype when others thought it would tank, and it paid off. Now they were the richest angel investors in the world.

Nikil's biography reads like a Silicon Valley archetype lured by money, meaning, and high hopes. He dropped out of Stanford in his first year, though his parents still don't know it, to work full time on a series of startups that all failed. Undeterred, he understands this is how it goes. Dropouts get rich here; everyone knows those stories. It just takes time and work. Prematurely silver-haired at the temples, he sees himself and those around him as part of a new California gold rush. But it's not money, exactly, that they're after. "We want something meaningful," he says, squinting into the setting sun, a moment that seemed like an outtake from the TV show *Silicon Valley*. "Something that's more than just money. That system doesn't work anymore."

But to succeed even on his own terms Nikil still needs money. He needs lots of money. In fact, he is here tonight looking to meet people like those gathered on the grounds below us, who will soon be on this balcony, as happens many Thursday nights. He and some friends have a virtual reality startup idea that desperately needs capital, but so far they have only been able to raise it from what are known as the Three Fs: friends, family, and fools.

"Some people come here to get laid, but I came to get paid," he says, laughing. Then he thinks a moment, and ads, "Both would be nice."

•

I CAME THERE in search of something too. Unlike Nikil, it was neither cougars nor capital. I came with a question: Why did we begin to search for meaningful work in the first place? To trace the history of an idea requires one to investigate the multiple headwaters of the stream. And I was convinced one ran through the Rosewood.

The clientele of the Rosewood stands in contrast to Thorstein Veblen's depiction of the wealthy in *The Theory of the Leisure Class*. His examination of turn-of-the-century wealth offered a vivid portrait of the rich committed to "conspicuous consumption," strategic buying practices that conferred on themselves status and honor. Whereas idleness and leisure were once markers of having made it, today the rich acquire prestige by flaunting their extreme commitment to work. Here was a group of relatively rich people, whose conception of self rested on their commitment to hard work, busyness, and long hours at the office. Veblen might suggest that today's well-off participate in a culture of "conspicuous busyness." When work was dirty, less was more; now that it's meaningful, more is better.

Douglas Coupland captured that kind of consummate passion for work in his prophetic 1995 novel, *Microserfs*, in which a group of nerdy engineers who hate their jobs at a fictional buttoned-down IBM move from Redmond, Washington, to Silicon Valley in search of more self-actualizing work. Their new home is literally the light of their life, constructed with just the right illumination streaming through plate-glass facades and spatial harmony to create beauty and intimacy. As they grow tired of chasing venture capital funding, which always seems just out of reach, one programmer has a startling revelation: "I would have come here for *nothing*. I never *had* to get paid. . . . It's never been the money. It rarely ever *is*. It wasn't with any of us—was it?"[2]

The real Google has never been far from Coupland's fictional world. "Do what you love" was the incantation I heard repeated ad nauseam, from low-level coders to more seasoned employees. Indeed, a growing trend among tech employers is to compete for recruits by offering nonmonetary perks, a practice that, according to industry insiders, is exactly what employees want. "We're seeing people taking a lower offer if the project they get to work on aligns more with their own goals," Rishon Blumberg, of the recruiting agency 10x Ascend, told CNBC.

Google is hardly a monolith, however. During my tour through tech country I heard more than a few dissenting voices. That night at the Rosewood I met a Google engineer named Mike, and I mentioned my run-in with his colleagues on the Google Bus. "Google thinks that if we have meaningful jobs we will prefer them to the other parts of our lives," he said. "Hence, more work. Everywhere you look you hear people talking about meaning. They aren't philosophers. They aren't psychologists. They sell banner ads. What do they know about meaning? I love this job. But that doesn't mean I need it to save my soul."

Mike has access to the company's "twenty percent program," which offers him the right to pursue side projects for one-fifth of his workweek. The idea is to allow employees to follow a degree of whimsy and their own curiosity. But he never uses that time. "That's for younger guys," he said, though he was not yet forty. "I clock in and clock out. It's not a popular view around here, but it works for me." Mike further emphasized that he's in the minority where he works: "You know what I'd like to do? I'd like to go home 20 percent earlier."

If much work is soul-crushing drudgery, meaningful work promises the opposite—work that is creative, artistic, and social. This seductive possibility calls to mind Karl Marx's remark about human nature, which he explains by noting the difference between the worst of architects and the best of bees—the former erects the structure first in the mind; the latter builds on instinct. The creative imagination at work is, in other words, the most fundamental hallmark of our humanity. Yet Marx was also concerned that work is necessarily alienating under capitalism, entailing for the worker a "labor of self-sacrifice," "the loss of his self," and "self-estrangement."

Meaningful work that engages a greater part of the self could resolve the jejune character of the modern workplace. But feminists have long claimed that the kinds of emotional labor that entail a fuller investment of the self are often even more alienating than those that allow us to draw a stark line between work and nonwork time.

Nevertheless, tech's prevailing ideology of meaningful work often appears genuinely revolutionary. What began as an ethos within the California counterculture—an understandable rejection of the alienating gray-green monotony of midcentury cubicle life—soon became a new spirit of capitalism. Employer strategies amplified by an army of human resource managers have developed workplace cultures that foster greater participation, input, and loyalty from workers, even as the workplace retreats from its commitments to them.

And we pay dearly for it. As the former head of People Operations at Google, Laszlo Bock, put it, "We [Google] shifted

programs from providing monetary awards to experiential
awards . . . [so that] recipients focus on the fact of what they get
to experience, rather than calculating values." "Money is fungi-
ble," he adds, "and fades from memory." Money has also faded
from paychecks, if not in Silicon Valley, then most everywhere
else. And the promotion of meaningful work by corporate executives has been a strategy to avoid giving it back. Which reminds
me of that verse from Ezekiel stickered to the laptop on the
Google Bus: "With their mouths they express devotion, but their
hearts are hungry for unjust gain."[3]

•

TECH COMPANIES DID not invent the idea that work should be
meaningful, but they certainly helped propel it into the mainstream. The concept, with its inherent desirability, is widely
accepted as an important goal across most industries today. But
that was not always the case.

Aristotle argued that leisure, not work, was the sphere of life
in which our true selves can be realized, where humans strive for
perfection. How to fill our free time had long been *the* question
of a purpose-driven life. The rise of capitalism gave way to a new
conceptualization of both work and the self. Well into the nineteenth century, the home and workshop were still central features of the economic landscape. Whatever else they produced,
they also created the moral vision for work in early modern
America. Self-employed farmers, artisans, shopkeepers, and mer-
chants labored largely without direct supervisors or managerial
oversight. The rise of these "masterless men," as the philosopher
Elizabeth Anderson calls them, undermined the legitimacy of
traditional authority based on divinity, blood, charisma, or inherited wealth. When self-employment was the dominant form, the
concepts of freedom and liberty were inherently linked to cottage
industry. There was nothing good about a job. "If any continue
through life in the condition of the hired laborer," Abraham

Lincoln argued, "it is not the fault of the system, but because of either a dependent nature which prefers it, or improvidence, folly, or singular misfortune."[4]

Then the factories came. The "satanic mills," as Marx called them, became a new symbol of economic progress. As large employers collected vast swaths under dark roofs, transforming independent laborers into wage workers, a new ethic was born. The romanticized world of the artisan was now mere nostalgia, and there soon emerged a new lust for the manager—the eyes, ears, and brains of a new kind of capitalism. The rising bourgeoisie in early capitalist countries distinguished themselves from the parasitic aristocracy by focusing on their own status as a productive class. Their sense of worth, and their claim to power, was predicated on their work ethic, which they saw as generating the true wealth of society. Working-class movements later took up nearly the same position. You had to sell your labor to survive, but that work also served a socially useful function by producing the things we need to live happy lives. Workers' meaning as a class was derived from their claim to being providers of the common good. These conceptions of work as including noneconomic markers of status are inherently social and class-oriented.

In the mid-nineteenth century, William Morris, the socialist champion of the Arts and Crafts movement, posed a famous dilemma: "meaningful work or useless toil?" Those were the choices afforded to a rich society. He believed the working class in general performed a socially valuable function, but derided the notion that all work was meaningful with a bitter aperçu: "a convenient belief to those who live on the labor of others." Yet there was indeed work, he said, that was "not far removed from a blessing." The crucial difference was that some work came with the hope, first and foremost, that it would ultimately bring well-deserved rest.[5]

Quite a different conception prevails today. Meaningful work isn't the guarantor of some hoped-for leisure, but rather a reason to work more. Moreover, the conception of meaningful work is far more focused on the significance that work bestows upon individuals, not classes. As work occupies more of our time, and leisure has become a self-indulgent luxury, we look to work for more individual meaning than we ever have before.

The graph below does not show the amount of meaningful work performed. That's impossible to quantify. It rather depicts how often the phrase "meaningful work" has appeared in English-language books in the past two hundred years. Until the early 1970s, it seems no one talked much about it. Then there was an explosion. Why?

The modern *search* for meaningful work, the notion that one *should* seek out work to fulfill an important part of oneself, is a recent phenomenon, and situates us squarely within the coordinates of neoliberalism. Sometime during the 1970s, a new kind of work ethic took shape, one that transformed work from a personal sacrifice into something we do for our own good. The overriding tension of the old work ethic was to strike the appropriate

FREQUENCY OF PHRASE
"MEANINGFUL WORK" IN BOOKS, 1800–2008

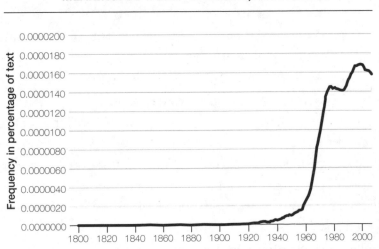

SOURCE: Google Books Ngram Viewer.

balance between leisure and employment, the self and self-denial. The sublime promise of the new work ethic is that there need not be any tension at all; work can fulfill the self.

The most popular explanations for this phenomenon today suggest that company culture has led us astray. In the *New York Times*, journalist Erin Griffiths says her generation "pretends" to love work. Lured by the vacuous promises of #hustleculture and the "do what you love" ideology, her fellow millennials foolishly waste the best years of their lives "performing workaholism." Derek Thompson, a writer at the *Atlantic*, argues that what he calls "workism" is "among the most potent new religions competing for congregants," a trend he says "defies economic logic." But what if it affirms economic logic? What if hustle culture is simply a corollary to hustle economics?

In 1972 the Senate Committee on Labor and Public Welfare convened a bizarre hearing on working-class alienation in American factories. Bizarre because it was usually Marxists, not the Senate, going on about alienated labor. The hearing addressed a countrywide crisis of worker discontent that involved detailed study of what came to be called the blue-collar blues. While white-collar workers were trying to revolutionize the office, industrial workers were demanding more engaging and personally satisfying work as well. Workers were overworked and, according to the committee, "increasingly dissatisfied by working conditions even if they are satisfied by their paycheck." The country outside the factory was "mesmerized by the industrial machine and unable to see the man behind the machine," which led to a situation in which "the non-economic needs of the worker have been forgotten . . . producing a class of angry and rebellious workers." The committee saw its job as to study this phenomenon and make recommendations that would "encourage the humanization of working conditions and the work itself," remedies that included more flexible schedules and a reduced workweek.[6]

At some point, the committee heard testimony from Dan Clarke, an autoworker from Lordstown, Ohio, site of famous wildcat strikes against speedups, long hours, and industrial monotony. Clarke addressed his union official, who was present at the hearing, and said that the UAW is "too concerned with wages and petty things. . . . They better start thinking of a man's mind and his relaxation."

Clarke's testimony is echoed by other workers, employers, and industrial experts whose names appear in the hundreds of pages of documents generated by the hearings. Together, they paint a picture of a restless working class, lobbying not for more money but for creative, engaging, meaningful, and fulfilling work.

The new ethos that work should be good for the self was not just the by-product of discontent, but of changes to the very structure of work itself. Over time, technological advances produced jobs that were less manual and routinized. With these

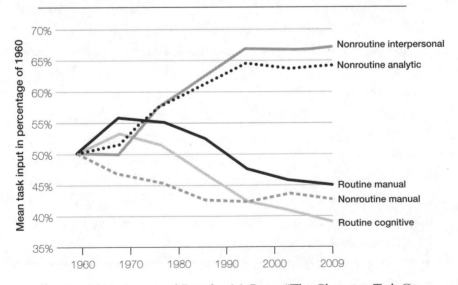

NONROUTINE TASKS ON THE RISE IN THE US LABOR MARKET

SOURCE: David H. Autor and Brendan M. Price, "The Changing Task Composition of the US Labor Market: An Update of Autor, Levy, and Murnane (2003)," MIT Mimeograph, Massachusetts Institute of Technology, 2013.

changes came a shift to a greater percentage of white-collar labor in the workplace.

The graph above indicates how nonroutine analytical and interpersonal work, as a percentage of overall employment, surpassed manual routine jobs in the early 1970s. As a result, over the past four decades work in general has required more human decision-making and cognitive input. A 1983 study by Daniel Yankelovich and John Immerwahr, conducted in the midst of these profound changes, found that increased job discretion—the degree of subjective input that workers have at work—helped give rise to the meaningful work discourse.[7]

"The move to a high discretion workplace has elevated the work ethic to a position of strategic importance," Yankelovich and Immerwahr write. "To the extent that managers can no longer stimulate effort through the existing reward system and through traditional methods of supervision, they must rely on the internal motivations of jobholders to guarantee high levels of effort and good quality work." In other words, when the economy was dominated by jobs in which one person could simply replace another on an assembly line, there was little rationale for looking for deeper meaning at work. But tasks that require initiative will only be completed if workers have a degree of buy-in and will do them without constant supervision. The new work ethic, replete with internal significance, arose when individual effort to master a particular task began to matter more in the production process.[8]

When a 1962 poll asked respondents to describe their "formula for success in today's America," a mere 6 percent cited a meaningful job. Twenty years later a similar question elicited 49 percent. Yankelovich made a career of documenting subtle changes in American public opinion, and he notes a clear trend toward "expressive" values, those that reflect a growing inwardness and introspection. In the mid-eighties Yankelovich found that "a significant number of jobholders now see self-development as their primary motivation for working."

The service sector expanded as the industrial factory landscape was under attack, and neoliberal elites broke the long-
standing practice of paying workers more money as they
produced more wealth. This is the signal achievement of business in recent American history. From the end of World War
II until 1973 gains in productivity were generally shared with
the workers who produced them. Relatively high wages and a
degree of shared prosperity meant that workers were motivated
first and foremost by money. Why did this matter for how we
think about work? As workers slowly lost their power, a historical bargain was broken, one where money was a "universal motivator" in exchange for arduous and routinized work.
That bargain has been slowly replaced with a new ideology of
meaningfulness.

In 1968, 58 percent of the public agreed that "hard work always
pays off." By the time Yankelovich and Immerwahr conducted
a similar survey in the early eighties, only one-third of workers endorsed this view. As the economic bargain began to break
down, so did the culture that connected work solely to money,
and thereby the work ethic in general.

Maybe that's why this joke was popular among midcentury business executives: "How many people work in your organization?"

"About half."

The quip may have been funny for a while, but by the early seventies, alongside a rising national anxiety about the work ethic,
it fell flat. Large macroeconomic changes can't be explained by
attitudinal shifts alone. Nonetheless, the idea that lazy or rebellious workers were making the country noncompetitive slowly
became widespread. Some of this thinking was just thinly dis-
guised capitalist shibboleth. "In their present temper," a report
by the American Management Association noted, workers
"would probably like nothing better than to down tools for a
rousing great strike."[9]

This certainly happened. Throughout the seventies, tens of thousands of workers took to the picket lines on wildcat strikes unsanctioned by even their own unions. A 1973 report published by the Department of Health, Education, and Welfare found that "dull, repetitive, seemingly meaningless tasks . . . are causing discontent among workers at all occupational levels. Worker dissatisfaction, measured by absenteeism, turnover rates, wildcat strikes, sabotage, poor quality products and a reluctance of workers to commit themselves to work tasks is crippling productivity in the workplace."[10]

Business leaders thus faced a double crisis. On the one hand, their profits had been declining after two decades of trade union activity limited the most excessive executive compensation schemes and kept regular people's wages up. On the other hand, their main assets for generating higher profits, regular workers, were too bored and alienated to be reliable. Lane Kirkland, then president of the AFL-CIO, captured this spirit of class struggle and resentment in one simple quip. "If hard work was so important," he told a reporter when asked about laziness on the job, "the rich would keep it all for themselves."

Frustrated by widespread reports of a crisis of the work ethic, William Batten, chairman of the New York Stock Exchange, declared that the "biggest challenge" business leaders faced was to "reorganize work in ways that will enable workers to derive satisfaction from it." Batten continued:

With dollar-compensation no longer the overwhelmingly most important factor in job motivation, management must develop a better understanding of the more elusive, less tangible factors that add up to "job satisfaction." . . . Perhaps the biggest problem today is to reorganize work in ways that will enable workers to derive satisfaction from it. . . . If we fail to develop the necessary philosophy and programs, we had better resign ourselves to coping with job tensions, attitudes and behavior that will limit productive output.

We typically assume that the search for meaningful work is the product of affluence. By the middle of the twentieth century it was self-evident that the specter of automation and declining hours would gradually erode our affection for hard work. Derek Thompson cites the writer Erik Barnouw, who argued in 1957 that "the increasing automatic nature of many jobs, coupled with the shortening of the work week [will lead] an increasing number of workers to look not to work but to leisure for satisfaction, meaning, expression." Today Barnouw's excessive optimism reads like a postcard from a quaint era of rising tides and shared prosperity. Moreover, the psychologist Abraham Maslow's pyramid of human needs tells us that before indulging our human desire for self-actualization, we must first attain a level of physical and economic security. This narrative is compelling because it suggests the search for meaningful work is the outcome of a historic achievement—economic and physical security—that prompted us to re-examine work for other kinds of rewards.[11]

But isn't it just the opposite? Workers' demand for meaningful, humanizing work emerged from the tiresome monotony of factories in the seventies, not in their comfortable affluence. And today, after decades of downward mobility, the unfulfilled promise of abundance defines our times. An increasing number of people are unable to find enough work to survive, and yet another cohort complains of overwork, a trend that mirrors economic inequality, not a rising prosperous tide. No, the popular search for meaningful work is the product of defeat, not victory. This attitudinal shift did not happen as work got better, but precisely when economic rewards for doing it began to decline, suggesting the notion of meaningful work, as we know it today, is thereby compensatory. The new work ethic saved capitalism from critique by reorienting its objectives toward the emotional and psychic needs of the self.

Management critics have long declared that strategies to motivate workers in a service economy are "surrogates for meaning." But they have it backward. Meaningful work wasn't eroded by high wages; meaning was introduced to make up for declining wages. In other words, managerial motivation was not a surrogate for meaning, but meaning was a surrogate for money. Career advice literature in the 1970s, beginning with Richard Bolles's *What Color Is Your Parachute?*, began encouraging workers to seek out professional paths that were basically secular versions of the Puritan's calling, stressing self-discovery and personal growth. By 1989, Marsha Sinetar's classic *Do What You Love, the Money Will Follow* laid out a plan for job seekers that prioritized the pursuit of passion above all else.

It is no coincidence that during a time of stagnating wages, the elite invocation to "do what you love" became, according to the writer Miya Tokumitsu, the "unofficial work mantra of our time." The directive to "take this job and love it" became so ingrained in our culture that the National Labor Relations Board tried to issue a legal ruling against it, in a case involving T-Mobile. The phone company had one rule preventing workers from saying negative things about the company and another prohibiting employees from arguing with one another. Nice try, said the NLRB, but its decision was later overruled by a court granting the company's right to enforce a "positive workplace environment."[12]

Lest you think preoccupation with meaning is merely a phenomenon among high-status workers, there are guides for workers in search of meaning in monotonous low-paying jobs. The business consultant Jessica Amortegui proposes that anyone can access the rewards derived from meaningful work as if it were a shot of wheatgrass. Feeling low about your job? She asks, "What could a boost of meaning at work do for you?" Strangely, there is some evidence that it's working. New research shows that younger Americans today tend to be more satisfied by their jobs than in the previous decade, even though hours have gotten worse and benefits and wages have barely budged. What seems to be happening, according to Gallup pollsters, is that after decades of disappointing work environments, we are simply lowering our expectations. Those polled claimed they were more satisfied with their jobs than they were a decade ago, even though they reported more complaints about the inflexibility of their hours and schedules.[13]

Workers in midcentury factories demanded more rewarding and meaningful jobs. Instead, they got a management culture that preached meaning but practiced a new kind of exploitation. Silicon Valley leaders rebelled against the man in the gray flannel suit. But it turns out that the man in the black turtleneck and the guy in the hoodie are just as committed to business discipline as their cultural forebears. Finding meaning at work, it turns out, is good for business. A study by economists Michael Kosfeld, Susanne Neckermann, and Xiaolan Yang confirms this belief. "Knowing that you matter really does matter," it finds, adding that "the provision of meaning can be a low-cost instrument to stimulate work effort."

The concept of meaningfulness has proven so attractive to employers that it survived even as what we used to call work has not. Nearly all of the ten million jobs created over the past ten years were temporary, reducing the American Dream to a part-time afterthought. While a yawning economic chasm further divides the rich from everyone else, employers stoke the emerging belief in our affection for meaningful work. This seismic shift signals a dismal paradox: the worse work gets and the less we are paid to do it, the more meaningful we are told it should be.

•

NEVERTHELESS, THAT so many people find meaning in their jobs makes it difficult to argue that meaningfulness is merely the product of an elite conspiracy. The great chronicler of the American worker, Studs Terkel, put it this way: "Work is about a daily search for meaning as well as daily bread; for recognition as well as cash; for astonishment rather than torpor; in short for a sort of life, rather than a Monday-to-Friday sort of dying." People tend to find "a meaning to their work over and beyond the reward of the paycheck."

Olivia Pei is a living illustration. She left a high-paying and stable job at Visa in Manhattan with great work-life balance and telecommuting possibilities to join an exciting startup venture in San Francisco. If you've ever rented one of those pay-by-the-minute electric scooters to get around, you might have her company, Lime, to thank, or one of the twelve competitors currently vying to dominate the alt-transport market. "I wanted to put myself into my work, for something I'm really excited about," she explained. Olivia is passionate about scooters, and views them as ecological and fun alternatives to Uber and buses. The move entailed a substantial pay cut—much of her compensation at Lime is in stock and could be worth either a lot or nothing—and a huge spike in hours. She estimates she works about seventy hours per week, yet doesn't really "feel like an employee" because the company is mission-driven and purposeful, encouraging its staff to identify as "participants in a movement." "I think it's sustainable to a point," she says. "Right now we're in a crunch period where we need to put in everything that we can, hopefully for a rewarding future in which we don't need to do that as much."

She describes it as a "9 a.m. to 10 p.m. kind of job." She spends the first eight hours of her day in meetings and then "from five onwards is when I get to actually do work. We also have food at the office, which kind of helps encourage me to stay in the office quite late." Olivia confirms the cynical suspicion that tech companies offer free meals and other amenities to encourage longer hours. "You could say that if you don't go to dinner [at work] you're kind of excluding yourself from social conversations or business conversations that happen over dinner." She noted that the broad assumption is that tech employees are searching for meaning. "It's almost like if you don't find your job fulfilling then maybe there's something wrong with you," she says, half laughing.

There was definitely something wrong with Sam Dunnington, but it wasn't his inability to find meaning in his job. It was that he had that job to begin with. Sam worked in Philadelphia as a fake shopper. He was hired through a temp agency by a company, undisclosed to him, to go into the Century 21 department store and pretend to shop—all day. "It was your basic 'warm body' kind of job," he said. He tried on clothes, perused merchandise, talked with salespeople, all without any intention of buying a thing—indeed, given his paltry wage, without the ability. The point of his job was to inspire customers to enter the store simply by his being inside it on the theory that real customers are turned off by an empty store. At times he and his fifty—repeat, fifty— fake shopping colleagues were told simply to walk laps around the block, going in and out of the store, or look through the windows from the outside, just to give the impression the store was worth entering.

He tried to derive some larger meaning from his duties, but it was impossible. "Any way that I could think of to make meaning in this job is unavailable to me," he said, because the pay was so low and he was discouraged from "engaging any mental faculty besides smiling and walking around." Sam was familiar with the argument in *Bullshit Jobs*, by the anthropologist David Graeber, who chronicled the lives of many well-paid professionals whose jobs provided no personal or social benefit. "This was a rung or two below that," he said, "because there was no living to be made."

The only thing more pointless than Sam's job was that of his supervisors, who also walked throughout the store incognito just to make sure none of the fake shoppers simply absconded mid-shift. It is hard to imagine a system that produces jobs so pointless in a culture that supposedly values meaningfulness. Sam says that his search for a better job was motivated by his desire to find meaningful work. "I think everybody wants that," he said, "and I think we deserve it, even if our jobs are for low pay."

My interviews suggest that low-wage workers like Sam, though hardly associated with high-status jobs or lofty ideals, routinely regard their work lives as about more than money. I met retail workers before, during, and after shifts and also between jobs. Many expressed understandable resentment at low pay and bad hours. But they also mentioned the holistic part of the job, the meaning they drew from it and the positive characteristics that they believed they brought to it.

This was Tatiana, a salesperson at H&M: "I think most people think we are stuck here. That we are here because we couldn't get something else. But . . . it's about the work. It's about working. Building yourself up. Making yourself better. More perfect. So you can take that to the next place [of employment]. It's about showing up for us. Not for them." With that, she looked over her shoulder and pointed to the store's managers. Nearly every retail clerk I interviewed reported some version of this same point.

That low-income workers seek out meaningful labor is surprising. Meaningfulness, after all, comes at a cost. A study by psychologists Jing Hu and Jacob Hirsh found that people who expect to find meaning in a job are willing to accept a salary approximately $20,000 less than if the job were "meaningless." A 2018 report by BetterUp Labs found that more than 90 percent of workers would give up some percentage of their earnings to have a more meaningful job, and workers who find their work meaningful take less time off. This is certainly true in Silicon Valley, where workers routinely report trading meaning for money when accepting offers from big companies. Moreover, the fact that a job is socially useful is often used as a justification for paying less. We wouldn't want public schoolteachers, whose pay on average has stagnated for two decades, to do their work just for the money, would we? Yet the opposite argument is made to defend high salaries for the most socially regressive labor. Why would corporate lawyers put in so many hours if we did not incentivize them with large paychecks? It's almost as if the meaninglessness of a job contributes to its economic value.[14]

But maybe those for whom jobs seem the least meaningful hold the key to reforming our working lives. The phenomenon of meaningless work illuminates the contradiction at the heart of capitalism itself. Long hours at tedious jobs could have been avoided, and yet here we are. Where's our sense of indignation? More importantly, where's our demand for change?

A celebrated myth has Milton Friedman, a leading proponent of free-market ideology, coming upon a construction site in China where workers are digging with shovels rather than with heavy equipment. "This is a work project," the local bosses told him when Friedman asked about the seeming stupidity of it. Friedman replied, "Then why don't they use spoons instead?" Friedman never actually said these words, but his joke could just as easily be directed at our society, where work is often said to be as much about producing an ethic as it is about accomplishing a socially necessary goal. In the United States a majority in polls say they are "actively disengaged" from their work, and a significant minority describe their jobs as "meaningless."[15]

This trend seems likely to continue, as most newly created jobs tend to be low-skill, low-paying, and low-status. Only 37 percent of the fifty million new jobs America will add by 2028 will require any education. So, while a small group of people can find fulfilling work, more and more jobs are likely to look like low-wage drudgery. This is bad news for lots of reasons, but it is particularly bad in an economy that increasingly defines work by its meaningfulness, because it will exacerbate inequality of both income and fulfillment.

"You want to enrich the job?" the unionist William Winpisinger famously asked. "Enrich the paycheck . . . decrease the number of hours." But if that is the only demand, we fail to take full advantage of the crisis of despair into which workers have fallen. The widespread alienation that so many express is an important critique of capitalism, and it's unlikely that workers would be suddenly mollified by a raise in pay, despite how important that would be. The failure to provide meaningful work to the vast majority of the population is a powerful indictment of our current system—one more promise capitalism makes but can't keep. Discovering a type of work and workplace organization that is truly engaging and empowering need not be a cynical or futile project, nor should it be dismissed as superficial. Rather, it carries with it the potential for larger political and social change.[16]

If we have to work to live, we should demand legitimately meaningful work as a fundamental social right. Such work should challenge and inspire our collective mental and emotional faculties and make a clear contribution to a better world. A demand for more engaging work can also accompany a demand for shorter hours. If some of our work is unable to meet the above criteria, and certainly we need to do things that do not, we should rightfully demand it be well paid and reduced to a minimum amount of time. Mechanization might focus on not just where the most profit can be made, but where the most meaningless toil can be reduced. And we should hold our workplaces accountable if they fall short on either of these counts, or if they try to peddle us meaning instead of money.

The roots of the meaningful work discourse lie in the blue-collar blues of midcentury factories, the white-collar woes of California's tech mecca, and the structural transformations that gave us the service economy. These trends reconceptualized our ideas about the meaning of work and the value we place on money.

Once management learned to make use of these new ideas, how-ever, legitimate demands for more fulfilling work were redirected into a probusiness ideology. As a result, the search for meaning-ful work has been more aspirational than reality. In other words, there's little evidence that we've created more meaningful jobs in the past few decades. The difference is that today we generally assume the added burden of having to look for meaning through work anyway, even if our jobs fail us. Another change was afoot at the same time the search for meaningful work went mainstream. Paradoxically, the rise of the meaningfulness discourse coincided with political changes that mandated absolutely meaningless work for millions of poor Americans. It's time to examine the policies that have blocked our ability to create better jobs and ensured that more time is filled with meaningless work.

CHAPTER 6

BACK TO WORK

THE ECONOMICS OF LONG AND UNSTABLE HOURS IS PROPPED UP by a widespread belief in the inherent goodness of hard work. Sometimes market pressures and poverty are enough to compel us to work, or the brass rings of bonuses lure us into the office on the weekends. At other times, long hours seem to be a measure of who we are, and more work confers more status. When the market and ideology fail to commit us to the daily grind, we have policies in place that force some of us back to work, with hardly any pay, at the least desirable jobs. We are told this not only builds character, but reinforces a society-wide work ethic, which some of us have to learn the hard way.

Conflicts over the hours of labor take many forms. Throughout American history, a consistent if shape-shifting policy has argued that almost everyone owes society their labor time, even those with unavoidable scheduling conflicts, mental and emotional health problems, or unavoidable responsibilities to children or other loved ones. Policies that make aid conditional on working are called workfare to distinguish them from welfare, and are usually debated on the basis of their morality. But workers typically experience them as conflicts over time, not ethics. That's because the policies are designed to control and monopolize the time of workers who either need or wish to remain detached from the paid labor market. To further understand the importance of workfare in a story about labor time today we need to brush up on some political background and dispel a few myths about welfare and those working for it.

Americans tend to view welfare and work as opposites, a clear demarcation separating the deserving (those who work or have worked) from the social parasites (those who don't). In reality, welfare and work are deeply intertwined. Welfare rolls expand and contract in response to labor market conditions, and policymakers routinely devise welfare policy to suit the needs of employers. Benefit levels are established at a low rate so as not to undercut regional labor markets, ensuring that work always seems like the preferable option. Workfare jobs aren't alternatives to the main labor market, but are deeply connected to it—the low wages and large supply of workers drag down standards across some major service industries. Since workfare replaced welfare, and a host of other work requirements have been tied to food, housing, and medical benefits, the boundaries of the labor market have been even more blurred. As a result, most welfare reforms today are directed at increasing potential workers' employability rather than offering poverty relief.[1]

Nevertheless, the contemporary attitude that regards work and welfare as discrete spheres has long-standing roots in our society. Early American colonists reproduced the workhouses of medieval England in the New World. British "poor laws" instituted workhouses in which poor people toiled in exchange for a pittance. Conditions were miserable by design to ensure that any job outside was better than ending up inside the walls of a workhouse. One report as late as the mid-nineteenth century said that workhouse workers were "reduced to sucking the marrow from the bones intended to be ground for fertilizer."[2]

In Massachusetts, Senator Josiah Quincy III argued that providing benefits to the poor would erode the work ethic by "destroying the economical habits and eradicating the providence of the laboring class of society." As an antidote, Quincy proposed "houses of industry," where "work is provided for every degree of ability in the pauper, and thus the able poor made to provide, partially at least, for their own support." Not far from where I live in Vermont there were "poor farms" full of the sick and disabled, who completed assigned work tasks to earn the right to reside there.[3]

Eventually, a clear political goal of work-for-welfare schemes materialized in midcentury America that was almost as punitive, if not as crass, as the earlier incarnations. Daniel Patrick Moynihan's 1965 report on "the negro family" can be said to offer a modern conceptual starting point. Moynihan, a sociologist serving in President Lyndon Johnson's Department of Labor, sought to "establish at some level of statistical conciseness what 'everyone knew': that economic conditions determine social conditions." But he said the evidence he collected, showing a widespread "culture of poverty" within the black nuclear family, showed the opposite.[4]

The Moynihan report inverted a long-standing postulate on the Left that capitalism, not individual behavior, is to blame for social ills. Over time this new behavioralism became dogma, and continues to shape public policy to this day. First, however, Nixon had to contend with rising discontent on college campuses, Martin Luther King's marches, summers of love, and the discordant clamor of rock 'n' roll. As the decade drew to a close, Nixon was on the verge of passing the most progressive redistribution policy in history, a guaranteed annual income for all poor families of $1,600 a year (about $11,400 in 2019). Fearing blowback to anything that sounded like a giveaway, Nixon called it the Family Assistance Plan, or FAP.

On the morning in 1969 the president was to announce this plan, his adviser Martin Anderson, a devoted follower of Ayn Rand, handed Nixon a memo. What happened next, according to historian Rutger Bregman, was one of the most shocking twists in public policy history. Nixon delayed his announcement and ordered his aides to do a study of an arcane eighteenth-century British welfare policy called the Speenhamland System. Much of what they found was written by Karl Polanyi in his classic *The Great Transformation*. Polanyi was a Christian and a socialist, but his conclusions that Speenhamland's generous entitlement program pauperized the masses by condemning them to sloth and indolence proved very useful to conservatives. To ease the concerns of congressional Republicans, Bregman shows, Nixon attached a provision to the bill that recipients of the basic income would have to register with the Department of Labor, a stipulation he thought would have virtually no effect. "I don't care a damn about the work requirement," Nixon said behind closed doors. "This is the price of getting $1,600."[5]

The next day, in a televised speech, Nixon repackaged "welfare" as "workfare." But what Nixon considered a mere rhetorical concession turned out to be the fatal blow of his original bill. Most people, it turned out, did give a damn about the work requirement. Nixon's basic income bill was gutted, and workfare became the preferred conservative policy goal.

The failure of Nixon's plan is more significant than a quirky anecdote about a corrupt conservative advocating a progressive policy. It is possible, after all, to conceive of welfare as a radical promise to end work as we know it. What is a robust basic income grant if not an inflated welfare check? In fact, that was the position of the National Welfare Rights Organization (NWRO), the movement of mostly black women on welfare in the early 1970s. They insisted on a "right to welfare" on the basis that it provided not just a survival mechanism but also a way to guarantee them the time to focus on things that mattered more to them. They demanded comfort, not simply a livable wage, a way to live apart from the necessity to work. Their campaign for a more robust basic income put them at odds with Nixon's plan, explicitly because of the work requirement. Their protests, which were wrongly blamed for the legislation's failure, promised to "Zap FAP."

Given the timing of the legislation, the work requirement was touted as an empowering possibility for women's liberation, a perversion of second wave feminism's belief in the value of work. But the NWRO was opposed to the more middle-class feminist analysis. Journalist Judith Shulevitz quotes Catherine Jermany of the Los Angeles County Welfare Rights Organization: "We thought white women were crazy to want to give up their cushiony Miss Cleaver life," she said. "We thought that was a good life." Whereas middle-class feminism saw welfare as preventing women from realizing their fuller selves in the labor market, working-class feminism understood the right to free time as the more radical potential.[6]

Regardless, by the time Reagan arrived in Washington, no one had any use for historical anecdotes or dog whistles. The right had won the argument. Lamenting the laziness of the lower classes, conservative scholar Lawrence Mead put it bluntly: "Low-wage work apparently must be mandated, just as a draft has sometimes been necessary to staff the military." There was no national emergency that required a reserve army of poverty-stricken workers. The unemployment rate had actually been declining for years when Mead wrote those words, and wages had risen as a result. Work had become the price of citizenship.

Extending that citizenship requirement was not ultimately the job of the right. It was Bill Clinton who made it into a national policy.[7] In 1996 Clinton made good on his promise to "end welfare as we know it" by signing a cornerstone piece of Republican-backed legislation called the Personal Responsibility and Work Opportunity Reconciliation Act (PRWORA). Colloquially known as welfare reform, the legislation was in reality welfare replacement. The act erased the New Deal–era Aid to Families with Dependent Children (AFDC) and created Temporary Assistance for Needy Families (TANF). Billed as a "reaffirmation of America's work ethic," the law required people to work in exchange for welfare benefits. With the stroke of his pen, Clinton transformed America's safety net into a low-wage work program.

Though delivered in Clinton's folksy drawl, it was a radical piece of legislation, breaking with party orthodoxy. Slashing eligibility for cash assistance, the bill established new five-year term limits on benefits and enforced strict work requirements as a condition for receiving aid. PRWORA also exempted some legal migrants from federal support like food stamps and Social Security.

Welfare reform was either a good policy implemented poorly or a bad policy implemented with cold-blooded efficiency, and there's far more evidence for the latter. If it was designed to mitigate poverty, it can surely be considered a failure. If, on the other hand, it was designed to end welfare, it was a smashing success. The graph below shows what happened. The welfare rolls expanded as the Great Society reforms attempted to contain mass unrest, plateauing during the onset of neoliberalism in the early 1970s, spiking again after the economic downturns in the late 1980s and the end of the Cold War. But Clinton's reforms ended that long-term trend, and subsequent administrations have continued his policy. By 2015 the number of people on welfare had fallen from a height of thirteen million in the mid-nineties to just over four million.

Despite these significant drops in welfare spending, the government didn't save any money. Instead, states redirected money from welfare caseloads to other programs, for education, infrastructure, and even to promote marriage. One report from 2014 shows that only about one-quarter of total TANF dollars went to cash assistance; another shows that Michigan used TANF dollars to fund college scholarships while Louisiana spent it on "abortion alternatives." Incentives to states to reduce their welfare caseloads had disastrous consequences. A report by the US

NUMBER OF FAMILIES RECEIVING
AFDC/TANF CASH ASSISTANCE, 1959–2018

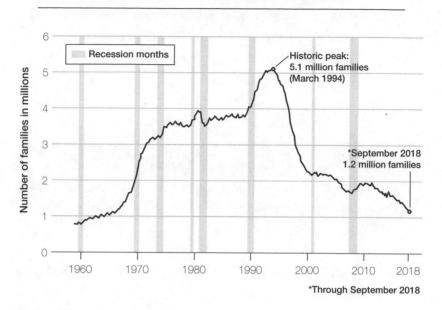

*Through September 2018

NOTES: Shaded areas denote months when the national economy was in recession. Information represents families receiving cash assistance from Aid to Dependent Children (ADC), Aid to Families with Dependent Children (AFDC), and Temporary Assistance for Needy Families (TANF). Figures for October 1999 through September 2018 include families receiving assistance from Separate State Programs (SSPs) with expenditures countable toward the TANF maintenance of effort requirement. SOURCE: Congressional Research Service, with data from the Department of Health and Human Services.

Commission on Civil Rights found significant evidence that money meant for childcare subsidies was being rerouted to other programs, amounting to widespread racist exclusion that disproportionately harmed poor families of color.[8]

Most damning of all, welfare reform barely affected the official poverty rate, which has stubbornly hovered around 13 percent for decades. Although child poverty has been somewhat mitigated, poverty among the unemployed and working poor has deepened.

The number of those in extreme poverty, a classification defined by those who live on two dollars or less per day, has doubled since 1996. Sociologists Kathryn Edin and H. Luke Shaefer find this level of degradation "has been concentrated among those groups that were most affected by the 1996 welfare reform."[9]

None of this was an accident or the result of a failed policy. Right after the legislation, Clinton's longtime friend and assistant director of Health and Human Services, Peter Edelman, walked off the job with a terse two-sentence resignation letter to his staff. "I have devoted the last 30-plus years to doing whatever I could to help in reducing poverty in America," he wrote. "I believe the recently enacted welfare bill goes in the opposite direction."[10]

Clinton signed the welfare reform bill on a sunny summer day on the White House lawn. But it was the woman standing over his right shoulder, Lillie Harden, a forty-two-year-old black single mother from Little Rock, who made the moment so profound. Harden's presence at the signing ceremony was no coincidence. Clinton had met Harden during a public discussion on workfare in Arkansas more than a decade earlier. After two years on welfare, Harden had secured a job at a local grocery store, and she had testified to the respect her job brought to her and her children, a theme she would repeat during her speech at the signing of the bill. Although some Democrats chastised Clinton for "caving" to Republicans by signing the legislation in 1996, he had actually been experimenting with similar programs for a long time in his home state.

This made Harden's conclusion in her speech all the more convincing. Identified as a "former welfare recipient," Harden introduced Clinton as "the man who started my success and the beginning of my children's future." Harden was the promise of welfare reform. By using her, Clinton cynically transformed Reagan's "welfare queen," a black unwed mother on public assistance, into an archetype of individual striving, the proud black working mom—hustling, holding it down all on her own.

As Hillary Clinton argued, they're "no longer deadbeats—they're actually out there being productive." A lot of those deadbeats had children, and Hillary was especially adamant about expanding punitive sanctions for not just failure to work outside the home but also poor parenting. "I've advocated tying the welfare payment to certain behavior about being a good parent," she said. "You couldn't get your welfare check if your child wasn't immunized. You couldn't get your welfare check if you didn't participate in a parenting program. You couldn't get your check if you didn't show up for student-teacher conferences."

These sanctions are heavily gendered, which is interesting given that they came from one of the most powerful liberal women in the country. But it's not surprising. Welfare reform targeted women, those who worked the least and, it was implied, could stand to work more. "Goodbye welfare queen, hello working mom" was a common refrain, signaling the racist and sexist language that characterized support for welfare reform. For much of American history, however, women, especially white middle-class women, weren't expected to work outside the home. Doing so, in fact, often brought its own kind of rebuke for violating traditional standards of womanhood. Welfare reform was predicated on the opposite assumption, that women were just as capable and willing to work as men. How did that premise come to be?

One uncomfortable answer is that the ideological groundwork for welfare reform was laid by midcentury feminists, who popularized the notion that women weren't truly free unless they could realize their full potential in the world of work. In 1963, Betty Friedan wrote in *The Feminine Mystique*, "Women as well as men can only find their identity in work that uses their full capacities. She cannot find it in the dull routine of housework."

In a 1987 interview in the *New York Times*, Maureen Dowd
asks Daniel Patrick Moynihan, seated amid a collection of rare
books, "Why is it essential in the current crop of proposals to
make mothers work?" Moynihan's response is shocking.

> When the original welfare program began, the family was seen
> as an arrangement where the husband went out to work and the
> woman stayed home and kept house and raised the children. It
> was before washing machines and refrigerators and vacuum clean-
> ers. So long as that assumption lasted, if you suggested that welfare
> recipients should work, you were suggesting that they be treated
> differently—and in some sense punitively—because you were say-
> ing, "All right, you are going to have to do what no self-respecting
> woman has to do." But then you looked up one day and women
> were working. Once it became a self-respecting thing to be in the
> work force, that changed the possibilities of discussing child sup-
> port in a mode that would include the income from the mother
> as well as the father.[11]

In other words, Moynihan thought that the middle-class feminist ideal of freedom through work had an unintended con-
sequence. It implied that women not only could work, but it
was good for them to do so. Had feminists unwittingly sent the
shock troops that were used to justify workfare? Decades later,
Moynihan's hunch seems confirmed by the cunning of history.
Feminist scholar Nancy Fraser argues that as second wave feminism arose alongside neoliberalism, their ideological messages
became inextricably entwined. "Feminists watched helplessly as
Bill Clinton triangulated their nuanced critique of a sexist and
stigmatizing system of poor relief into a plan to 'end welfare as we
know it,' which abolished the Federal entitlement to income support," she writes. As middle-class women moved decisively into
paid employment in the seventies and eighties, American bosses
faced a new landscape and a new opportunity. Policymakers

slowly realized that it was okay—even feminist!—to put women to work in the paid labor market.

Over the next three decades working mothers were dropped from the welfare rolls, but they did not rise out of poverty at corresponding rates. Today, one-third of children are raised in single-parent households, which are predominantly headed by women. And about one-fifth of low-income moms remain "disconnected," the term researchers apply to those not in the labor force or receiving benefits. Yet as this demographic has exploded, the funds to support them have dwindled. A study by the Urban Institute found that these single mothers survive by relying on informal social networks to manage their precarious lives and take care of their children.[12]

If women should work, why not children? Such is the logic that has occasionally gained popularity among the defenders of workfare programs. While on the road to his losing bid for the Republican Party's nomination for president in 2012, Newt Gingrich unveiled his plan to replace unionized adult janitors with young schoolchildren, calling laws prohibiting child labor "truly stupid." "The kids would actually do work, they would have cash, they would have pride in the schools," he said. The plan was intended to indoctrinate poor youth into a world of work, which, even by Gingrich's own admission, conferred no status and wasn't worth it in economic terms. It was the inverse of the meaningful work discourse explored previously. "Get any job that teaches you to show up on Monday," he said, "any job that teaches you to stay all day even if you're fighting with your girlfriend . . . the whole process of making work worthwhile is central." These policy proposals weren't taken very seriously, but they underscore the fact that workfare was designed less to provide opportunity than to "teach" about the value of work.

Lessons from Lillie Harden's story are far more important. After a stroke in 2002 left her unable to work, Harden asked the *New York Times* writer Jason DeParle to "ferry a message back to Clinton." In *American Dream*, DeParle recounts how Harden wanted Bill Clinton to help her receive Medicaid, which she had gotten while on welfare but had recently lost. As her monthly prescription drug bills reached $450, she needed extra help. She said of the job she got after welfare, "It didn't pay off in the end." When another journalist sought to interview Harden for a feature on the twentieth anniversary of PRWORA, he learned she had died the year before at the age of fifty-nine in North Little Rock, a community where more than one-fifth of the population lived in poverty, just across the Arkansas River from where Clinton first began experimenting with workfare as governor.

Today North Little Rock is significantly more impoverished than the national average. I spent time there interviewing workfare participants when 2019 legislation expanded the work requirements for those receiving aid. Arkansas had recently become the first state in the country to mandate a work requirement for healthcare benefits. Other states had tried, but the Republican-controlled legislature there had moved the Trump administration policy through rather smoothly. Arkansas quickly became the leader of a conservative movement to further eviscerate welfare and force people to work.

On April 1, 2016, Donna, who wished to be identified only by her first name, went to a North Little Rock grocery store to shop with food stamps, as she had for years. But her electronic card was denied. "I knew it was no April Fool's joke," she said. She marched out of the store and walked miles back to her friend's house, where she was staying, and didn't leave for three days.

Donna was one of 18,000 food stamp recipients who lost their benefits for failing to meet new state work requirements. In subsequent months, during which time she went without the vital benefits she needed to avoid long bouts of hunger, she was able to restore her benefits after proving she actually had been meeting the work requirement all along. The requirement is, in many ways, a reporting requirement, as most food stamp recipients already work in paid employment. Donna didn't work regularly, but she cobbled together what she could. A few shifts at Walmart, the state's largest employer, were usually supplemented by other informal jobs. She'd worked at laundromats and, as an animal lover, volunteered at a humane society shelter. But a lack of affordable or dependable public transportation—she usually walked, hitchhiked, or got rides from neighbors—made it difficult to commute from North Little Rock. She found it hard to hold down a job, though she did not have a diagnosed mental or physical disability that could have excluded her from the population of able-bodied adults who had to meet the new work requirements.[13]

Meeting the work requirement was difficult for Donna, but the state also had trouble administering it. A 2018 study by the Kaiser Family Foundation found that transforming healthcare into a work program proved exceedingly difficult. Medicaid clients who lost their coverage had either not heard of the work requirements, and, therefore, failed to comply, or were in compliance but could not accurately report their work hours.[14]

Internet access is limited among low-income rural Arkansans, but initially the only way to log your work hours was online. Tomiko Townley, a social worker at the Arkansas Hunger Relief Alliance, recalls talking with Medicaid recipients who had met the minimum work rules but couldn't properly report them. Even those with internet access sometimes had trouble because the online form clients used to report their hours was mysteriously unavailable between 9:00 p.m. and 8:00 a.m. The government actually made it difficult for people to meet its own reporting requirement, which, at the time, was the only mechanism to ensure continued access to healthcare. But the most damning part of the report was that work requirements only intensified the stress, anxiety, and fear that already course through the lives of the impoverished. "The new requirements are not incentivizing new work or other activities in which enrollees were not already engaged, but are layering on one more thing to deal with in enrollees' already complex lives and causing added stress because no one wants to lose their coverage," the report concluded.[15]

"It's a cure for a disease that doesn't exist," Townley told me. "And it will only exacerbate the problem." The disease that does exist, poverty, is in desperate need of a cure, and is on quick display throughout Little Rock. The problem I encountered while there was not that people don't work or don't want to work. Even those with myriad physical, emotional, and mental health problems report desperately seeking work hours to stay alive, keep their medication, or support a family member.

The free breakfast at River City Ministries—old pizza, piles of chicken cutlets, baked ziti, and watered-down coffee—attracted a group of early birds even before the doors opened at 7:30. Townley, who was there to register people for food stamps, has just informed Stacy Eslinger of a ray of hope. A federal judge had struck down the state's work requirement for Medicaid the day before, arguing that the state hadn't "adequately considered whether the program 'would in fact help the state furnish medical assistance to its citizens, a central objective of Medicaid.'" Eslinger had fled to Little Rock after escaping an abusive husband in Texas, saving her life and the lives of her two kids, she said. But the move hardly solved her problems. An unrelated violent altercation between her and the police landed her in jail for seven months.

"No one's hiring me after that," she said. She left jail sick, destitute, and without any social connections. Sometimes she panhandled for money as tourists walked across the Clinton Bridge to get a panoramic view of the city. She works informally—odd jobs, off-the-books eldercare, and some housecleaning for a man she affectionately referred to as Grandpa. "I was working forty hours," she said. "Just not the right kind of work, I guess." Eslinger lost her medical coverage not because she wasn't working, but because she had no idea how to report her hours. Penniless, she had no way to get to and from her house, on the outskirts of Little Rock, and a job or an interview unless a neighbor drove her.

And reporting complications were the main obstacle to her qualifying for aid in the first place. For the 18,000 people already kicked off Medicaid, social service workers know the process to get them back will be made purposely difficult. When I checked, the website that receives applications didn't even mention Medicaid on its home page.

•

THE ARKANSAS SITUATION is profoundly dispiriting. And although workfare programs have long provoked animosity, unrest, conflict, and protest, only in New York City has that energy translated into concrete reforms. As anomalous as it is, the story of how those reforms came to pass could serve as a model for other states looking to reverse their workfare laws too.

In the late 1980s a throng of putrid fish called mossbunkers began washing up dead on the shores of Long Island beaches in Larchmont, Mamaroneck, and Rye. No one knew where the fish were coming from or why they were dying in such large numbers. But some smelled an opportunity.

Mary Glass, commissioner of social services in Republican-controlled Westchester County, devised a plan to dispatch welfare recipients to clean up the mess. To ensure compliance with the work requirement, she also enlisted a small army of case managers to ferret out those who were trying to escape work by lying about their address or hiding stashes of cash to appear impoverished. If welfare recipients didn't show up, their benefits were cut. If they called in sick, the county had a doctor examine them to see if they were lying. Eligibility requirements were also raised. A routine door-knocking schedule by case managers ensured that able-bodied adults were living at their stated residence.

But the program to surveil and litigate alleged fraud was so cumbersome and expensive that the mossbunkers rotted on the

beach. Caseloads dropped precipitously, and the policing bureaucracy increased to the point that there were either not enough
eligible people to clean up or enough city officials to oversee
the work. Nonetheless, the Pride in Work program, as it was
known to the public, or Operation Mossbunker, as Glass and
her colleagues called it privately, inspired New York City Mayor
Rudolph Giuliani to expand workfare across the entire city a few
years later.

The fish problem was old news by then. But the city's parks
were awash in crack pipes and heroin needles, detritus from the
ballooning drug epidemic. Who better to clean them up than
welfare recipients? Giuliani hated welfare. He thought it undermined the industriousness of the city's base, prohibiting recipients from realizing, as he put it, the "self-worth that comes from
having a job." To stimulate that entrepreneurial spirit, he gave
welfare recipients the worst jobs in the city and barely paid them.
He called it the Work Experience Program, or WEP. These jobs
were not intended to lift WEP workers out of poverty. They were
intended to discipline workers by controlling their time. More
time at work meant less time for drugs and other forms of bad
behavior, so the logic went. Giuliani distinguished WEP workers with special uniforms and occasionally restricted them from
using the same bathrooms and cafeterias as regular employees.
To safeguard the careers of corrupt union leaders, who viewed
WEP workers as second-class citizens, Giuliani agreed to segre-
gate WEP and non-WEP work crews on public projects, even
though both did the exact same work.[16] Strict work rules and
higher eligibility requirements conspired to eliminate a significant number of welfare recipients from the rolls. Relief dropped
precipitously, from 1,160,000 in 1995 to 437,500 in 2005, a
63 percent decrease.

Tyletha Samuels was one of those eliminated. When she was
fifteen, her mother dragged her to the welfare office to pick up
their check. She didn't like going there, finding it undignified

and chaotic. Tyletha can't remember a time when her mother was not on welfare. Still, there was always a degree of confusion about how to apply for and receive the assistance her family needed because the rules were always changing. On this occasion, they had been back to the same office for three consecutive days trying to submit the necessary paperwork to qualify. That day, after being refused service by the social service clerk, an argument started about her family's eligibility, and it seemed they were going to leave empty-handed again. A supervisor was called to mediate, which had the opposite effect.

"The welfare lady called my mama a 'B,'" Tyletha explained. "So I picked up a credenza, and I hit the lady with it." Such was her fury that battering someone with furniture qualifies as a fond memory. The office erupted in a brawl. The police arrested Tyletha but released her later that day with no charges, plus a complimentary order from Burger King. Over the next few years, Tyletha said she went back to the office looking for that same social service worker, seething with vengeful rage. "I thank God I never saw her again," she said, adding, "She should too."

Tyletha's anger wasn't uncommon, even if acting on it was. Dispatches from welfare offices often suggest a simmering discontent that threatens the veneer of bureaucratic civility surrounding the administration of poverty relief.

Twenty-five years later, instead of fighting for her welfare check, she was working for it, answering phones and filing paperwork for Medicaid clients as a WEP worker. Welfare reform meant that Tyletha's family went from receiving assistance to giving their labor. Whereas society once viewed them as deserving a little something for their bad luck (Tyletha herself is disabled), the new rules meant that she owed the rest of us her most precious resource—her time. Workfare is a policy to fill up the time of the poor with pointless jobs at poverty wages. That, policymakers allege, teaches the value of hard work. It's the kind of thing that's not supposed to happen in a capitalist economy. For half of the twentieth century Americans had criticized their communist rivals for make-work jobs that existed merely to ensure "full employment." Yet with the Cold War scarcely over, a Democratic president in the wealthiest country in world history set about ensuring no one was allowed to survive without giving over their time. It was as cruel as it was ineffective.

Tyletha earned a $68.50 welfare check every two weeks, a standard workfare rate, in addition to food stamps and a Section 8 housing subsidy. But her coworkers on either side of her desk made a decent salary for the exact same job. Her job in the Medicaid office opened old wounds as well, as she was suddenly forced to confront the denial of benefits to needy people in ways that reminded her of her childhood. "You had people coming there who couldn't afford toilet paper, with children, working full time on WEP, being told they weren't going to receive any extra help. I hated every minute of it," she said.

Soon after the WEP started, Tyletha began fighting it. She was connected to Community Voices Heard, a grassroots organization in New York City, through a friend. For the next two decades it became a home base for her, a launchpad for the anti-workfare movement. Though she began by fighting the new Republican regime of Rudolph Giuliani, Tyletha recalled that it was Democrats who proved to be savvier opponents. "At times you really couldn't tell the difference on this issue," she said. "They were just as bad."

Despite there being fewer people on welfare and more at work, the percentage of impoverished New Yorkers has only recently declined. In 2003, Action for a Better Community and the city's Department of Human Services conducted a study on the status of former welfare families a year after their cases had closed. The study found that the majority of the families did not earn enough to put their household income above the federal poverty level. The average respondent had three children and worked thirty-four hours a week at a job that paid $9.80 an hour, or

$17,327 a year. The WEP also had the effect of driving down the wages of nonwelfare workers too. By 1997 there were more than 38,000 WEP workers who needed to fulfill a work requirement to receive benefits. But they were legally owed only two dollars a day, making them highly desirable for city contracts. Quickly, Giuliani began to replace high-paying union jobs with WEP workers.[17]

Workfare supporters stressed that work requirements entailed the classical Republican values associated with full citizenship—liberty, freedom, responsibility, dignity, civility, etc. But the jobs that WEP workers landed had hardly any hope of providing those virtues. City officials maintained a distinction between workfare workers and regular employees, referring to WEP workers as "participants," denying them even rhetorical inclusion in a community of laborers.

Studies found that the Giuliani administration circumvented due process rights, which led to a lawsuit that found the city's workfare program in violation of the 1964 Civil Rights Act. In *Citizens and Paupers*, sociologist Chad Goldberg compared WEP to the Freedmen's Bureau, established by Lincoln during Reconstruction. "Just as the bureau sought to remake its clients into self-disciplined workers fit for citizenship in a free-labor society, the WEP aimed to instill a 'lost' work ethic in clients who were overwhelmingly people of color."[18]

This helps explain what Tyletha was doing in 2009 in Union Square, dressed as an American plantation slave, with a chain gang of welfare recipients in tow. Tyletha and a group of Community Voices Heard activists were dramatizing what was by then a common refrain among critics of the program—workfare was modern slavery. "I looked like Harriet Tubman or Aunt Jemima," she said, laughing, though it was clear her rage was real. "They called it the Work *Experience* Program," she said, stressing the irony. "Nobody was getting a work experience the way regular people get it. This was a slave-type experience."

At New York City's 1997 Labor Day Parade, WEP workers came together for one of the first large demonstrations opposed to workfare. Almost immediately the activists seized upon their misclassification as "welfare recipients" or "participants," rather than as full-fledged workers, as their primary grievance. Forming a coalition of grassroots groups from across the city, they called themselves WEP Workers Together, and sought recognition on the basis of their status as deserving, contributing, socially useful citizens. It was the expectation that work, not the right to welfare, offered them a route to full social citizenship. Therefore, they argued that city officials should finish what they started. "They wanted us to work, so we said, 'Treat us like workers,'" Tyletha said. "And while you're at it, pay us like workers too."

By 1998 more than 17,000 WEP workers had signed union cards collected by ACORN, a progressive community organization. But the votes were routinely rejected by courts and labor relations boards across the country, which held that workfare participants had no right to collectively bargain with the state, upholding the legal limbo that industrial workers suffered under until the New Deal.[19]

ACORN's efforts did, however, spur unions to get involved in organizing WEP workers once they felt the nonprofit had encroached on their turf. District Council 37, the largest municipal union that had initially engaged in some backroom deals with Giuliani to avoid WEP replacements, discovered a newfound interest in representing all the city's park cleaners, not just those on the official payroll. DC37's efforts inspired the AFL-CIO to take up workfare organizing more seriously in an effort to "change the traditional definition of who is a worker."[20]

This activism was familiar to Steven Banks. As head of the Legal Aid Society, he sued the government six times on behalf of the city's homeless and poor. Lawsuits alleged that the Human Resources Administration (HRA) had illegally denied people lifesaving benefits like food stamps and Medicaid, a violation of its own charter. An in-depth examination by the nonprofit news organization City Limits argued that the HRA assumed "the main reason that so many New Yorkers were poor was that they were lazy," which meant that "the very agency tasked with lifting New Yorkers out of poverty all-too-often pushed them deeper into destitution."[21]

Today, as HRA commissioner, Banks finds himself at the helm of the institution he once attacked. Banks is soft-spoken and humble. When we met, he waved his hand toward the stunning view of Lower Manhattan from a conference room at the HRA, an apologetic gesture that indicated he was uncomfortable in such swank environs. Banks was appointed by Mayor Bill de Blasio in 2014 to attend to the problems that Tyletha and others experienced. He estimated that approximately one-third of the clients HRA placed in a job were back on the rolls a year later, a persistent problem in desperate need of a solution. But instead of merely attending to that deadlock, he solved the larger problem. In 2016 he quietly ended the Work Experience Program and replaced it with a robust social safety net.

Banks's phaseout of the WEP required hundreds of legislative changes to the social services for poorer New Yorkers. The new system replaces a work-or-nothing plan with a variety of supportive programs—an expanded job-training program in coordination with the City University of New York, more than triple the number of contracts with employers, and the ability to attend a four-year college without losing benefits. Moreover, for the first time in twenty years, unemployed New Yorkers no longer have to work for food stamps, a policy change that will help tens of thousands of hungry residents, according to activists. And although workfare has been eliminated, there are now far greater services available to help people find and keep jobs, including services tailored to youth, gays and lesbians, and those with criminal records. The most significant change is that welfare recipients who are seeking employment are now funneled into union-wage jobs through a partnership with District Council 37. Critics said welfare rolls would go up if the WEP was ended, but Banks proved them wrong. The latest data has shown virtually flat welfare enrollment annually. "I've been doing this a long time," he said. "People don't respond well to punishments and sanctions. . . . If you want to get people back on their feet, then help them. That's what we're doing."

Ending the WEP was a heroic effort. Yet it happened very quietly, because Banks and others wanted to experiment with a new modus operandi while provoking as little backlash as possible. And just as Banks received very little public credit for doing it, he was quick to point out that neither did people like Tyletha. All these changes mean that the assessment of clients is now far more comprehensive and individualized. Banks admits the new system is more complicated to administer, but the complexities of peoples' lives aren't easily managed by a one-size-fits-all model. "We take each case seriously now. You know why?" he asks, smiling wryly. "Because cases are people."

"WEP ended because we didn't quit," Tyletha told me. She noted Banks and a few others "get it." They understood how bad the system was and had some ideas about how to transform it. "But the ones who 'get it' usually got their hands tied," she said. "This time was different. Hallelujah."

The discourse of workfare was ingenious because the champions of the policies could be seen as giving us more of something we already liked—work—and removing the free ride and idle hands associated with welfare. Resistance to it has been consistent over time, even though the outcome of Tyletha's story is anomalous. But she's hardly alone. It's time to examine those leading individual and collective struggles to win better jobs and take back their time.

CHAPTER 7

WE CONTROL THE CLOCKS

WORKFARE LAWS ENSURED THAT LOW-WAGE JOBS REPLACED THE old social safety net. In the private sector, the gig economy is the new social safety net. There's nothing glamorous about being pushed into long hours for below-poverty wages, fulfilling a requirement imposed by the government. But the gig economy comes replete with the high-tech functionality of app-based labor and the oft-repeated promise that you can be your own boss. If managerial power is, as I've argued, a major impediment to control over one's time, the gig economy, with its myriad scheduling possibilities, seems to offer a ready-made solution. Work when you want, at the pace you want, and regain control over your life. Childcare conflicts? Just work when they sleep! Already have a low-paying job with short hours? Pick up the slack after work, before work, or on the weekends, with a side hustle. The choice is yours.

The superficial modernity of app work actually harkens back to a past when workers had no rights. Even the central promise of flexibility isn't as tangible as the industry advertises. The sociologist Alexandrea Ravenelle points out that TaskRabbit's workers have to respond to clients' emails within thirty minutes and agree to do at least 85 percent of the gigs they are offered to maintain good status on the platform. Likewise, many ridesharing platforms require drivers to accept a large portion of the requests they receive and impose big penalties for canceling rides. Thus, "the autonomy they expected—work when you want, doing what you want—has been usurped by the need to maintain algorithm-approved acceptance and response rates," Ravenelle writes. "The gig-economy offers 'flexibility,' but if they spend too much time away from the platform, they may discover they've been 'removed from the community,' or 'deactivated.'"

Platforms turn a long-established trade-off on its head: in traditional work arrangements, employees work when their bosses tell them to in exchange for some measure of stability and economic security. Independent contractors and freelancers, on the other hand, have more freedom to choose when and how to work, but they lack the certainty provided by employee protections and benefits. Giggers, taskers, Turkers, and ridesharers have the worst of both worlds because they lack the protections that can come from employment regulation *and* the freedom of a genuinely independent service provider. Overall, there's much evidence—including the stories below—that it isn't just services that are "on-demand," but workers themselves. Just ask Rebecca Wood.

At a certain point, Rebecca began sending me screenshots of her nightly earnings as an Uber Eats driver. The text messages arrived late, often after midnight. Sometimes she would check in even before she called it a night—"at 17 runs so far, gonna shoot for 20," which had the unintended effect of keeping me up to see if she reached her goal. In fact, over the course of several weeks I found myself adjusting my sleep habits, waiting up later than usual to see what she had made or if she had any unusual stories to tell about the late-night delivery scene. Sometimes I didn't last, but would wake up to a text declaring victory or a sense of frustration. Though I hadn't yet met her, this made for a strange kind of intimacy. Americans don't like to talk about how much money they make, yet she made a point of it—usually about eleven dollars an hour. On weekend nights, if she started at five and drove until two, she could make $150. During the week, she'd work from five until about 11:30 and make roughly ninety dollars. But the screenshots weren't just pay stubs; they showed a breakdown of how much she earned per trip, plus bonuses she accrued every time she passed a certain point. After twelve runs, she received a seven-dollar bonus; after fifteen runs, nine dollars. After twenty runs, going for a bonus wasn't worth it.

Occasionally, I found myself responding with what I thought were words of encouragement. "You got this!" or, trying to match her own dark sense of humor, "It's only midnight, don't stop already!" But I sometimes felt a pang of guilt for even trying to be supportive. She worked harder than she should have had to and wasn't alone on those long nights. Her seven-year-old daughter, Charlie, rode along in the back seat night after night, a steady copilot who, when she wasn't dozing off, helped pick up and deliver orders with her mom in and around Charlottesville, Virginia.

When she was twenty-six weeks pregnant, Rebecca was diagnosed with preeclampsia, a disease that is potentially fatal to both mother and child. Charlie was born shortly after, the size of Rebecca's hand. The birth took place under general anesthesia, and both nearly died. Rebecca woke up in an intensive care unit after the birth, and Charlie was three days old before Rebecca first saw her. "I watched you fight and I cheered you on," she would write later on her blog. "On your difficult days, I prayed and begged. Sometimes you would forget to breathe. I gently nudged you as a reminder."

Rebecca quickly jettisoned her plans to go to graduate school in public health and became Charlie's full-time caretaker. For four years she did physical therapy with Charlie every day. Charlie has cerebral palsy. She was in diapers until she was six years old. She was formula-dependent for three years until she had a feeding tube put in, which needed constant monitoring. It was difficult to find a professional and affordable caretaker who could handle the various challenges Charlie's health problems posed. Local schools didn't have specialists who could accommodate her, so she had to start school late, even though she was cognitively capable. But Charlie's health problems weren't her most formidable challenge.

The 2016 elections gave so much power to the right that Rebecca had good reason to fear Charlie would lose her most vital healthcare coverage, so they packed up and moved to Charlottesville. Even with private health insurance, Charlie relies on a Medicaid waiver for most of her care. Occupational therapy gave her the use of her hands. Physical therapy made it possible for her to run and jump. Speech therapy enabled her to speak. Yet all of it came at a cost, and her family's finances were destroyed. Without health insurance Rebecca would not have been able to afford the significant costs of feeding Charlie through the G-tube.

Even with healthcare, their young family was barely scraping by. Their plans of homeownership were crushed. Vacations or some kind of break were out of the question. Yet Rebecca made far graver sacrifices. "It cost me all of my teeth. And part of my jaw," she said, with a flatness that must come from not quite being able to believe what you're saying, all the while knowing it's too real. By the time Charlie was three, she was finally starting to communicate verbally beyond grunts and gestures. Rebecca didn't want Charlie to miss any of her speech therapy appointments, so she chose to forgo her own dental procedure until the next pay period. "It was an easy choice, to go without my care and pay for hers. But I shouldn't have had to make it. No one should."

During that time an infection spread through her mouth that nearly cut off her airway. She had emergency surgery that required the dentist to pull some teeth, but it was too late. She endured a six-hour procedure with only general anesthesia because it was all she could afford. "They started pulling teeth, and they kept pulling them until I didn't have any more. And then there was scraping as they were scraping parts of my jaw away, and it turns out I lost a good portion of my face too." Rebecca was left with, by her own admission, "crappy ill-fitting dentures" that continue to cause pain and other problems to this day. Sometime after that, her marriage fell apart and she suddenly became a single mom. Unable to work a traditional job because she couldn't afford childcare, she found herself falling back on America's new social safety net: the gig economy. I came across her Twitter posts one day, and gave her a call right then, and she shared her story as Charlie slept in the back seat.

Rebecca began delivering food for Uber Eats at night and for Instacart during the day, carrying Charlie along with her, trying to save enough money to move to Boston, where she had a community of friends and could take advantage of higher-quality healthcare. Eventually she quit Instacart because after the company's pay structure changed, she was earning below minimum wage. "I tried to make it fun like we are playing the Amazing Race. But I feel horrible that she has to do it. I feel like a shitty parent as I juggle a sleeping child in 1 arm and a carry out order in another," she posted to Twitter. The job was hard on her body, and her chronic pain flared up often. She worried her car might give out before she could save enough money for the move. "Nobody goes to school to schlep food back and forth in the evenings carrying a small child," she told me. "But you do what you gotta do."

The late-night delivery circuit contains some kind of camaraderie, because everyone is hustling. "Everybody who's driving is desperate," she explained. "It's a way to get cash immediately. You got that car payment due? Shit, gotta go drive for Uber." Moreover, the hours are hardly as flexible as it seems, because it's not worth it to drive during nonpeak hours. This left her work schedule at the whim of user demand and Uber algorithms, instead of her own availability. Accordingly, she was virtually constrained to late nights.

Then one night she had a revelation. She ordered food delivery from home with a gift card when Charlie fell asleep early. When she went outside to receive the order, she noticed the driver was a mother with a young child riding along. "I'm not the only one," Rebecca thought, "and that is horrifying." But there wasn't resignation in her voice—it was anger. "When I saw the other mom delivering food, I was like, Holy crap, there are more of us. We need to be talking about this."

The first time I spoke with Rebecca, there was one thing she made clear: she's not an activist. "I'm a mom," she said, "doing what any mom would do for their daughter." It would be a forgivable mistake, however, if you thought she was an activist because both Charlie and Rebecca are fixtures on Capitol Hill, with Charlie sporting a T-shirt that reads, "I am a pre-existing condition." They make the rounds to meet with policymakers and just about anyone who will listen to their story. When they crashed a 2018 holiday party to talk to lawmakers about healthcare, Nancy Pelosi took the mic at one point to shush the crowd. "I just want you to know the party can officially start now," she said. "Charlie's here."

Defending the Affordable Care Act was a matter of life or death, and Rebecca committed herself to reform. Once, while on a trip to Austin, Texas, she decided to pay Senator Ted Cruz a visit to tell him why she supported the ACA. Cruz's staffers barred her entry from the building. Later, she reflected on the experience: "It dawned on me that in order to have healthcare justice, the guys writing the policy have to live by it."

It was an aha moment that transformed her into a militant voice for universal healthcare. Suddenly, meeting legislators in their offices wasn't enough. She was arrested a short time later for civil disobedience while protesting proposed repeals of the ACA, and she said she was thinking of Charlie the whole time.

I wanted to tell her that I did everything within my power if it got repealed. My daughter's future is in this. What choice do I have as a parent? Am I going to just sit back after everything we've sacrificed? The work and energy she put into it? Because you know what? It's not easy to will parts of your body to move when they don't want to. None of her therapy was fun for her. So it's like, I'm not going to sit back and let them line their pockets with her future."

Rebecca kept fighting. In 2018, you might have seen her on CNN being dragged out of the tax bill hearing by police, screaming, "Don't steal my baby's future!" Or maybe you saw her speaking alongside Bernie Sanders, supporting his Medicare for All campaign. Or on stage at the Women's March in Roanoke, Virginia. Raising Charlie is isolating, and her own health problems compounded that sense of embarrassment and hardship. But she found her community in an odd place: on buses bound for jail on Capitol Hill.

When Rebecca was arrested for the first time, she was sitting in the holding pen her fellow protesters nicknamed the Barn, because it was where the police horses were usually kept. That day it was filled with people in plastic handcuffs who had just been arrested for protesting against changes to the ACA. "Suddenly everyone started chanting, 'Chuckie! Chuckie! Chuckie!' and they walked him off in *real* handcuffs and took him to *real* jail," she recounted to me. Chuck Denison had accumulated too many arrests—he estimates about thirty—to be let off as easily as everyone else. "They banned me from the whole district for six months. Not the federal, not the Senate building, from the whole District of Columbia," he said, with a bit of pride. After all, this was the plan—retire early, fight like hell.

Chuckie grew up in Germantown, Ohio, a small homogenous town outside Dayton. He dropped out of college midway through his freshman year and took a job at a General Motors brake plant

in the industrial zone on Needham Road. Here he first encountered racial diversity, which made the experience, in addition to
the high wages, incredibly appealing and interesting. But then
the plant closed, and in 2003 Chuckie was transferred to a GM
factory in Shreveport, Louisiana.

The plant was a state-of-the-art, billion-dollar general-
assembly factory that produced trim, chassis, and final-line on
Hummer H3s and GMC Acadias. The job was good, but the
transfer left him feeling isolated, far from family and friends.
When that plant faced a downturn as a result of the 2008 economic crisis, he was sent back to Ohio and ended up working
on the Lordstown assembly line, about four hours from where he
grew up. Lordstown was luring workers because high gas prices
meant the small cars it produced, like the Chevrolet Cobalt, were
becoming popular alternatives to the large vehicles Americans
had gotten hooked on. Moreover, GM had invested $350 million
in the five-million-square-foot plant to upgrade its robotics, and
boasted it could produce as many as seven models on one assembly line, making it resistant to downturns in finicky consumer
demand. So GM created a third shift of one thousand additional
workers, including Chuckie, to accommodate the greater efficiency. Cheryl Jonesco also worked the third shift. Cheryl grew
up in Youngstown and had been stuck in the "waitressing trap"
for a while before landing at GM in 2008.

"He's always been a fighter when he was at the plant," Cheryl
told me. "When I met him, he was not afraid to speak up if he saw
something that's not right." It was an appealing quality to her,
as Cheryl had also been active in the union at Lordstown. They
began a life together, working the line and organizing the union.

Chuckie was accustomed to moving around, so when he sensed
that a slight downturn was coming as the Chevy Cruze began to
tank among car buyers, it was time to move again. He requested
a transfer to a plant in nearby Parma, but Cheryl stayed at
Lordstown. Chuckie was right. The Monday after Thanksgiving

in 2019, GM announced it was idling 14,000 workers at a number of plants across the United States and Canada, including
Lordstown, to invest money in autonomous vehicles. For Cheryl
it was the death knell of the American Dream. "People's lives
changed because of the Lordstown plant," she said. "We workers, we built something here." But Wall Street celebrated as the
company got rid of pension obligations and healthcare associated with its heavily unionized workforce, and its stock closed
5 percent higher the day GM CEO Mary Barra announced the
shutdown.

The Lordstown plant had supported the community for fifty
years, and people were devastated. Wages had declined by 6 percent since 2014, but the plant generated $250 million in salaries
for workers in 2018 alone, fueling the regional economy. Its closure rippled through the Mahoning Valley, costing eight thousand additional jobs, including in Parma, where Chuckie worked.
A study by the Center for Economic Development at Cleveland
State University found that $8 billion would be lost in the local
economy. Falcon Trucking, which helped supply and deliver for
Lordstown, alerted its 585 employees via text message that it was
shuttering operations immediately. Drivers who were on the road
were left stranded, as their company gas cards were reportedly
canceled midshift.[1]

"These are the only good jobs that you have for people like me
that came out of the high school that wasn't cut out for college,"
Chuckie said, his voice trailing off. "The steel mills are down, the
tire factories are down, and now General Motors. So there is no
opportunity for these kids coming out of the high school to get
a good job to take care of their families if they're not cut out for
college."

The disaster of the closing has been felt more acutely given all
that workers and local residents gave up to avert it—significant
concessions in bargaining and local tax breaks that were supposed
to prevent this very fate. In 2007 workers accepted a contract

that created a tiered system in which new hires went without a pension and accepted wages that were about half of what older workers made. Two years later, GM received a $50 billion gift from American taxpayers as part of the post-crash bailout package, none of which, of course, was shared with average GM workers. Finally, in 2017, Lordstown workers accepted concessions worth $118 million just to keep up production of the Cruze.[2]

At a rally in Youngstown in 2017, President Trump advised Mahoning Valley residents not to sell their houses because "we're going to fill those factories back up," echoing claims he'd made while campaigning for president in Youngstown that helped him win Ohio, Pennsylvania, and Michigan. Trump also personally attacked local union president Dave Green on Twitter, telling him to "get his act together and produce," though Green was obviously not responsible for closing the plant. Chuckie credits Green, whom he describes as a fighting unionist, with helping to promote the "Drive It Home" campaign to generate community support for laid-off workers.

Facing unemployment and loss of healthcare, Cheryl accepted a forced transfer to a GM facility in Spring Hill, Tennessee, nine hours from where she lived with her daughter, Marissa, who stayed behind to finish her senior year of high school. Cheryl got an apartment and tried to adjust to a new reality. She suffered during the move almost immediately. I corresponded with her from her hospital bed, where she was recovering from colon surgery for a problem she chalks up to the stress of the move. Far from her family, she missed home, but also struggled with the hope the company held out that it might restart production at Lordstown. The plant had been technically "unallocated," not closed outright. This limbo gives the company the opportunity to negotiate big concessions with the UAW that might lure another product and jobs back. Or it could run the plant entirely nonunion.

"That's not gonna happen," said Chuckie, with a sliver of bravado. He and Cheryl and others have started organizing via

Bernie Sanders's Our Revolution to preemptively block a return of the company unless it is fully unionized, just as it was when the plant was shut down. Yet both Democratic and Republican lawmakers have supported union givebacks to bring the plant back online.

The Lordstown plant has a vaunted place in American labor history because of its role· as a trial balloon for class-struggle unionism. A notorious strike in 1972 lasted twenty-two days and cost GM $150 million. It was an early battle in what came to characterize a rank-and-file rebellion throughout the decade. Workers walked off the job to protest the mandated speedup of the line and the monotony of deskilled work routines. But they were also fighting back against their own union leadership, which tried to negotiate sweetheart deals with management to restart production. Yet the Taylorist factory wasn't the only inspiration for the walkout; workers wanted control over the production process, greater input in factory design, and fewer hours without a reduction in wages. The Lordstown strike has occasionally been read as a strike against work, but in many ways it was a strike to control time and demand more meaningful, fulfilling work.

After Chevrolet introduced the Vega, in 1971, GM consolidated two plants into the General Motors Assembly Division (GMAD), which came to be affectionately known among workers as "Get Mean and Destroy." The consolidation included significant layoffs, but the company still managed to meet its increased production targets by speeding up the assembly line. The factory had produced sixty Chevy Impalas every hour, but increased quotas meant it was soon churning out one hundred Vegas per hour. This meant workers had thirty-six seconds rather than sixty to complete each highly routinized task. The cars were produced but were often missing so many key elements they were unsellable. Workers simply refused to complete them. Plus, the well-documented youthful culture of the shop floor meant that not working hard became righteous and dignified. Workers smoked pot and drank on the job, worked slow, called in sick, and filed thousands of grievances through their union, making industrial jurisprudence a burden on the company. The strike embodied the countercultural spirit that defined the blue-collar blues that beset American factories and earned Lordstown the moniker of "Industrial Woodstock." The twenty-nine-year-old local union president, Gary Bryner, testified to the post-Vietnam era politics that governed the shop floor. "The young black and white workers dig each other. There's an understanding. The guy with the Afro, the guy with the beads, the guy with the goatee, he doesn't care if he's black, white, green, or yellow. . . . They just wanted to be treated with dignity. That's not asking a hell of a lot."[3]

But they were actually asking for a lot more—fewer hours and lower productivity, without wage reductions, plus a more humane and engaging workplace. Workers often expressed disdain for the automatic nature of the work, which degraded their skills and was interminably boring. It was a new movement, but one that recalled labor's classical tradition of wanting more for less, in addition to work worth doing. The strike ended without a clear victory for the union, but it put worker resistance on the map. It inspired other autoworkers across the country, who were diagnosed in the popular press as having contracted Lordstown Syndrome. The strike also initiated a larger national conversation about workplace alienation, meaningful work, automation, and job quality.

"People definitely talk about it," Cheryl said. "I know back in the day it was very radical in the seventies. I loved hearing what the workers went through and did. People weren't afraid to stand up. I feel like we kind of need to bring that back because it's slowly being taken away from us."

"Whatever happened to your brother's keeper?" Chuckie asked. "You know, where there's an autoworker, a truck driver, a teacher, a garbage guy, white-collar worker, you know . . . we haven't united to fight back in a way that we should."

It's impossible to know if such a movement would have saved jobs at the plant, but it certainly doesn't exist today. And that's exactly what frustrates Cheryl and Chuckie. When the Parma shop looked as though it might put Chuckie out of a job, he couldn't bear yet another transfer. He'd been in a plant since he was barely an adult. He decided to retire early, at forty, sold his boat and Harley, and settled for an old Chevy S-10 to get around. It wasn't an easy decision, but not because he had to get rid of his toys.

"It was one of the hardest things I went through in my life-time," he said, explaining how, after twenty years in factories, his measure of self-worth was determined by how long and hard he worked. But he's hardly slowed down.

Chuckie retired to commit himself to the labor movement, to join workers like Cheryl who were organizing from the inside. Can the unemployed be part of a labor movement? Chuckie is living proof that they can. He joined the team that will nego-tiate the next contract as a retiree. Chuckie started at fourteen dollars an hour in the mid-nineties, almost the exact starting wage Cheryl made in 2009—with a union. In addition to rais-ing wages, his mission is the same as Rebecca's: Medicare for All. Government-funded universal healthcare is good for union-ized workers in a number of ways. If employers don't have to pay expensive healthcare costs, workers can bargain for higher sala-ries or time off. "If you take healthcare off the negotiation table, now you're talking about wages, hours, safety, job security, and keeping plants open," he explained. Moreover, universal health-care would make it easier for workers to quit a bad job because they would not be reliant on their employer for healthcare. "Exit options" are essential to democratic economies because they offer more freedom for workers to choose their employer and incentiv-ize employers to raise standards.

Soon Chuckie began touring the country with Good Jobs Nation, a grassroots organization of workers looking to build a more progressive electorate throughout the Midwest. Once Trump's campaign got wind of what they were doing, anyone who showed up at a Trump rally in a Good Jobs Nation T-shirt was denied entry. Chuckie decided to join them at the next Trump rally to talk to red state voters about union issues. So he buzzed his long hair, shaved his bushy beard, donned a flannel shirt to cover up the words "union thug" tattooed on his forearm, and ended up touring around the country talking to Trump support-ers, trying to turn them blue. He even brought back a handful of success stories.

"A lot of it is just trying to get their anger off of where Trump is pushing their anger to, and redirecting it towards the corpora-tions, the hedge fund managers, the banks, and the billionaire class," Chuckie told me. "That's who they need to be angry at." Once Chuckie realized whom *he* was angry at—Trump, milque-toast Democrats, most employers, private insurance companies, union busters—he never missed an opportunity to let them know. "I'm busier than ever now that I'm retired," he said, laughing. He divides his time between organizing in Ohio, the wider Midwest, and taking the fight to Washington, DC. Plus a few hobbies: "I play guitar now, I started painting, drawing, writing. And these are things I've never done in my life. . . . Imagine if we didn't have to work hard labor jobs. And people could do what we were meant to do, spend time with your family, start up a small busi-ness, not just work our ass off eight to twelve hours a day."

Chuckie and Cheryl were both walking GM picket lines in 2019, less than a year after Cheryl moved to Spring Hill. As contract negotiations stalled, fifty thousand GM workers staged the largest strike in half a century. Immediately, the company stopped paying healthcare benefits to its workers, which was the main reason Cheryl relocated in the first place. "It was that or lose my healthcare," she said. And now the only reason she still has it is because the UAW paid for its members' medical cover-age while they were on strike. Most Spring Hill workers, some of whom were arrested for a civil disobedience protest during the strike, ultimately voted against ratifying the GM contract, but it passed anyway.

•

CHUCKIE'S SIX-MONTH BAN from the District of Columbia was ending just as Rebecca's was beginning, so they only overlapped briefly on the civil disobedience circuit. But if both of their professed visions for social change are expanded, they'll meet sooner rather than later. Chuckie's strategy to win universal healthcare would be cheaper for everyone, including employers. But if Antonia Crane and Nicole Moore get their way, and it increasingly looks like they will, some major employers will soon have to fork over a lot more to cover a host of expenses that are owed to all legal employees in California—healthcare assistance, paid parental leave, unemployment insurance, overtime, workers' compensation, and a twelve-dollar minimum wage. This would be a stunning blow to the gig economy model that prospered even before the gig economy as we now know it came to be.

Antonia is a veteran stripper and a college-level English teacher in Los Angeles. Nicole drives for Uber in the same city. Like Chuckie and Rebecca, they are on the periphery of each other's worlds, yet their lives are intertwined by the shifting structure of the American political economy. A recent court case could change their lives by reclassifying them as employees, a shift from their status as independent contractors, which would grant them the right to unionize and make it harder for their employers to evade labor laws.

A groundbreaking California Supreme Court decision, *Dynamex Operations West v. Superior Court*, would make it nearly impossible for companies to treat workers as independent contractors rather than employees. Hundreds of thousands of workers would be reclassified under the bill. The ruling, which clarifies existing law, requires that businesses determine whether or not a worker qualifies as a contractor by using the so-called ABC Test. Businesses must prove that the worker (a) is free from company control, (b) is doing work that isn't central to the company's business, and (c) has an independent business in that industry. It's all or nothing—if an employer fails to meet one of the criteria, the worker must be considered an employee. There's a strong legal precedent here, as strippers in Florida, New York, and Georgia have all won lawsuits defending their rights as employees, even when workers signed contracts with management that alleged they were independent contractors. What makes a worker an employee by law is a matter of what dancers can and cannot do, or how much control bosses have over their time. The law is especially salient in California, where half the state's workers struggle with poverty and an incredible 10 percent work in the gig economy.[4]

Antonia began stripping in the mid-nineties, when "sex workers were the VIPs of San Francisco." A punk rock feminist sensibility ruled the counterculture, one at odds with the so-called second wave of Gloria Steinem's cohort. Under those conditions, the Exotic Dancers Union at the Lusty Lady peep show seemed like the logical extension of a generation raised on *Our Bodies, Ourselves* and Bikini Kill. In the early 2000s I did a stint as a union organizer and even found myself walking their picket line in solidarity, chanting, "Five, six, seven, eight! Don't come here to masturbate!" The Lusty Lady eventually closed and the union disbanded, but Antonia, who also worked there, thinks it's time for the movement's rebirth.

Over the past few decades, prostitutes, strippers, cam girls, and dominatrices have largely won the battle to redefine sex work as work. The next logical step is to grant them workers' rights. Antonia cofounded Soldiers of Pole to do exactly that. The intergenerational group of dancers seeks to educate workers and punish rule-breaking clubs. In the 1980s, the Mitchell Brothers O'Farrell Theatre in San Francisco began charging "stage fees" for dancers just to show up at work, a practice that became generalized across the industry, much the way a hairdresser "rents" a chair in a salon. The fees have gotten higher and higher. Since the *Dynamex* decision, clubs have increased stage fees and are using dancers' money to subsidize higher wages, new taxes, and fees. "The way they're implementing the law is that they're charging us to pay our own wages," Antonia told me. Soldiers of Pole has held a number of protests against this practice and is seeking to reach an agreement with a major union to represent dancers. Because of her political stances, Antonia has been blacklisted from dancing at many clubs in LA. The only upside to this, she says, has been more time to organize. She says the main skepticism dancers have about legal employee status is that managers will have control over their time, and could force them to come in during off-peak hours. She advises them that the opposite is true; a union will mean more control over the way they work, including when they work. In fact, a union contract could give dancers the ability to stipulate their right to work only when they want. This isn't to say a union automatically guarantees total control, but it's a necessary starting point from which to challenge the complete discretion of management.

Stormy Daniels, the porn actress who was once poised to save the United States from the nightmare of the Trump presidency, has come out against the unionization effort, adding her celebrity status to a well-funded anti-union campaign. By contrast, in an online guide she published, Antonia urged regular clients to support their favorite dancers as they organize. Rule Number One: "Treat her like a Teamster."[5]

Just like Teamsters, strippers benefit greatly from the security and high wages that unions can bring. Just like Teamsters, most dancers are there first and foremost for the money—so tip well. "It's a great blue-collar job," Antonia said. "I'm there for the money. There is something about being a sex worker that makes people think I should be happy doing my job. But people don't insist that secretaries are happy every day of their lives, so why do they insist that I be happy giving hand jobs? I'm happy leaving with $950 on a Tuesday night." And just like Teamsters, strippers also have one another's backs. "We all need to stand together," Antonia said, "so it doesn't really matter if you're sucking dick or gyrating on a lap. That's my coworker, and that's my sister or brother."

By far the most contentious debate around *Dynamex* centers on the fate of rideshare drivers. By classifying drivers as independent contractors instead of employees, Uber and Lyft aren't required to pay certain taxes, benefits, overtime, or wages to their grow-ing fleet of one hundred thousand drivers. And just like strippers, self-employed contractors don't have a legal right to join a union or bargain collectively with an employer. They're on their own. For more than half of Uber's short existence, its drivers have been challenging their misclassification status in court. They argue, quite sensibly, that Uber fails the ABC test because transport-ing passengers in cars is certainly a central facet of the company's stated mission. The organizing efforts against Uber and Lyft are central to creating a new temporal condition for workers because the gig economy is premised on schedule flexibility for workers and on-demand services for users.

The stakes are high for companies like Uber, which has acknowledged the problems it would face if it followed the law. As the company explained in a statement filed with the Securities and Exchange Commission, "If, as a result of legislation or judicial decisions, we are required to classify Drivers as employees . . . we would incur significant additional expenses for compensating Drivers, potentially including expenses associated with the appli-cation of wage and hour laws (including minimum wage, over-time, and meal and rest period requirements), employee benefits, social security contributions, taxes, and penalties." The state of California estimates this kind of misclassification law-dodging costs it $7 billion per year in lost tax revenue.[6]

Nicole Moore works a good job at the health department in Los Angeles County. But a few days a week she walks out to the parking lot at 5:00 p.m., gets in her car, and starts driving for Uber late into the night. A few years ago, her mortgage tripled as a result of a bad loan. "We cut all of our expenses down to nothing, and we still couldn't make it," she said. "We had to figure out how to close the gap or lose the house." The conclusion that she and her husband landed on was to start driving for Uber. The extra cash was necessary, even if she was gambling that her car would last long enough, and even if it meant spending fewer evenings with their ten-year-old daughter.

The extra cash made a difference at first. However, her ability to earn declined as Uber and Lyft began cutting mileage reimbursement rates by as much as 25 percent around the major markets in the country. Drivers began getting restless, but more importantly they began to get organized. Nicole was one of them. It began at the airport, because that's where drivers actually see one another and communicate, waiting in lines to pick up fares. Using the functionality of the app against itself, drivers turned off their apps at once and waited for "surge pricing" to kick in, which caused the algorithm to bump up the cost of a ride. Then they all turned the apps back on at once and made more money with the jacked-up fares. But these kinds of job actions were restricted to the few hundred drivers at the airports; there are approximately one hundred thousand Uber drivers in Los Angeles. Drivers even began developing their own app, which helps them track ride fares around the city, but also allows them to reach out to new drivers, have conversations, and recruit them into an organization, Rideshare Drivers United. "The industry works very hard to keep us isolated from each other. We're doing the opposite," Nicole said.

Uber, Lyft, Postmates, and other gig economy companies see the *Dynamex* decision as a death sentence for their business model, which allows them to extract maximum effort while exerting maximum control, all without a legal responsibility to pay basic benefits like healthcare and workers' compensation. Instead, they skate by while taxpayers subsidize those costs. Yet they have put those cost savings to use in a campaign against the *Dynamex* decision. Gig companies are the sleazy club owners of the on-demand economy, and for years they have gone to great lengths to fight any hint at unionization. Yet at times it seems that they've been aided by labor's traditional forces—the same kinds of unions Chuckie and Cheryl see as vital to a thriving economy—as some major unions have made overtures to sign contracts with Uber and Lyft that would retain drivers' status as independent contractors. Drivers have thus looked instead to "alt-labor" groups like the one that Nicole is spearheading.

Nicole got involved when she began talking to drivers and saw the struggles they endured, even as the titans of the tech industry seemed to grow only wealthier. "The reason that I'm willing to do it is because when you see somebody hungry, and they have to decide whether they use the ten dollars in their pocket to buy a sandwich or put gas in their car so they can work, that's when you know that the system is wrong. If we don't do something about it, our future is so dire." She also noticed her own earnings dwindle as the app began to send her to high-traffic areas, like the airport, where there was already a line of drivers waiting. But she was quoted lower rates than they were. She was, in a sense, being sent to scab. "They are tricking out these algorithms to figure out how little drivers are willing to work for. . . . People talk about video games and how manipulative they are, and they pull you in—that's exactly the same kind of technology Lyft has. But they're pulling people into a cycle of poverty."

Committed to breaking that cycle, Uber and Lyft drivers went on strike in ten cities across the country in the spring of 2019 to coincide with the companies' IPO announcements. At Los Angeles International Airport strikers waved banners that read,

"Regulate Rideshares" and "Uber and Lyft Stop Stealing from People." Striking is literally the drivers' only recourse if they disagree with their terms of employment—clicking "no" to the contract terms just deactivates an account. A major demand of the strike was to implement the $27.86 per hour minimum guarantee that rideshare drivers won in New York City. The drivers also demanded that the companies allow drivers to take home more of the money from each fare. Nicole said that when she signed up for the app, Uber advertised she would make 80 percent of each ride, but sometimes that number is as low as 40 percent.

The strike was the top trending item on Twitter, even as it contended with the royal baby's birth in the United Kingdom. The strike targeted lawmakers more than the companies, in a bid to pressure them to respect the *Dynamex* decision and classify rideshare workers as employees, thereby granting them rights to organize and bargain with their employers. There are some signs the PR strategy worked—Uber went public with an astounding $82.4 billion IPO, but that was significantly less than what was anticipated. "What it means to be deployed by an app is the same thing it means in hospitals when the head nurse has a schedule on a piece of paper," Nicole told me. "And we have to create labor standards around it. We can't let the tech companies run circles around us. We're working with not a penny to our name, we have no staff, and we're trying to save the fucking labor movement. We organize or we die—we control the clocks or they control us."

•

REBECCA WOOD, THE Uber Eats driver in Charlottesville, often felt like she was losing that battle. A text message from her came in one night, but it wasn't as late as usual. "Charlie's had it, goin home early tonight," it said. I responded predictably, saying I wish there was something I could do to help.

"Come to Virginia," she responded, "if you're serious."

A few weeks later I was on my way to Charlottesville. We began driving after dinner. We made the usual rounds—delivering food to drunk college kids or, occasionally, some grateful travel-weary visitors from out of town. Rebecca is as well known as a late-night delivery worker as she is on Capitol Hill. Occasionally sympathetic restaurants offered her a complimentary extra drink out of solidarity. The Uber Eats app alerts drivers to new delivery jobs even before they've completed the delivery at hand. The catch is that you can only see the job after you've accepted it, which is, by any reasonable standard, an odd way to work. Rebecca accepted the job and then sighed once the details popped up on the screen. "Great, right back from where we just came from," she said.

Driving for Uber Eats delivers the same insults to one's pride as other kinds of low-wage work. The shiny veneer of technological mediation may make it seem more sophisticated or less degrading, but drive around with Rebecca for a night and you'll get a different perspective. "It's the same shitty work poor people have always been doing. It's not any different just because we have smartphones," she said.

Just a few years ago, she could have been on the other side of the app, ordering food from the comfort of her late-night couch. She had an easy life and a clear future. She was a hopeful expectant mother, without challenges arrayed before her like an obstacle course. "I'll see families that are in restaurants while I'm picking up an order or I'm dropping food off at a family's home and I'm thinking, 'That's where I'm supposed to be. That's where I was supposed to go, and instead, I'm here.' But it's gotta be done."

She believes anyone who wants to understand the struggles of the working poor should learn from them face to face, so she invited me to join her for a few days in Virginia. "I really want to see the poverty conversation opened up because I don't think they get it on Capitol Hill," she told me. Her time meeting with elected officials showed her how sheltered they are from the policies they enact for everyone else. "I really think people need to step outside of their bubbles and see what the lives of other people are like. Travel, and see what other parts of the country are like. Because the people writing policy right now just don't get it. Most people, in fact, don't get it." Since she had become an expert on healthcare, she had started Healthcare Now Virginia to educate people from the rural, often reddest, parts of the state on ways to gain access to better care. Her main takeaway from this experience became something of a mantra for her. Conservative voters really wanted universal healthcare, and they deserved it, but it was often centrist elected Democrats who were the major obstacle. "Our enemies are those who pretend to be our friends," she said, "not just conservatives." She thought a weekend in rural Virginia might show me what she meant.

After delivering past midnight, the next morning we found ourselves driving into the sunrise through rural Virginia, closing in on Chesapeake. There we began setting up the Remote Area Medical clinic. RAM began providing care in 1985 as a pop-up medical service in impoverished countries. But it quickly discovered its services were just as crucial in the United States. It now operates dozens of free clinics each year throughout rural America.

Rebecca began volunteering after her dental surgery. "Horrific and brutal as it was, at least I had somewhere to go in the midnight hour," she told me. A lot of people don't, and so I wanted to make something good come out of my nightmare." The clinic, which we set up inside a Hindu temple in Chesapeake, had eighteen dental chairs, six eye exam areas, a women's health clinic, preventive care stations, orthopedists, and pulmonary specialists— all staffed by local doctors and medical students volunteering their time. Over the course of the week, one RAM coordinator estimated that dentists pulled hundreds of teeth. Rebecca had initially signed up to work in dental, but she was assigned instead to the vision lab, a truck in the back of the clinic that manufactured glasses. Over the past few years she had become a lay expert, and led the team that ground lenses and fitted them into frames for hundreds of people.

A winding line of families waited overnight to get a spot near the front for the 8:00 a.m. opening, some coming from neighboring states. Nearly everyone I spoke with worked a minimum wage job or had a side hustle in addition to a main occupation. They did the things policymakers say you should do to lift yourself out of poverty. Most even had some form of healthcare plan. But their jobs paid pitifully, and even though they hated them, they wanted more hours. Their insurance was too expensive to use. Natalia Floris risked losing her job as a travel agent by taking the day off to come to RAM, but she said she'd been painfully ignoring her dental problems for years because of the expense. Princeton Carpenter, from nearby Virginia Beach, said his insurance co-pays were too high and his job didn't offer any assistance. One could survey the landscape at the clinic and appreciate the outpouring of mutual aid. Hundreds of medical professionals plus ordinary residents took time to patch desperate holes in our broken healthcare system for the weekend. Emotions ran high at times. One man I spoke with, who goes by Spike, said he would finally be able to kiss his grandchildren now that the pain from his chronic toothaches would subside, his voice jumping and catching as he spoke.

When I recounted some of these scenes to Rebecca, who was stuck in the vision lab truck all day, she snapped. "It's not fucking inspiring," she said, in her plainspoken manner. "It's poverty. It's a disgrace. None of this should even be happening. I hate it when people feel inspired by this. It's grotesque."

Because poverty is so prevalent, it's easy to see it as ordinary, a natural feature of our economic landscape. The same could be said about the kinds of exploitation that Antonia sees regularly in the clubs—dancers being drugged, assaulted, battered, or pimped out by clients and employers. Cheryl and Chuckie had suffered the indignities and health consequences of being moved around the country at their employer's whim, a routine experience of manufacturing workers throughout US history. Uber drivers often appear as though they're their own bosses, but some of the drivers I met on the picket line with Nicole regularly slept in their cars, unable to afford basic accommodations—a segment of the working homeless amid the glitz of the tech boom. A common theme throughout these stories, in fact, is the refusal of organizers to accept the status quo. In each case, workers were moved to action not because their rights on the job were violated or a specific grievance drove them over the edge. Rather, it was the basic structure of the job that often made it so unlivable. "Nothing happened, actually, to make this job so shitty," said Rebecca, about Uber Eats. "It's just the job itself, and there's a million more just like it. My life is governed by shit work."

Terrence Wiggins, the Target employee we met in Chapter 1, also knew the indignities of being pushed around for low-wage work. Though he was initially hired full time, his hours were quickly reduced. Soon he had too many hours one week, and not nearly enough the next. As his schedule became increasingly erratic, he tried to solve it by appealing to friendly managers for more hours at more convenient times, all the while rearranging family obligations. He talked about his situation with others and soon started hearing they suffered the same problems. "We all wanted regular hours, better schedules," he said. "Some of my friends had houses or apartments that they couldn't even pay rent for because of the simple fact that they're getting their hours cut."

These scheduling practices are a persistent complaint of millions of Americans. Workers are expected to be "flexible" and accept whatever schedule they're given. They're sent home in the middle of shifts or threatened with termination if they don't stay for overtime. On top of that, wages are abysmal, the industry average hovering around thirteen dollars an hour. Terrence's life began to intersect with this combination of temporal instability and poverty pay. At some point a coworker showed him an article about a community group called One Pennsylvania, which was fighting for fair scheduling for retail workers, and he immediately became involved. He thought the legislation they were proposing, which would make it mandatory for employers to give workers their schedules with greater advance notice, would allow him to keep his job.

Pretty soon he was attending two organizing meetings per day. He testified at public hearings about what a fair workweek would mean to him and found himself sharing others' stories too. "Fighting for a fair workweek wasn't just for me," he said. "It was for all the people who were scared to stick up for themselves. It was a whole bunch of people in different retail stores. . . . One Pennsylvania is all about fighting for what's right, and not because they help you, but because we help others. I feel like this is a major part of economic justice and worker justice. I feel like helping people is everything."

Terrence wasn't asking for much: two weeks' notice of his schedule. But it would make all the difference. "I can make doctors' appointments, I can pick the days I need off, without worrying about retaliation, someone being on your back, in case something might come up, like a funeral," he said. "I love my family to death, so I'd love to be around them when they need me. You can do a lot with two weeks."

Eventually Terrence's story found YouTube, and a video of him giving a speech went viral. "I got to work one day and everyone had seen it," he told me, laughing. "Instagram was crazy with it." He was afraid Target would retaliate, but the opposite happened. Target began to give him better hours, inching toward the schedule for which he was originally hired. "Once I felt that energy it was like, Oh, so in order for people to get respect in here, they have to fight back." Terrence felt emboldened.

In December 2018 his effort paid off. The Philadelphia City Council passed the Fair Workweek Employment Standards

Ordinance, which required large retail, hospitality, and food service establishments to offer more regular schedules to workers, including two weeks' advance notice; to provide "predictability pay" to make up for departures from posted schedules; and to guarantee a nine-hour rest period between shifts. One Pennsylvania estimates these changes will affect 130,000 workers. Philadelphia became the eighth city to pass a scheduling law, along with San Francisco, San Jose, and Emeryville in California; Seattle and SeaTac in Washington; Portland, Oregon; New York City.

Terrence was a leader but hardly a pioneer in the movement. I interviewed dozens of retail workers across the country who suffered the same work conditions as he did and saw the fair scheduling movement as the pathway to change their industry. In 2013 workers launched a nationwide movement to win fair scheduling legislation that would allow them a greater degree of control over their time. Noemi Castro, for example, was literally the face of the movement in Los Angeles. Her likeness was used in ads and on banners during the fight to win fair scheduling legislation there. Despite offering Kmart "open availability," industry parlance for being able to work at any time of day, she was assigned thirty hours some weeks but only four hours other weeks. For three years. Some of those hours came in the form of exhausting "clopening shifts," which meant she would close the store one night at ten and leave the house by five the next morning to open the store at six.

The first victory came in 2014 in San Francisco County, where the Board of Supervisors passed a landmark Retail Workers Bill of Rights that covers the city's "formula retail" stores, which employ about half of all retail workers there, and guarantees similar rights as those Terrence helped win in Philadelphia. Defending such legislation without a unionized workforce has already hampered the real viability of the movements in some places, however, so we should see these legislative battles as beginnings, not ends.

Fair scheduling matters a lot to workers, but losing even a shred of managerial control over workers' time is a big deal for employers too. Already, twelve states have passed legislation preempting local fair scheduling laws. These places don't even have fair scheduling laws on the books yet, but employers have already found ways to block them. That means if you work at Target, Staples, Kmart, or some other retail firm in Alabama, Arizona, Arkansas, Georgia, Indiana, Iowa, Kansas, Michigan, North Carolina, Oregon, Tennessee, Texas, or Wisconsin, you don't have the right to have the right to a fair schedule.

The fair scheduling movement is the clearest way workers are struggling to control time today. Even though they are occasionally asking for *more* hours, a "time agenda" for labor must include a way for workers to reliably meet their basic needs. Implicitly, however, the notion of a "fair workweek" means that everyone gets the right amount of work. And because we have too much already, the best plan is to reduce hours across the board and more equitably share what's left.

Most jobs can be good jobs, with decent wages, high safety standards, and a strong voice for workers. But even the best jobs at long or irregular hours can't always fit into our lives the way we need them to. The first step toward more good jobs is to reduce our need to work so much in general. As a nation, we have paid an enormous price for allowing the hours of labor to become unnecessarily long, unpredictable, and unmanageable. The next chapter examines remedies that could reduce work time to a minimum.

CHAPTER 8

LABOR'S FORGOTTEN FIGHT

FREE TIME IS AN OBJECTIVE GOOD IN AND OF ITSELF, AND WORK-
ers clearly deserve more than they're currently getting. Benjamin
Kline Hunnicutt, a professor of leisure studies at the University of
Iowa, refers to the search for free time as the "forgotten American
Dream." Before Americans promoted the work ethic and upward
mobility as our national theology, we professed allegiance to an
entirely different, more enlightened ideal: "Higher Progress," a
term Hunnicutt borrowed from Walt Whitman. Higher Progress
mixed religious and early Romantic notions of freedom, painting
a picture of humankind as fundamentally burdened by work and
liberated at rest. The reward for our labor isn't money, in this
case, but the ultimate peace.

But rest and respite are hardly the only benefits, and free
time can't be defined simply as the absence of work. Free time
is an essential facet of democratic society. It gives us the ability
to exercise our rights and enjoy the freedoms we already have.
Voting is hardly democratic if people can't get to the polls. Who
needs national parks if there's no time to pitch a tent and do a
little stargazing? Free time is also a necessary component of any
movement for social change. As every activist knows, time scar-
city is one of the largest impediments to ordinary people becoming politically engaged. Without time to contemplate the world,

how can we expect to change it? We need to carve out free time to organize, plot, conspire, and fight.

Early labor history is littered with bloody battles over the physical control of clocks and violent episodes to win the eight-hour day. Yet reducing labor time was less an insurrection and more of a century-long grind. Concern over time has largely been forgotten, pushed aside by demands for higher wages, healthcare, safety, and job security. But we've forgotten this concern at our peril: a major worsening condition for workers has been the intensity, duration, and unpredictability of their working life. When we work, for how long, and at what point in the day or week, is usually beyond our grasp today. The historic struggle for shorter hours isn't just about leisure—it's about control.

According to the Economic Policy Institute, only 15 percent of workers say they are "free to decide" their work schedule. This instability is a growing problem, associated with mental and physical stress, unstable income, emotional turmoil, family conflicts, gender inequity, ecological instability, and overall personal unhappiness. We seem to want the opposite. A YouGov poll in 2015 found that only 15 percent of workers would choose to work a day less in exchange for losing that day of pay. However, if workers could take a day off with no corresponding change in pay, 78 percent would do it. It's not that we don't want to work less; it's that we live in a society where not all of us can afford to do so.[1]

Popular solutions to the time crunch are typically predicated on individuals' making new lifestyle choices, and are geared toward the upper echelons of the labor force. "Downshifting" to less rat-race careers, a white-collar take on voluntary simplicity, enjoyed a high-profile moment in the early nineties. Then "work-life balance" became the watchword for overworked professionals. Today, the FIRE movement—financial independence, retire early—promises more leisure through better money management for those who can afford to save.

A more structural demand is that employers consider employ-ees' lives outside their jobs by offering flexible work arrange-ments to give workers options about where and when to work. This would be a welcome enhancement to many workplaces, but depending on benevolent bosses doesn't give workers more control over their time. We should simply reduce hours instead. Decreasing hours would bring a number of benefits besides merely reducing the amount of time we have to spend working. It would help create a smaller national ecological footprint, for example, one part of a larger movement to reverse the climate catastrophe.[2]

Many countries, though not the United States, have managed to attain fewer working hours through provisions for guaranteed family and medical leave. This has led some to argue that merely copying and pasting European policies is a strategy for shorter hours, a position with some merit. If we had more legally man-dated vacation time, more sick leave and time to care for chil-dren and the infirm, and greater unemployment benefits, work time *could* go down. Overall hours reduction is key to developing effective means of care, a particularly time-consuming form of labor, and would recognize that care is a socially important pub-lic resource.

More time for care is absolutely essential. One in four mothers returns to work two weeks after childbirth, a dangerously early time for both mother and child. More paid leave to devote to care could help combat gender inequality because most care and domestic labor is unpaid, and time-use studies have indicated that women spend nearly twice as much time as men engaged in these activ-ities. Though women have dramatically increased their hours in recent decades, their overwork in the home generally pushes them out of high-income occupations that require and reward extensive hours. This economic penalty against women incentivizes married fathers to work longer hours, often resulting in an even greater gendered division of labor within the home. One major study by Harvard economist Claudia Goldin on the "last chapter" of gender inequality found that "the gender gap in pay would be considerably reduced and might vanish altogether if firms did not have an incentive to disproportionately reward individuals who labored long hours and worked particular hours."

Those advocating these policies do so under the banner of "choice." If we give people more options for care and family time, the logic goes, we can empower them to control their own time as they see fit. It's important to remember, however, that care work is work, even if it doesn't appear in government statistics. Freeing up hours for parents to do more unpaid childcare does not necessarily increase our sense of free time. Moreover, the political freedom to choose a policy advocating shorter hours does not resolve the fundamental problem. Millions of workers could never afford to choose fewer hours in exchange for more time at home. Choice is only useful if the options are realistically available.

An agenda to reduce hours overall is more effective. To realize this possibility, workers must regain the power to control, reduce, and improve the quality of the time we work. We need a mass movement to win particular policy changes that can allow us to exercise greater collective control over work time—a return to labor's forgotten fight. Such a movement would be aimed at not only reducing but also controlling the time we already work, a quantitative and qualitative shift. Now, what might such a time agenda look like today?

In a precarious economy with a dwindling safety net, hours reduction represents an issue with the potential to cut across race, gender, and age lines, even uniting unions with community and social justice groups, thereby presenting strategic opportunities for workers to build a new social movement unionism. A shorter hours movement—with no or very little reduction in pay—would require a few related puzzle pieces to come together. The foundation would be an active workers' movement that can sustain a long struggle. It's a high bar. Working people's organizations are severely weakened, yet they are still our best hope for large-scale social change. Workload is a constant concern of average workers, though it almost never makes the agenda of the trade union movement, pushed out by other important concerns such as pay and benefits. Marx argued that high levels of economic prosperity—as we have here in the United States—would lead societies to define real wealth as free time, or "disposable time." Unfortunately, workers too often feel that their lives are disposable, useful only so long as they generate profit. It's about time we take up the fight to reduce work time, and in the process to revalue workers' lives. Below I suggest a few ingredients that might form a kind of recipe for work time reduction.

Spread It Around

Work-sharing programs constitute the most robust policy vehicle to spread work around, maintain or elevate workers' incomes, reduce unemployment, and avoid layoffs. We have far too much work already, so let's spread it around. Work-sharing policies could redistribute our unfair allocation of work time. If many in one group are overworked but those in another group are demanding more hours, as stories throughout this book demonstrate, then work-sharing is well suited to address the problem. The idea is simple enough. During economic downturns, employers and employees agree to reduce the labor hours of a firm's workers as opposed to laying off a select few. Such programs essentially spread the income losses that occur during recessions or downturns across a wider group of people, preventing more damaging consequences, like the loss of a job. The practice dates back to the campaign to win the eight-hour day. Samuel Gompers, president of the American Federation of Labor, said, "So long as there is one man who seeks employment and cannot obtain it the hours of labor are too long."[3]

At various crisis points throughout history, the US government imposed work-sharing programs to guard against widespread unemployment. Such policies were hotly debated in public, placing work time closer to something we can control on a large scale. The practice was a common antidote used by the Hoover administration to combat joblessness and underemployment amid the Great Depression. In 1938, the Fair Labor Standards Act attempted to spread out employment by mandating a forty-hour workweek for most nonfarm industries, plus time and a half for overtime. Then in the 1960s, fear of automation and the large baby boomer generation caused another uptick in bargaining down hours to avoid unemployment.[4]

Work-sharing has occasionally been not just a policy instrument but an act of solidarity. Labor organizer and writer Sam Gindin recalls that work-sharing was a common response to any proposed layoffs in automobile manufacturing. In the late 1970s, the auto unions in the United States and Canada negotiated significant work reductions through paid holidays and four-day weekends, which allowed plants to employ more people, even as they operated six days per week. By the 1990s, the unions were fighting for even greater reductions in work time, occasionally at the expense of wages. Gindin told me,

> In our early agreements at Ford, if there was a layoff, everybody would just go down to working 20 percent less. You'd all work four days a week instead of five, instead of some people being laid off. And it was a sense of solidarity that was kind of emerging out of the organizing. Whereas the companies had been arguing that

higher wages threatened jobs, that it is the companies who create jobs and the workers who are the barrier, we said, "We're creating the jobs, you guys are just laying off people all over the place." And we got a lot of public support because of that emphasis on work time.

But work-sharing is better as a law than as a private bargaining issue. As the Great Recession struck, work-sharing claims increased tenfold, and between 2010 and 2014 eleven states created new programs. As a response to increased need, the Obama administration passed a federal work-sharing program in 2012 that sought to increase these programs by ensuring that employees whose workweeks were reduced by at least 10 percent would be eligible for a proportional amount of unemployment compensation, encouraging employers to shorten workers' hours rather than reduce the number of workers.

Overall, however, work-sharing programs have been underutilized in the United States, compared to Europe, during corresponding periods of economic distress. In Germany, for example, the *Kurzarbeit* system enabled German firms to avoid layoffs and promote legitimate flexibility of hours to save jobs in 2008 and 2020, insulating workers from some of the crash-induced financial pains of the Great Recession and the coronavirus crisis. Rather than allowing widespread layoffs, the federal government in the United States should have utilized existing legislation to subsidize work-share programs as soon as the magnitude of the COVID-19 pandemic became known. Work-sharing legislation is a clear tool in crisis management and a pathway to better hours, but, as a temporary measure, it can't be the horizon of hope for dealing with work time.[5] Rather than just reallocate work time, we need a bold plan to reduce it, which will require more people being able to live with much less of it.

Universal Basic Services

In order for significantly shorter hours to be feasible in the long run, they must be implemented in conjunction with other policies that create a foundation for all Americans, working or not. A Universal Basic Services (UBS) platform would provide free, unconditional access to healthcare, education, childcare, transportation, shelter, and adult social care. Rather than relying on profit-based, private companies to meet shared human needs, UBS would create public systems focused on efficiency and collective well-being.[6]

The recent fascination with universal basic income has prompted a renewed interest in ways to increase social well-being by decoupling income from work. A more cost-effective and fair way to do this would be simply to fund universal access to social services with our taxes—let's make survival an unconditional social good. A report by Autonomy, a think tank based in the United Kingdom, suggests the "economic security" of accessible basic services creates a "social wage" that "could allow for the voluntary reduction of working time on the part of individuals." Currently, employment and wages largely determine workers' ability to gain access to and pay for basic services that they need to survive. If services like food and medical care were guaranteed, there could be more opportunity to reduce work hours because we would need to work less to pay for our essential life maintenance. A comprehensive UBS program may seem like magical thinking, but it's not a zero-sum game—and part of the groundwork is already in place. There have long been experiments across the world, including in the United States, that enacted fare-free transport, and many places offer free healthcare and education.[7]

Medicare for All in the United States was perhaps the most divisive plank of the progressive 2020 Democratic hopefuls, even though the majority of Americans on the left and right now support it. During a 2019 meeting on Medicare for All, Michael Lighty, a leading expert on healthcare policy, asked the question with which he begins most such gatherings: "How many of you would like to avoid ever talking to a health insurance agent again?" Predictably, every hand went up. Yet many raised concerns that included comparisons to other countries with free healthcare systems. "They say Canadians hate their public system," Lighty countered, "but you don't see them marching in the streets for Aetna." When pushed on the cost of free care, Lighty provided data that showed universal healthcare is $5 trillion cheaper than our current system, and provides a far higher quality of service.[8]

A Medicare for All program is a strategic part of the fight for shorter work hours and better schedules. Healthcare is closely tied to work hours, as 49 percent of Americans get healthcare through their employer. Minimum hour eligibility requirements for coverage and high out-of-pocket expenses keep workers locked into long-hour work schedules just to receive medical care. As the coronavirus pandemic began taking its toll, many low-wage workers lost their healthcare as a result of losing their jobs. They were then forced to risk their own health, and that of others, by looking for more work under dangerous conditions. Amid the chaos of those early days of the outbreak in the United States, many people quickly realized that paid sick leave, work sharing, banked vacation time, fair scheduling laws, basic income, and Medicare for All would be necessary to save lives and stave off complete economic ruin. Employers and government agencies typically viewed these things as temporary solutions to an emergency, but they are exactly the policies that should be permanent features of our economy.

Bargaining over healthcare and related benefits is a driver of stagnating wages and long hours. Since the seventies, unions have negotiated higher benefits, such as healthcare, instead of wages, driving up the fixed cost per worker. This incentivizes employers to press for longer hours from workers rather than hire more workers who require benefits. The value of fringe benefits ballooned over the second half of the twentieth century, rising from 17 percent of pay in 1955 to 36 percent in 1987. As of 2018, fringe benefits make up an average of 46.6 percent of pay. And in some cases, when benefits are scaled back by management, we are forced to work longer to pay for basic needs.[9]

For the past two decades, healthcare has been a constant drag on contract negotiations, as employers continue to shift health-care costs onto workers. Healthcare disputes have thus become the leading instigator of strikes, lockouts, and concessionary bar-gaining. During strikes, employers often freeze health insurance and pension benefits to try to force workers to concede, as hap-pened to Cheryl during the GM strike. And as Chuckie noted in the previous chapter, when unions are forced to bargain over maintaining workers' health coverage, they lose opportunities to get higher wages and other benefits.[10]

A Medicare for All system would cost employers the powerful leverage they hold by controlling access to workers' healthcare, and unions could focus on bargaining for other benefits such as higher pay and shorter hours. Workers who want to transition to shorter hours would not have to worry about losing coverage or not being able to afford out-of-pocket expenses, as medical care would be guaranteed. Historically, unions have often opposed universal healthcare because they've held out the prospect of coverage as a benefit to attract new members. Yet, as veteran labor journalist Steve Early notes, workers have also struck to fight for a tax-supported universal healthcare system, not merely coverage for their own members, and there's no reason why they can't again. What a boon it would be to the labor movement if unions fought for, and won, a society-wide gain. "Universal" means everyone in, no one out. For this reason, campaigns for universal services incubate strong movements to defend the commons. Nowhere is this more visible than in recent teacher strikes to improve public education.[11]

Striking for the Common Good

As always, we should learn from our teachers. In 2018 teachers in Mingo County, West Virginia, began to shut down their schools, demanding higher pay. Eighth-grade history teacher Jay O'Neal remembers the moment vividly. "We were trembling, some of us excited, some of us afraid, all of us a little unsure what might happen."

What eventually happened was something none of his colleagues had imagined—a wave of strikes broke out in schools across the nation, concentrated in rural Trump country, earning the movement the moniker Red State Revolt. One by one, schoolteachers in West Virginia, Oklahoma, Colorado, New Mexico, and Kentucky began walking out. As the strikes kept going through the end of the school year, I interviewed teachers in North Carolina.

One Wednesday in late April, Kristin Beller, a kindergarten teacher and president of the Wake County branch of the North Carolina teachers' union, called her school's central office to check on the number of personal days teachers had requested that week. It was three hundred, a normal amount. When she called back on Monday, there were eight hundred requests. The next day there were 1,200, at which point she was told the office was no longer allowed to speak with her. Three weeks later, on May 16, the first day of the legislative session, around thirty thousand teachers were marching on Raleigh, each having requested a personal day to attend the protest. The annual "advocacy day" held by the North Carolina Association of Educators (NCAE) typically draws about four hundred people.

That year, so many teachers requested the day off that superin-
tendents in 42 of the state's 115 districts were forced to close
schools, a movement that piggybacked on months of strikes
across the country.[12]

What do these upsurges have to do with movements for shorter
hours, which none of the strikes were explicitly demanding?
Common to all the strikes was an attempt to use unions as vehicles to intervene in political debates outside the workplace. In
North Carolina teachers began organizing at the Moral Monday
protests, which brought tens of thousands of citizens to the statehouse in Raleigh each week to participate in civil disobedience
actions. The premise of Moral Mondays was to unite a spectrum
of political viewpoints under a universalist agenda for healthcare,
education, voting rights, and reproductive freedom. Local teachers began independently canvassing at the events and built a list
of hundreds of rank-and-file educators. A core of that group was
largely responsible for the success of their mass sick-out. Virtually
every strike has examples like this.

In Kentucky, Tia Kurtisnger-Edison had buried one of her own
students, who was killed in a drive-by shooting in 2018. As a
teacher and member of a local Black Lives Matter chapter, she
appealed to her union in Jefferson County, where more than
half the students are black and brown and 70 percent are on free
lunch, to oppose a local stop-and-frisk "gang bill" that was making its way through local government. When her union said no,
she organized her fellow teachers to walk out anyway and shut
down their schools—six times. "We knew how to sick out," she
said, referencing lessons learned from other teacher strikes. Her
union's president appeared on local news shaming teachers for
the unauthorized strike, and the governor has subpoenaed the
names of all those who took part. "There's more of us than them,"
she said, seemingly confident in the ability of her coworkers to
keep the pressure on the bill.

Gillian Russom is a history teacher in Los Angeles. Her union, the UTLA, thinks it's no coincidence that the anti-tax policies that made California schools forty-fourth in the nation for funding coincided with an influx of students and teachers of color since the 1970s. This is exactly why her union has developed a racial justice platform that uses the school as a launchpad for addressing issues related to racism in the community.

When a father of one of her students was detained by immigration police as he dropped off his daughter at school, the union immediately joined a successful campaign to save him from deportation. "Our union organizing doesn't happen in a silo," Gillian said, explaining that her union also worked alongside student organizers. In a public setting, it's technically illegal to have "nonmandatory" demands on the table when workers vote to strike. After they're on strike, however, workers can make any demands part of the conditional deal to go back to work. "They will tell you that you can't bargain over this or that demand," Gillian said at a public forum in Chicago. "You can get 'em if you go on strike for 'em."

When their contract was settled and teachers went back to work, they had successfully baked into their contract a set of policies that supported issues in their local community—ending random searches of students by school police, starting an immigrant justice fund to support families facing deportation, freeing up public green space for local families on their school campuses, and creating affordable housing out of unused district buildings. Bargaining for the common good recognizes that schools are social and political institutions embedded in communities that can choose to either support or oppose local reform movements.

The overarching demand made by striking teachers was to reclaim funding for public education. On the surface, this would appear to have nothing to do with control over time. However, teachers have longer workweeks (around fifty-three hours) than most Americans. Teachers typically log seven of those hours at home, long after they've left the classroom, often fulfilling duties imposed upon them because of a lack of school funding. Almost all teachers in the United States report buying school supplies for their students, attempting to fill in the gaps left by slashed education budgets.[13]

Many teachers across the country were pushed to strike because they were unable to survive by working only one job. I interviewed a handful who moonlighted as salesclerks, waitresses, or Uber drivers, or who ran small businesses out of their homes just to get by. It has long been common for teachers to take summer jobs, but juggling multiple jobs at once is new. During the 2015–2016 school year, almost 20 percent of public school-teachers worked another job, according to the National Center for Education Statistics. That's an even higher percentage than what was reported at the peak of the Great Recession in 2008. Teachers are now about five times more likely than the average full-time US worker to hold down a part-time job.

Shorter hours is a perfect "common good demand," associated with a range of benefits beyond the workplace. Common good bargaining views unions as powerful social institutions that are accountable to more than just their own members, championing universalist demands.

In 2018, the German trade union IG Metall struck to win a twenty-eight-hour workweek for its members, in part by operating under the framework of the common good. Union leaders argued that shorter hours would allow them to spread the work, as well as to confront "social problems," such as providing childcare and caring for sick family members. A similar rationale informed the strikes at the start of the coronavirus pandemic. As a few large firms retaliated against workers for wearing protective clothing or for unionizing at their workplaces, resentment quickly turned into action. Thousands of workers went on strike throughout March and April 2020 to enforce public health guidelines in their workplace and keep essential services flowing safely—for the good of all of us. This example is one to follow as it explicitly embeds concerns about work time with a concern that transcends the workplace in collective bargaining agreements. We should do the same for concerns about technological innovation.

Robots for the Common Good

Concerns about "the future of work" are of a speculative nature: what will the future look like? A focus on the "future of workers" instead tries not to predict the future, but to restructure it. Robots won't liberate us from toil or save us time unless society has greater control over their use and technological innovation is explicitly geared toward social good. Automating jobs away is not the same thing as saving time or reducing work. The reason the full potential of automation can be best realized under actual democracy is that the gains to be had from replacing workers would be shared society-wide, whereas capitalism limits automation's applicability only to where it can make companies more profitable.

One way to do this might be to link robot-induced productivity to a "leisure dividend." During the midcentury decades, technology-driven productivity increased faster than today, but lower-wage workers reaped the gains from it even more than those at the top thanks to strong unions. In this way, we reduced overall inequality and helped truncate the workweek. In 2019, the AFL-CIO tepidly advocated a proposal for a four-day week at thirty-two hours, based largely on a leisure dividend from technology.

Workers could bargain for contracts that guarantee a wage increase and/or the option to receive productivity gains in paid time off. As firms become more automated and productive, and therefore profitable, workers would have a solid justification to demand a greater portion of the surplus. But automation doesn't equal work reduction unless workers have a union or some other time-sharing mechanism. And productivity alone isn't the best bet if the goal is shorter hours. The overall sluggish growth of productivity throughout the seventies and eighties, alongside the intensified deployment of labor-saving technology, presented a curious paradox, which famously prompted economist Robert Solow to quip, "You can see the computer age everywhere but in the productivity statistics." This doesn't mean that productivity isn't important. If all of our productivity gains could be converted into time off instead of pay and consumption for the next twelve years, we could reduce our standard workweek by 20 percent. We would maintain, not improve, our current standard of living, but produce it quicker. This would be a welcome decline in hours, but the change is not significant enough.[14]

There are drawbacks to tying leisure to productivity increases, however. Some sectors of the economy are easier to make more productive than others. Producing more widgets per hour seems like a good thing. But making nursing or teaching more productive—by treating more patients or teaching more students per hour—has obvious risks. It would be unfair to reward only people in the most productive industries with more free time. This inequity could be mitigated through a federal policy to distribute productivity gains broadly, not just to those workers who happen to be in firms or sectors that are well positioned to increase efficiencies. The Alaska state government pays each of its citizens a dividend from its oil reserves, though not everyone, obviously, works in the petroleum industry. Alaskans consider it a public resource.

Using productivity gains to produce leisure can be part of a strategy to reduce our workload. But for it to be most effective, it must be tied to a larger political movement to transcend the limits of capitalist society. Demanding shorter hours should help us decide when and how much we want to work, and also animate a vision of the future in which work plays a wholly different role in our lives. The logical conclusion of the demand for shorter hours is not zero work—it's control over labor time. For this reason, champions of automation usually have a lot in common with democratic socialists. Shorter hours is a bridge to larger political change, which is the real reason elites oppose it so vigorously. I'd like to elaborate this final point by way of a brief anecdote from my own life.

Time After Capitalism

In my early twenties I did a short stint as a longshoreman, unloading cargo containers on the Seattle shipyards. My designation as a "casual" required me to show up at the hiring hall hours before the shift, and then wait to see if my number was called. Seattle longshoremen had struck several times against the maritime companies to try to regain control over the hiring process and stop casuals from working on ships because we were nonunion, at-will employees. My very presence there was the product of a historical defeat, though by that time it was recognized as the industry's modus operandi. It was the only job I ever had that required a strength test, and to this day I can't believe I passed.

One day we had to recover some debris from the top of a shipping container that had been stacked on top of another one. It was miserable, with rain and cold wind, a quintessential Seattle morning. I volunteered to take the ladder up, eager to prove myself worthy to my coworkers, all of whom could probably tell that I was not cut out for this work and would not last long. (They were right.) As I approached the middle of the ladder I could feel it bow under my weight and sway in the wind. I paused for a split second.

"You got this!" one of the guys yelled from below.

I made the first recovery pretty quickly, came back down, and immediately got back up to continue the job. I repeated this a number of times with Stakhanovite exertion, hoping to impress the guys holding the ladder. After a few ups and downs, someone grabbed my arm when I touched the ground. "Relax," he said. "Take it slow."

"I'll be careful," I said, assuming he was looking out for my safety.

"I mean we're paid for our time here," he explained, "not for the work." Others were watching our interaction and nodded approvingly.

In an instant I could tell I had simultaneously violated an important code of their workplace and embarrassed myself. Despite the burly builds that predominated, strength and physical prowess were hardly the main points of pride on the docks. There was a larger principle at play—not being a sucker. We were hired for eight hours, not to complete a set lump of work. If we worked too quickly, the company would give us more work to do without extra pay, or reduce our hours or threaten layoffs. If we worked too slowly, we would stand out and face reprimand. What fundamentally distinguished experienced workers from newbies like me was not only a physical capability or technical competency but an understanding of the entire work and management process. What many would have identified as a poor work ethic and classic foot-dragging was actually a strategy to retain a sense of dignity, to maintain safety, and exert a degree of control. I was not only endangering myself by working unnecessarily fast— I was a sucker.

The philosophy on the docks was not so much a work ethic as it was a time ethic. There was the coveted night shift, colloquially known as the hoot owl, where wages were such that it was commonly said you worked five but were paid for eight. There was even a movement within the rank and file to get rid of overtime on the basis that it was "scabbing on the unemployed," a solidaristic impulse that harkened back to the heyday of communist labor radicalism. And there was a plodding rhythm to the workday, not a frenzied race.

About a decade later I found myself risking my safety again, this time in actual race mode, as a bicycle messenger. The job entailed the opposite kind of time-consciousness. More deliveries meant more money. And speedier riders received larger tips. There was, therefore, an obvious incentive to ride dangerously through Manhattan's treacherous streets, dodging taxis, buses, garbage trucks, and pedestrians. The work philosophy and point of pride was completely individualistic. The job rewarded those who worked the fastest, took the biggest risks, yet managed to survive the inevitable roadway mayhem. By and large, the modern workplace produces the second philosophy, a work ethic. But it is the first, an ethic of collective time-consciousness, that we should rediscover. The docks provide a good place to start.

In Tony Kushner's play *The Intelligent Homosexual's Guide to Capitalism and Socialism with a Key to the Scriptures*, an Italian American dockworker from Brooklyn, Gus, invites his adult children back to their home in Carroll Gardens to explain why he is going to kill himself. A committed communist until the end, Gus helped longshoremen win a guaranteed basic income, a struggle based on the real history of the East Coast dockworkers' union. But it wasn't enough; he's got the old-time religion. Gus has been increasingly plagued by the fact that the working class was unable to fulfill its historic mission as the handmaiden of proletarian revolution. To make matters worse, his children are in fealty to a system he spent his entire life trying to destroy. "What you call progress, I call the prison rebuilding itself," he tells his daughter, Empty, a labor lawyer. Toward the denouement, he delivers a righteous panegyric that captures his sense of accomplishment, even in defeat: "We did something that no one appreciates. It was working class guys, working class, with no politics, no training, facing down their own fears of being called bums and featherbedders, and crooks! And insisting not only on a worker's right to a wage! But a right to a share in the wealth! A right to be alive! A right to control time itself!"

The demand to "control time itself" is a double entendre. The longshore unions were shockingly successful at winning vacation days, long weekends, overtime pay, and even a basic income that allowed laid-off union members to continue drawing a wage, thus avoiding poverty. In general, my experience of the time-consciousness of my coworkers on the docks bears out in the larger ethnographic studies of this workforce. But Gus's demand also refers to the destiny of humankind under worker control. Those on the Left understand the working class to be the historical agent of change that will transcend capitalism. With their hands on the instruments of mass production and service provision, they are particularly well positioned to launch a revolution against business owners, a battle that will literally change the course of human history and the type of society in which we live. Gus feels it is the right—no, the *duty*—of his coworkers and others like them to fulfill this sacred mission. And when it appears that it will fail, when the forces arrayed against them are too strong, he simply cannot bear to watch the alternative ending.

The starring role in which workers have been cast in this historical drama—both in Kushner and Marx—has often perpetuated the great misunderstanding that socialists fetishize hard work. This is not the case. Marx argued, "The realm of freedom actually begins only where labor which is determined by necessity and mundane considerations ceases . . . the shortening of the working day is its basic prerequisite." Never one to shrink from a contradiction, Marx thought that workers should abolish work. Should we?

"Fuck work!" is often the clarion call today from the antiwork Left. The phrase evokes a transgressive desire that derives its power from wishing to undermine an unjust social convention. Most of us can, even on good days at the office, empathize with "fuck work." But the stance would be greatly aided by an in-depth analysis of a mass movement struggling against work in general. The problem is that work abolition tends to glorify the possibility of free time yet sidestep the issue of controlling it. In that sense, being antiwork offers a kind of psychic release, an escape from the mess of social life, but it does not offer a vision beyond work. A push for shorter hours, by contrast, tries to build an alternative from the inside out. "Fuck work!" is a better bumper sticker than a clarion call. Shorter hours are something that workers can really fight for.

After seeing Kushner's production, I was finally able to digest the lesson the docks had to teach: time isn't money; it's power, control, and justice. And those with the power to control labor also control time. Throughout this book are stories of workers fighting back. They rebelled against Taylor's stopwatch. They resisted algorithmic domination. They fought in welfare offices and in the streets to end brutal workfare policies. They turned the tools of the gig economy against itself, and struck to control the uses of automation in the heart and soul of the old industrial factories. Sometimes they won, making small advances against all odds. Just as frequently they were blacklisted, beaten, dragged off in handcuffs, or threatened with unemployment. This generalized resistance, sometimes called class struggle, has shaped how and how much we work. Although a movement for shorter hours has been off labor's agenda for some time, there's plenty of evidence that workload is a major problem, and much to suggest that if workers controlled labor time, the world would be a better place to work and live. I'd like to propose a return to a movement for work reduction, the initial inspiration for trade unionism—a movement to control time itself.

•

STRUGGLES FOR CONTROL of labor time have a common ancestor in the politics of socialist unionism. The ceaseless conflict between work time under capitalism and the time necessary to satisfy human needs provides an opening for an alternative politics of time. "A political strategy centered on the reduction of working hours may be the main lever with which we can shift the balance within society," wrote the philosopher André Gorz, who saw shorter hours as the basis for socialist revolution. "And this would mean the extinction of capitalism."

It was socialists within the rank and file of the trade union movement who originally fought for the ten-hour day, the eight-hour day, the weekend, and increased paid holidays. This was not won by tying free time to productivity but by fighting for the widespread redistribution of wealth. Exhausted workers wouldn't revolt, they thought. Historian Benjamin Kline Hunnicutt quotes the socialist Mary Marcy: "It is obvious that men or women working from ten to sixteen hours a day have little strength or leisure for study, or activity in revolutionary work. . . . The eight-hour day . . . would insure us leisure for study and recreation—for work in the Army of the Revolution."[15]

Today, socialism is back. At least forty-six democratic socialists won primary elections in 2018, and the membership of the Democratic Socialists of America went from seven thousand members in 2016 to almost sixty thousand in 2020. The socialist revival has come with a wave of support among young people for unions and greater economic democracy.

Record levels of inequality, economic backsliding among millennials, a not insignificant number of Leftist memes, and the popularity of Bernie Sanders, the avuncular radical from Vermont, have spurred a renewed interest in American socialism. A recent Gallup poll shows that 43 percent of Americans think "some form of socialism" would be a "good thing for the country." Moreover, our understanding of socialism is slowly becoming more sophisticated. A Gallup poll found that in 1949, 34 percent of respondents thought socialism meant "government ownership or control"—of businesses, utilities, and "everything." Only 12 percent associated socialism with "equality." In September 2018, Gallup found that the percentage of respondents who associated socialism with equality had gone up to 23 percent, while only 17 percent said they viewed socialism as signifying government ownership or control. Additionally, 10 percent of respondents said they associated socialism with benefits like free social services and universal access to medicine—that same number was only 2 percent in 1949. And yet the primary fear of those opposed to socialism, according to a 2019 Pew survey, isn't Venezuela or bread lines or Stalinist labor camps—it's anxiety about a declining work ethic.[16]

Years ago I set up a weekly Google Alert for the phrase "work ethic." This service monitors the web for mentions of the phrase in English-language newspapers, magazines, and other formats, and then sends them as an email digest once per week. I have read thousands of these articles over the years. As individual stories, they are only moderately interesting. A significant percentage of the stories written in American newspapers and magazines that contain the phrase "work ethic" are about sports, as star athletes are routinely praised for their tireless practice-makes-perfect commitment. Others say the same about politicians, and a good portion are op-eds by elected officials or business leaders complaining about the pathetic state of the work ethic among today's youth.

Taken as a whole, however, they illuminate a severe anxiety about a fundamental precept of the American civil religion. The work ethic is a tent pole of national identity politics. Reading between the lines, across the media, or even just skimming the headlines, gives one the impression that we are a nation under attack. And socialists are often considered the front line of assault.

But the work ethic wouldn't necessarily diminish in a socialist America. After all, if workers had more control over production and services, and profited more from it, they'd likely invest far more interest in making sure it was done right. Capitalism wastes our energy and steals the fruits of our labor. Socialism would allow workers to plan out how much work needs to be done to satisfy not corporate greed, but human need. We need a new kind of work ethic that values our labor for how it can satisfy our needs most efficiently, not one that lionizes a commitment to overwork.

In a socialist system, the productive capacity of society is our commonweal. Such an organizational structure could provide workers with a degree of control to effect changes in work hours if they so choose. Today's employee-owned firms still need to compete in the capitalist market and could potentially be at a competitive disadvantage if they decide to lower hours but their peers do not. For this reason, expanding the density of worker ownership within certain sectors would be a strategy to offset the problem of competition, allowing firms to experiment with new work schedules as an industry rather than just as a company.

Technically, small business owners already enjoy the autonomy to decide their hours, and most data suggests they work, on average, more than nonbusiness owners—sometimes twice as much. Simply having discretion over their time isn't enough to lower hours. That's because their autonomy is constrained by factors outside their discretion, such as competition and the costs of having employees. Our choices, in other words, are only as real as society permits. If we want individual autonomy, we need a large-scale change that promotes shorter hours as a collective good.[17]

Let's return to Marx's famous remark about free time and the need to work: "The realm of freedom actually begins only where labor which is determined by necessity and mundane considerations ceases." He further argues this realm is realizable only under conditions in which workers themselves can regulate the working day, "bringing it under their common control, instead of being ruled by it." Only beyond the "realm of necessity," during which time we must produce what we need to survive, can true freedom "blossom forth." He then seems to put a point on it, saying, "The shortening of the working-day is its basic prerequisite."

The logical conclusion is pretty seductive: human freedom means the progressive abolition of work to its barest necessity.

There's a definite virtue to that possibility. But the real power of Marx's formulation is not that it provides answers, but that it raises the questions that any truly democratic society must grapple with: What are the things we can't go without—food and shelter, or also education, art, and travel? What makes life worth living? Who decides? How can we spend our days? These are exactly the questions we can't answer in capitalist society because human needs and desires are subordinated to the dictates of the owner-ship class, for whom we must work when they want us to work. Marx's distinction between freedom and necessity is helpful, but it nevertheless poses a profound quandary: since we must labor to sustain life, how can we get free?

One final allegory from labor history is instructive. In 1912 a strike broke out in Lawrence, Massachusetts, a mill town where immigrant women were predominant. A local law had reduced the workweek from fifty-six to fifty-four hours for women, but unlike previous such reductions, it included a proportional pay cut. The subsequent strike soon grew to twenty thousand, unit-ing workers from forty nationalities, as workers in other mills walked out in solidarity. Strikers, who went without pay for nine frigid winter weeks, shipped their hungry children to sympathetic families out of state, partly to care for them, partly to humiliate the local government. It worked, and management eventually settled for a 20 percent pay increase. The event became known as the Bread and Roses strike, because the workers' demands included more than just wage increases, but respect, dignity, and more free time. James Oppenheim's eponymous poem inspired the slogan:

Our lives shall not be sweated from birth until life closes;
Hearts starve as well as bodies; give us bread, but give us roses!

The point was that the *necessities* of life aren't just for survival under socialism, but for human flourishing in a broad sense—roses. Capitalism has managed to define "necessity" as the requirements of a growing economy, rather than about human need. Socialist time-consciousness is different because it allows us to redefine the realm of necessity, rather than have it dictated to us. The need to work isn't actually the limit of freedom, but the condition that allows us to consider the society we must fight for to be free. The blurriness between the realm of necessity and freedom doesn't negate the goal of vastly reducing drudgery and unpleasant work, which is an absolute good. The blurriness does challenge the notion of freedom as merely the absence of work. Free time is the presence of collective control—the real autonomy to decide what we do and when.

Three-quarters of the way through Kushner's play, Gus's son, Pill, looks at his father. "In some way, history's just another kind of timetable, just, you know, another clock we have to punch, or break. Maybe the socialists felt free of that pressure in Marx and Lenin to force the revolutionary moment, to disrupt history?" He continued, "I've wanted to ask you: in 1973 when you guys won the Income, you must've felt . . . Free of the clock, for the first time in your lives . . . That must've felt amazing."

"It was. We had . . . so much time on our hands," Gus said. "To talk about stuff, to think over stuff. For a remarkable moment."

Withholding labor, as in a strike, is a form of power, but one that is exercised only intermittently. Real control of work time changes the quotidian experience of daily life, and that's why socialist politics offers such transformative potential. While reducing our workload to a minimum is indeed a goal, we must reorganize and control that which remains, exercising degrees of freedom within the realm of necessity. Doing so brings us far more control over our time, an essential condition of freedom in a real democracy.

ACKNOWLEDGMENTS

I first became interested in writing about labor time as an attempt to reconcile my intense personal work ethic with my political conviction that the shortening of work hours is a central goal of social justice. I'm grateful to everyone who has, in their own way, helped me explore the issue.

I began by asking workers about their jobs. I watched them while they worked, met them during breaks, visited them on strike, told their tales, and kept their secrets. We talked while they were at their pinnacles of success and at their weakest points. I traveled far and wide to meet them, yet some were my neighbors. I'm forever grateful that so many took the time to share their stories with me. Without them this book wouldn't exist, and I hope that some of its ideas will one day help support a movement for greater worker control over time.

I'm indebted to Brian Distelberg and Alex Colston at Basic Books, who helped transform my little mountain of stories, anecdotes, data, archival discoveries, and theory into a coherent narrative. I'm also thankful to the staff and production team at Basic who helped bring this book to life.

Over the years my research was aided by a scrappy band of student assistants. I'm so lucky to have worked with Sarah Koch, Marcella Maki, Tim O'Donnell, Abby Dennis, Ivy Geilker, Ari Grant-Sasson, Sophie Vaughan, and Maria Bobbitt-Chertock. Special gratitude goes to Adriana Ortiz-Burnham, who made honest assessments of my worst ideas over a number of years, and who helped me rethink the qualitative meaning of work. Carmen Sanchez Cumming, the Michael Jordan of research assistants, carried this whole book in her head, and talked me through the hostile jungle of conflicting quantitative data whenever I needed it, which was far too often.

I benefited greatly from feedback from friends and colleagues across the country. Kim Voss hosted me at the University of California, Berkeley, during my research sabbatical, and Chris Kapka opened his home to me for weeks on end, providing convenient access to Mission burritos. In Vermont, my friends Dave Weston and Alexander Wolff provided thoughtful feedback and editorial changes. Daniel Schneider at Berkeley, Matthew Lawrence at Middlebury, and Rachel Swaner at New York University all helped me navigate some vexing quantitative research problems. I'm especially thankful to Adam Dean for inviting me to workshop the book with the DC Area Labor and Working-Class History Seminar at George Washington University.

Work is our main source of conflict when it comes to spending time with friends and caring for our families. Leaving mine from time to time to research and write was necessary, but always involved sacrifices on their part. As important as solitude is to write, it was actually being enmeshed in their lives that allowed me to finish. My parents provided endless support, especially Dad, my perennial editor, who set aside his own work to improve mine. My brother, Chris, made comments on early chapter drafts too.

I owe a lifetime of gratitude to Erin, who was smart enough to let me pick the music and cook the food, and generous enough to do pretty much everything else while I was "too busy" researching ways we can all work less. A fierce devotee of play, she called bullshit on my paradoxical love and hatred of long hours at work, a tension that inspired me to write this book in the first place. Sweet Asa, to whom this book is dedicated, is a bottomless well of mystery, intrigue, and laughter— the most wondrous distraction a writer could ask for. He was also the first person to persuade me to take extended time off from work, and commit myself to a higher purpose: being his dad. I hope his life is full of love and free time.

NOTES

Introduction: One Nation Under Work

1. Mika McKinnon, "What Drives an Astronaut to Strike?" *Gizmodo*, November 18, 2015, gizmodo.com/what-drives-an-astronaut-to-go-on-strike-1732239226.

2. Paul Vitello, "William Pogue, Astronaut Who Staged a Strike in Space, Dies at 84," *New York Times*, March 10, 2014, www.nytimes.com/2014/03/11/science/space/william-r-pogue-astronaut-who-flew-longest-skylab-mission-is-dead-at-84.html.

3. "SP-4208 Living and Working in Space: A History of Skylab," NASA History Division, history.nasa.gov/SP-4208/ch17.htm.

4. Barbara J. King, "The Astronaut Who Went on Strike," *NPR*, March 14, 2014, www.npr.org/sections/13.7/2014/03/14/290093752/the-astronaut-who-went-on-strike.

5. Vitello, "William Pogue."

6. Joan C. Williams et al., "Stable Scheduling Increases Productivity Sales," Center for WorkLife Law (report), 2016, worklifelaw.org/publications/Stable-Scheduling-Study-Report.pdf.

7. Harriet B. Presser, *Working in a 24/7 Economy: Challenges for American Families* (New York: Russell Sage Foundation, 2005).

8. Raj Chetty et al., "The Fading American Dream: Trends in Absolute Income Mobility Since 1940," NBER (working paper no. 22910), December 2016 (revised March 2017), www.nber.org/papers/w22910.pdf.

9. Lydia Saad, "The '40-Hour Workweek' Is Actually Longer—by Seven Hours," Gallup, August 29, 2014, news.gallup.com/poll/175286/hour-workweek-actually-longer-seven-hours.aspx.

10. "The American Exception," *The Economist*, June 27, 2019, www.economist.com/business/2019/06/27/the-american-exception; Paul Muggeridge, "Which Countries Work the Longest Hours?," World Economic Forum, August 20, 2015, www.weforum.org/agenda/2015/08/countries-working-the-longest-hours/.

11. John McCormick, "Most Agree with Trump on America's Lost Greatness," *Bloomberg*, September 24, 2015, www.bloomberg.com/news/articles/2015-09-24/most -agree-with-trump-on-america-s-lost-greatness-bloomberg-poll-finds.

12. Gordon S. Watkins, *Labor Problems* (New York: Thomas Y. Crowell, 1929).

13. Richard M. Boeckel, "The Thirty-Hour Week," *Editorial Research Reports 1936* 1 (1936): 33–51, library.cqpress.com/cqresearcher/document.php?id=cqresrre 1936011700; Benjamin Kline Hunnicutt, *Work Without End: Abandoning Shorter Hours for the Right to Work* (Philadelphia: Temple University Press, 1988).

14. Daniel Hamermesh and Elena Stancanelli, "Americans Work Too Long (And Too Often at Strange Times)," VoxEU.org, September 29, 2014, voxeu.org/article /americans-work-long-and-strange-times; Daniel Schneider and Kristen Harknett, "Consequences of Routine Work-Schedule Instability for Worker Health and Well-Being," *American Sociological Review* 84, no. 1 (2019): 82–114.

15. Marianne Levine, "Behind the Minimum Wage Fight, a Sweeping Failure to Enforce the Law," *Politico*, February 18, 2018, www.politico.com/story/2018/02/18 /minimum-wage-not-enforced-investigation-409644.

16. Integrity Staffing Solutions, Inc. v. Busk et al., 574, U.S. (2014), www.supreme court.gov/opinions/14pdf/13-433_5h26.pdf.

Chapter 1: The Hours of Inequality

1. Diana Farrell, Fiona Greig, and Amar Hamoudi, "The Online Platform Economy in 2018: Drivers, Workers, Sellers, and Lessors," JPMorgan Chase Institute (report), September 2018, www.jpmorganchase.com/corporate/institute/document /institute-ope-2018.pdf.

2. Angus Maddison, "Growth and Slowdown in Advanced Capitalist Economies: Techniques of Quantitative Assessment," *Journal of Economic Literature* 25, no. 2 (1987): 649–698; Angus Maddison, "The World Economy: A Millennial Perspective," Organisation for Economic Co-operation and Development (paper), 2001.

3. Simona E. Cociuba, Edward C. Prescott, and Alexander Ueberfeldt, "US Hours at Work," *Economics Letters* 169 (August 2018): 87–90, doi.org/10.1016/j.econlet .2018.05.021.

4. Juliet Schor, "The (Even More) Overworked American," in John de Graaf, ed., *Take Back Your Time: Fighting Overwork and Time Poverty in America* (San Francisco: Berrett-Koehler Publishers, 2003).

5. Juliet Schor, "Sustainable Consumption and Worktime Reduction," *Journal of Industrial Ecology* 9, nos. 1–2 (2005): 37–50.

6. Juliet Schor, "Assessing the Controversy About Trends in Time-Use," in Deborah Figart and Lonnie Golden, eds., *Working Time: International Trends, Theory and Policy*, (London: Routledge, 2000).

7. Lawrence Mishel, "Vast Majority of Wage Earners Are Working Harder, and for Not Much More," Economic Policy Institute (report), January 2013, www.epi.org/pub-lication/ib348-trends-us-work-hours-wages-1979-2007/; Economic Policy Institute, "Annual Wages and Work Hours," State of Working America Data Library, 2019.

8. Valerie Wilson and Janelle Jones, "Working Harder or Finding It Harder to Work," Economic Policy Institute (report), February 22, 2018, www.epi.org/publication /trends-in-work-hours-and-labor-market-disconnection/.

9. Ariane Hegewisch and Valerie Lacarte, "Gender Inequality, Work Hours, and the Future of Work," Institute for Women's Policy Research (report), November 14, 2019, https://iwpr.org/publications/gender-inequality-work-hours-future-of-work/; Eileen Appelbaum, Heather Boushey, and John Schmitt, "The Economic Importance of Women's Rising Hours of Work: Time to Update Employment Standards," Center for American Progress and the Center for Economic and Policy Research (report), April 4, 2014, https://cdn.americanprogress.org/wp-content/uploads/2014/04/WomensRisingWork v2.pdf; Jasmine Tucker and Kayla Patrick, "Low Wage Jobs Are Women's Jobs: The Overrepresentation of Women in Low-Wage Work," National Women's Law Center, August 2017, https://nwlc.org/wp-content/uploads/2017/08/Low-Wage-Jobs-are -Womens-Jobs.pdf.

10. Ryan Cooper, "The Leisure Agenda," People's Policy Project (report), 2019, www.peoplespolicyproject.org/projects/the-leisure-agenda/.

11. Matt Bruenig, "Top 1% Up $21 Trillion. Bottom 50% Down $900 Billion," People's Policy Project, June 14, 2019, www.peoplespolicyproject.org/2019/06/14 /top-1-up-21-trillion-bottom-50-down-900-billion/.

12. "Productivity Pay Gap," Economic Policy Institute, July 2019, www.epi.org /productivity-pay-gap/; Lawrence Mishel and Jessica Schieder, "CEO Compensation Surged in 2017," Economic Policy Institute, August 16, 2018, www.epi.org/publication /ceo-compensation-surged-in-2017/.

13. John DiNardo, Kevin Hallock, Jorn-Steffen Pischke, "Unions and Managerial Pay," NBER (working paper no. 6318), December 1997; Rafael Gomez and Konstantinos Tzioumis, "What Do Unions Do to Executive Compensation?," Center for Economic Performance, London School of Economics and Political Science, 2006.

14. Frank Runnels, "All Unions' Committee to Shorten the Work Week," Walter Reuther Library, Wayne State University, Accession Number 880, April 11, 1978, https://reuther.wayne.edu/files/LR000880.pdf.

15. Ann Skelton, "Going into Classrooms with Our Story," UAW Region 8 (timeline), n.d., www.uawregion8.net/UAW-History-timeline.htm.

16. Jeffrey M. Jones, "As Labor Day Turns 125, Union Approval Near 50-Year High," Gallup, August 28, 2019, news.gallup.com/poll/265916/labor-day-turns-125 -union-approval-near-year-high.aspx.

17. Wilson and Jones, "Working Harder or Finding It Harder to Work"; Mark Carely, "Industrial Relations in the EU, Japan, and USA, 2002," European Foundation for the Improvement of Living and Working Conditions (report), February 23, 2004, www .eurofound.europa.eu/publications/article/2004/industrial-relations-in-the-eu-japan -and-usa-2002; "State of American Vacation 2018," Project Time Off, www.ustravel .org/sites/default/files/media_root/document/2018_Research_State%20of%20 American%20Vacation%202018.pdf.

18. Sarah Jane Glynn, "An Unequal Division of Labor," Center for American Progress (report), May 18, 2018, www.americanprogress.org/issues/women/reports/2018 /05/18/450972/unequal-division-labor/.

19. Edward Salsberg and Robert Martiniano, "Health Care Jobs Projected to Continue to Grow Far Faster Than Jobs in the General Economy," *Health Affairs*, May 9, 2018, www.healthaffairs.org/do/10.1377/hblog20180502.984593/full/.

20. Lonnie Golden, "Flexibility and Overtime Among Hourly and Salaried Workers," Economic Policy Institute (briefing paper), September 30, 2014, www.epi.org/publication/flexibility-overtime-hourly-salaried-workers/; Ginger Moored, "D.C.'s Low-Wage Workers Have the Longest Commutes," District of Columbia Office of Revenue Analysis, *District, Measured* (blog), August 28, 2015, https://districtmeasured.com/2015/04/28/d-c-s-low-wage-workers-have-the-longest-commutes/.

21. Lonnie Golden, "Still Falling Short on Hours and Pay," Economic Policy Institute (report), December 5, 2016, www.epi.org/publication/still-falling-short-on-hours-and-pay-part-time-work-becoming-new-normal/; Robert Valletta, "Involuntary Part-Time Work: Yes, It's Here to Stay," Federal Reserve Bank of San Francisco, *SF Fed* (blog), April 11, 2018, www.frbsf.org/our-district/about/sf-fed-blog/involuntary-part-time-work-here-to-stay/; Daniel Schneider and Kristen Harknett, "Consequences of Routine Work-Schedule Instability for Worker Health and Well-Being," *American Sociological Review* 84, no. 1 (2019): 82–114.

22. Gérard Duménil and Dominique Lévy, *Managerial Capitalism: Ownership, Management, and the Coming New Mode of Production* (London: Pluto Press, 2018).

23. Peter Kuhn and Fernando Lozano, "The Expanding Workweek? Understanding Trends in Long Work Hours Among U.S. Men, 1979–2006," *Journal of Labor Economics* 26, no. 2 (2008): 311–343.

24. Thomas Lemieux, W. B. Macleod, and Daniel Parent, "Performance Pay and Wage Inequality," *The Quarterly Journal of Economics* 124, no. 1 (2009): 1–49; Linda A. Bell and Richard B. Freeman, "The Incentive for Working Hard: Explaining Hours Worked Differences in the US and Germany," *Labour Economics* 8, no. 2 (2001): 181–202; "Nice Work If You Can Get Out," *The Economist*, April 22, 2014, www.economist.com/finance-and-economics/2014/04/22/nice-work-if-you-can-get-out; Kuhn and Lozano, "The Expanding Workweek?"

25. Bell and Freeman, "The Incentive for Working Hard."

26. Kuhn and Lozano, "The Expanding Workweek?"

27. Wilson and Jones, "Working Harder or Finding It Harder to Work."

28. Wilson and Jones, "Working Harder or Finding It Harder to Work"; "The Distribution of Household Income, 2014," Congressional Budget Office (report), March 2018, www.cbo.gov/system/files/115th-congress-2017-2018/reports/53597-distribution-household-income-2014.pdf.

29. Elsie Gould, "Millions of Working People Don't Get Paid Time Off for Holiday or Vacation," Economic Policy Institute (report), September 1, 2015, www.epi.org/publication/millions-of-working-people-dont-get-paid-time-off-for-holidays-or-vacation/; Wilson and Jones, "Working Harder or Finding It Harder to Work."

30. "Emerging and Developing Economies Much More Optimistic Than Rich Countries About the Future," Pew Research Center, October 9, 2014, www.pewglobal.org/2014/10/09/emerging-and-developing-economies-much-more-optimistic-than-rich-countries-about-the-future/; "Pervasive Gloom About the World Economy," Pew

Research Center, Global Attitudes Project (report), July 12, 2012, www.pewresearch
.org/global/2012/07/12/chapter-4-the-casualties-faith-in-hard-work-and-capitalism/.

31. Todd Gabe, Jaison R. Abel, and Richard Florida, "Can Low-Wage Workers Find
Better Jobs?," Federal Reserve Bank of New York, Staff Report no. 846, April 2018,
www.newyorkfed.org/medialibrary/media/research/staff_reports/sr846.pdf.

32. David H. Autor, "Work of the Past, Work of the Future," AEA *Papers and
Proceedings* 109 (2019): 1–32.

33. Emmanuel Saez, "Income and Wealth Inequality: Evidence and Policy Implications," *Contemporary Economic Policy* 35, no. 1 (2017), eml.berkeley.edu/~saez/Saez
CEP2017.pdf.

34. Annette Bernhardt et al., "Broken Laws, Unprotected Workers: Violations
of Employment and Labor Laws in America's Cities," National Employment Law
Project (report), 2009, www.nelp.org/wp-content/uploads/2015/03/BrokenLawsReport
2009.pdf.

Chapter 2: Nickel and Timed

1. Max Weber, *The Protestant Ethic and the Spirit of Capitalism*, trans. Stephen
Kalberg, revised ed. (Oxford: Oxford University Press, 2010).

2. Weber, *The Protestant Ethic and the Spirit of Capitalism*.

3. Frederick Winslow Taylor, *Principles of Scientific Management* (New York: Harper
& Brothers, 1911), at www.marxists.org/reference/subject/economics/taylor/principles
/ch02.htm.

4. Vladimir Lenin, "The Immediate Tasks of the Soviet Government," *Pravda*, no.
83, April 28, 1918, in *Lenin's Collected Works* (Moscow: Progress Publishers, 1972), at
www.marxists.org/archive/lenin/works/1918/mar/x03.htm.

5. Robert Kanigel, *The One Best Way: Frederick Winslow Taylor and the Enigma of
Efficiency* (New York: Viking Adult, 1997).

6. Lillian Moller Gilbreth, *The Psychology of Management: The Function of the Mind
in Determining, Teaching and Installing Methods of Least Waste* (New York: Sturgis &
Walton, 1914).

7. Blanche Halbert, *The Better Homes Manual* (Chicago: University of Chicago
Press, 1931).

8. "Dr. Gilbreth's Kitchen," National Museum of American History, http://american
history.si.edu/ontime/saving/kitchen.html; Harry Braverman, *Labor and Monopoly
Capital: The Degradation of Work in the Twentieth Century* (New York: Monthly Review
Press, 1998).

9. Melissa Gregg, *Counterproductive: Time Management in the Knowledge Economy*
(Durham, NC: Duke University Press, 2018).

10. Elton Mayo, "Industrial Peace and Psychological Research III: The Mind of the
Agitator," *Industrial Australian and Mining Standard* 67 (1922c): 111.

11. Daniel T. Rodgers, *The Work Ethic in Industrial America, 1850–1920*, reprint ed.
(Chicago: University of Chicago Press, 1979).

12. Leon Trotsky, "The Growth of Inequality and Social Antagonisms," *The Revolution Betrayed* (1937), at www.marxists.org/archive/trotsky/1936/revbet/ch06.htm #ch06-2.

13. Noam Scheiber, "How Uber Uses Psychological Tricks to Push Its Drivers' Buttons," *New York Times*, April 2, 2017, www.nytimes.com/interactive/2017/04/02 /technology/uber-drivers-psychological-tricks.html.

14. Oliver Burkeman, "Why Time Management Is Ruining Our Lives," *The Guardian*, December 22, 2016, www.theguardian.com/technology/2016/dec/22/why -time-management-is-ruining-our-lives.

15. Gregg, *Counterproductive*, 54.

16. Yusuf Mehdi, "Empowering a New Era of Personal Productivity with New Surface Devices," Microsoft, *Windows Blogs*, October 2, 2018, blogs.windows.com /windowsexperience/2018/10/02/empowering-a-new-era-of-personal-productivity-with -new-surface-devices/.

17. Lisa Wade, "Luxury and the Consumption of Labor," *The Society Pages*, December 26, 2011, thesocietypages.org/socimages/2011/12/26/luxury-and-the-consumption -of-labor/.

18. Taylor Lorenz and Joe Pinsker, "The Slackification of the American Home," *Atlantic*, July 11, 2019, www.theatlantic.com/family/archive/2019/07/families-slack -asana/593584/.

Chapter 3: The Electronic Whip

1. Colin Lecher, "How Amazon Automatically Tracks and Fires Warehouse Workers for 'Productivity,'" *The Verge*, April 25, 2019, www.theverge.com/2019/4/25 /18516004/amazon-warehouse-fulfillment-centers-productivity-firing-terminations; Karen Weise, "Somali Workers in Minnesota Force Amazon to Negotiate," *New York Times*, November 20, 2018, www.nytimes.com/2018/11/20/technology/amazon-somali -workers-minnesota.html; *Integrity Staffing Solutions, Inc. v. Busk*, October 2014, www .supremecourt.gov/opinions/14pdf/13-433_5h26.pdf.

2. Elizabeth Tippett, Charlotte S. Alexander, and Zev J. Eigen, "When Timekeeping Software Undermines Compliance," *Yale Journal of Law and Technology* 19, no. 1 (January 14, 2018), https://digitalcommons.law.yale.edu/yjolt/vol19/iss1/1.

3. Jonathan Vanian, "How Unions Are Pushing Back Against the Rise of Workplace Technology," *Fortune*, April 30, 2019, www.fortune.com/longform/unions -workplace-technology/.

4. Shoshana Zuboff, "Surveillance Capitalism and the Challenge of Collective Action," *New Labor Forum*, January 2019, https://newlaborforum.cuny.edu/2019/01/22 /surveillance-capitalism/.

5. Zuboff, "Surveillance Capitalism."

6. Sam Adler-Bell and Michelle Miller, "The Datification of Employment," The Century Foundation (report), December 19, 2018, https://tcf.org/content/report /datafication-employment-surveillance-capitalism-shaping-workers-futures-without -knowledge/.

7. John Boudreau, "Predict What Employees Will Do Without Freaking Them Out," *Harvard Business Review*, September 5, 2014, https://hbr.org/2014/09/predict-what-employees-will-do-without-freaking-them-out.

8. US Congress, Office of Technology Assessment, *The Electronic Supervisor: New Technology, New Tensions*, OTA-CIT-333 (Washington, DC: US Government Printing Office, September 1987), https://ota.fas.org/reports/8708.pdf.

9. "SHRM Research: Flexible Work Arrangements," Society for Human Resource Management (report), 2015, www.shrm.org/hr-today/trends-and-forecasting/special-reports-and-expert-views/Documents/Flexible%20Work%20Arrangements.pdf.

Chapter 4: Time Machines

1. Carl Benedikt Frey and Michael A. Osborne, "The Future of Employment: How Susceptible Are Jobs to Computerisation?" ("Machines and Employment" workshop, University of Oxford, September 17, 2013), www.oxfordmartin.ox.ac.uk/downloads/academic/The_Future_of_Employment.pdf; Daron Acemoglu and Pascual Restrepo, "Robots and Jobs: Evidence from US Labor Markets," NBER (working paper no. 23285), March 2017, www.nber.org/papers/w23285.

2. Thomas B. Edsall, "Robots Can't Vote, but They Helped Elect Trump," *New York Times*, January 11, 2018, www.nytimes.com/2018/01/11/opinion/trump-robots-electoral-college.html.

3. Nicholas Bloom, Charles I. Jones, John Van Reenan, and Michael Webb, "Are Ideas Getting Harder to Find?" *American Economic Review* (forthcoming), www.aeaweb.org/articles?id=10.1257/aer.20180338&&from=f; Lawrence Mishel and Josh Bivens, "The Zombie Robot Argument Lurches Onwards," Economic Policy Institute (report), May 24, 2017, www.epi.org/publication/the-zombie-robot-argument-lurches-on-there-is-no-evidence-that-automation-leads-to-joblessness-or-inequality/.

4. Lewis Krauskopf, "Cheaper Robots Could Replace More Factory Workers: Study," Reuters, February 9, 2015, www.reuters.com/article/us-manufacturers-robots/cheaper-robots-could-replace-more-factory-workers-study-idUSKBN0LE00720150210.

5. A. W. Geiger, "How Americans See Automation and the Workplace in 7 Charts," Pew Research Center, *Fact Tank* (blog), April 8, 2019, www.pewresearch.org/fact-tank/2019/04/08/how-americans-see-automation-and-the-workplace-in-7-charts/.

6. Peter Frase, "The United States Makes Things," *Peter Frase* (blog), April 4, 2011, www.peterfrase.com/2011/04/the-united-states-makes-things/.

7. "Father of Cybernetics Norbert Wiener's Letter to UAW President Walter Reuther," Libcom.org, January 24, 2011, libcom.org/history/father-cybernetics-norbert-wieners-letter-uaw-president-walter-reuther.

8. Robert Asher and Ronald Edsforth, "The 1949 Speed Up Strike and the Post War Social Compact, 1946–1961," in *Autowork* (Albany: SUNY Press, 1995), 142.

9. Matt Novak, "Will Robots Make People Obsolete?" *Gizmodo*, May 20, 2008, paleofuture.gizmodo.com/will-robots-make-people-obsolete-1959-512627356; Daniel Akst, "Automation Anxiety," *Wilson Quarterly*, Summer 2013, archive.wilsonquarterly.com/essays/automation-anxiety; Isaac Asimov, "Visit to the World's Fair of 2014," *New*

York Times, August 16, 1964, archive.nytimes.com/www.nytimes.com/books/97/03/23 /lifetimes/asi-v-fair.html.

10. "Prepared Statement by Frank Runnells," Hearings before the Subcommittee on Labor Standards of the Committee on Education and Labor, 96th Congress of the House of Representatives, first session on HR 1784, 1979.

11. Christoph Hermann, *Capitalism and the Political Economy of Work Time* (London: Routledge, 2014); Ricky Cove, "Manufacturing Workers' Increasing Work Hours," *Market Realist*, April 24, 2018, marketrealist.com/2018/04/manufacturing-workers -increasing-work-hours/; "Prepared Statement by Frank Runnells."

12. Deborah Sunter and Rene Morissette, "The Hours People Work," *Perspectives on Labour and Income* 6, no. 3 (Autumn 1994).

13. Lydia DePillis, "Minimum-Wage Offensive Could Speed Arrival of Robot -Powered Restaurants," *Washington Post*, August 16, 2015, www.washingtonpost.com /business/capitalbusiness/minimum-wage-offensive-could-speed-arrival-of-robot -powered-restaurants/2015/08/16/35f284ea-3f6f-11e5-8d45-d815146f81fa_story.html ?noredirect=on.

14. Aaron Smith and Monica Anderson, "Automation in Everyday Life," Pew Research Center (report), October 4, 2017, www.pewinternet.org/2017/10/04 /automation-in-everyday-life/.

15. R. J. Reinhart, "Most U.S. Workers Unafraid of Losing Their Jobs to Robots," Gallup, February 8, 2018, https://news.gallup.com/poll/226841/workers-unafraid -losing-jobs-robots.aspx.

16. Sarah Kessler, "Amazon's Massive Fleet of Robots Hasn't Slowed Down Its Employment of Humans," *Quartz*, February 3, 2017, qz.com/885425/amazons-massive -fleet-of-robots-hasnt-slowed-down-its-employment-of-humans/.

17. Kotaro Hara, Abi Adams, Kristy Milland, et al., "A Data-Driven Analysis of Workers' Earnings on Amazon Mechanical Turk," *ArXiv* (unpublished paper), December 2017, arxiv.org/abs/1712.05796.

18. River Donaghey, "Robot Strippers Are Here," *Vice*, January 10, 2018, www .vice.com/en_us/article/xw45az/there-are-robot-strippers-in-vegas-now-vgtrn.

19. Thomas Kochan, Adrienne Eaton, Robert McKersie, and Paul Adler, "Partnership and HealthConnect," in *Healing Together: The Labor-Management Partnership at Kaiser Permanente* (Ithaca, NY: Cornell University Press, 2009).

20. The Undercommons, "No Racial Justice Without Basic Income," *Boston Review*, May 3, 2017, bostonreview.net/class-inequality-race/undercommons-no-racial -justice-without-basic-income.

21. Judy Wajcman, "Automation: Is It Really Different This Time?" London School of Economics and Political Science, 2017, http://eprints.lse.ac.uk/69811/1/Wajcman _Automation%20is%20it%20really%20different%20this%20time.pdf.

22. Richard L. Trumka, "Technology Must Be Used for Good, Not Greed," remarks at the opening meeting of the Commission on the Future of Work and Unions, Washington, DC, May 3, 2018, https://aflcio.org/speeches/trumka-technology -must-be-used-good-not-greed.

Chapter 5: More Than Money

1. Larry Magid, "Zuckerberg Claims 'We Don't Build Services to Make Money,'" *Forbes*, February 1, 2012, www.forbes.com/sites/larrymagid/2012/02/01/zuckerberg-claims-we-dont-build-services-to-make-money/#66722ffd2b11.

2. Douglas Coupland, *Microserfs* (New York: Harper Perennial, 2008).

3. Laszlo Bock, *Work Rules! Insights from Inside Google That Will Transform How You Live and Lead* (New York: Twelve, 2015).

4. Abraham Lincoln, "Address before the Wisconsin State Agricultural Society," September 30, 1859, at www.abrahamlincolnonline.org/lincoln/speeches/fair.htm.

5. William Morris, *Useful Work vs. Useless Toil* (London: Hammersmith Socialist Society, 1893), at www.marxists.org/archive/morris/works/1884/useful.htm.

6. US Congress, Senate Committee on Labor and Public Welfare, Subcommittee on Employment, Manpower, and Poverty, Worker Alienation, second session, on S. 3916 (Washington, DC: US Government Printing Office, 1972).

7. Daniel Yankelovich and John Immerwahr, *Putting the Work Ethic to Work: A Public Agenda Report Restoring America's Competitive Vitality* (New York: The Public Agenda Foundation, 1983).

8. Yankelovich and Immerwahr, *Putting the Work Ethic to Work*.

9. Richard F. Hamilton, *State of the Masses* (New York: Aldine, 1986), 22.

10. Cy Gonick, *The Great Economic Debate: Failed Economics and a Future for Canada* (Toronto: James Lorimer, 1987), 209.

11. Stephanie Buck, "Our Parents Discovered Leisure. We Killed It," *Timeline*, September 2, 2016, https://timeline.com/hobby-career-b5d199b0df18#.3c9t8ark6.

12. Kane Russel Coleman Logan, "Court Upholds T-Mobile's Positive Workplace Environment Rules," *Lexology*, May 24, 2019, www.lexology.com/library/detail.aspx?g=0ee0668f-aa38-4d35-ade3-a3b88f5ab265.

13. Morten Hansen and Dacher Keltner, "Finding Meaning at Work, Even When Your Job Is Dull," *Harvard Business Review*, December 20, 2012, https://hbr.org/2012/12/finding-meaning-at-work-even-w; Rich Bellis, "The Unlikely Reasons Why We're More Satisfied at Work," *Fast Company*, September 16, 2015, www.fastcompany.com/3051044/the-counterintuitive-reasons-why-were-more-satisfied-at-work.

14. Jing Hu and Jacob Hirsh, "Accepting Lower Salaries for Meaningful Work," *Frontiers in Psychology* 8 (2017): 1649; Andrew Reece, Gabriella Kellerman, and Alexi Robichaux, "Meaning and Purpose at Work," white paper (BetterUp Labs, 2018); Jennifer Liu, "Tech Workers Are in the Position to Negotiate for High Pay, but It's Not Always the Perk They Want Most," CNBC, November 17, 2019, www.cnbc.com/2019/11/07/tech-workers-command-high-pay-but-its-not-always-what-they-want-most.html.

15. Amy Adkins, "Majority of U.S. Employees Not Engaged Despite Gains in 2014," Gallup, January 28, 2015, https://news.gallup.com/poll/181289/majority-employees-not-engaged-despite-gains-2014.aspx; Peter Moore, "One Quarter of Americans Think Their Jobs Are Meaningless," YouGov, August 14, 2015, https://today.yougov.com/topics/lifestyle/articles-reports/2015/08/14/one-quarter-americans-think-their-jobs-are-meaning.

16. David Lewin, *The Impact of Unionism on American Business: Evidence for an Assessment* (New York: Columbia University Press, 1978).

Chapter 6: Back to Work

1. Jane L. Collins and Victoria Mayer, *Both Hands Tied: Welfare Reform and the Race to the Bottom of the Low-Wage Labor Market* (Chicago: University of Chicago Press, 2010).

2. "Workhouse," in *New World Encyclopedia*, August 2013, www.newworldencyclopedia.org/entry/Workhouse.

3. Desmond King, "Welfare as Workfare in the USA," in *In the Name of Liberalism: Illiberal Social Policy in the USA and Britain* (New York: Oxford University Press, 1999), 263.

4. Daniel Moynihan, *Miles to Go: A Personal History of Social Policy* (Cambridge, MA: Harvard University Press, 1996), 170.

5. Rutger Bregman, "The Bizarre Tale of President Nixon and His Basic Income Bill," *de Correspondent*, May 17, 2016, https://thecorrespondent.com/4503/the-bizarre-tale-of-president-nixon-and-his-basic-income-bill/173117835-c34d6145.

6. Judith Shulevitz, "Forgotten Feminisms: Johnnie Tillmon's Battle Against 'The Man,'" *New York Review of Books*, June 26, 2018, www.nybooks.com/daily/2018/06/26/forgotten-feminisms-johnnie-tillmons-battle-against-the-man/.

7. Lawrence Mead, *Beyond Entitlement: The Social Obligations of Citizenship* (New York: The Free Press, 1986).

8. Jordan Weissmann, "The Failure of Welfare Reform," *Slate*, June 1, 2016, https://slate.com/news-and-politics/2016/06/how-welfare-reform-failed.html; Bryce Covert, "Mississippi Refuses to Use Money That Would Give Poor Families Child Care," CLASP, March 3, 2016, www.clasp.org/mississippi-refuses-use-money-would-give-poor-families-child-care.

9. Kathryn J. Edin and H. Luke Shaefer, *$2.00 a Day: Living on Almost Nothing in America* (New York: Houghton Mifflin Harcourt, 2016).

10. Alison Mitchell, "Two Clinton Aides Resign to Protest New Welfare Law," *New York Times*, September 12, 1996, www.nytimes.com/1996/09/12/us/two-clinton-aides-resign-to-protest-new-welfare-law.html.

11. Maureen Dowd, "Washington Talk: Q&A: Daniel Patrick Moynihan; Welfare and the Politics of Poverty," *New York Times*, February 19, 1987, www.nytimes.com/1987/02/19/us/washington-talk-q-a-daniel-patrick-moynihan-welfare-and-the-politics-of-poverty.html.

12. Pamela J. Loprest and Austin Nichols, "Dynamics of Being Disconnected from Work and TANF," Urban Institute (report), September 12, 2011, www.urban.org/research/publication/dynamics-being-disconnected-work-and-tanf.

13. Jennifer Wagner and Jessica Shubel, "States' Experiences Confirming Harmful Effects of Medicaid Work Requirements," Center on Budget and Policy Priorities (report), October 22, 2019, www.cbpp.org/health/states-experiences-confirming-harmful-effects-of-medicaid-work-requirements.

14. MaryBeth Musumeci, Robin Rudowitz, and Barbara Lyons, "Medicaid Work Requirements in Arkansas: Experience and Perspectives of Enrollees," Kaiser Family Foundation (issue brief), December 18, 2018, www.kff.org/report-section/medicaid-work -requirements-in-arkansas-experience-and-perspectives-of-enrollees-issue-brief/.

15. Musumeci, Rudowitz, and Lyons, "Medicaid Work Requirements in Arkansas."

16. Chad Goldberg, *Citizens and Paupers: Relief, Rights, and Race, from the Freedmen's Bureau to Workfare* (Chicago: University of Chicago Press, 2007), 203.

17. New York State Assembly, Standing Committee on Social Services, *An Evaluation of Welfare Reform Policy in New York State*, February 2006, https://assembly.state .ny.us/comm/SocServ/20060316/; John Krinsky, *Free Labor: Workfare and the Contested Language of Neoliberalism* (Chicago: University of Chicago Press, 2007), 1; Douglas Besharov, *Family and Child Well-Being After Welfare Reform* (London: Routledge, 2004), 75–76.

18. Goldberg, *Citizens and Paupers*, 201, 212.

19. David Firestone, "Public Lives: He Fights, Patiently, for Workfare Laborers," *New York Times*, January 16, 1998, www.nytimes.com/1998/01/16/nyregion/public-lives -he-fights-patiently-for-workfare-laborers.html.

20. Steven Greenhouse, "Wages of Workfare," *New York Times*, July 7, 1997, www .nytimes.com/1997/07/07/nyregion/wages-of-workfare.html.

21. "LSNYC Files Lawsuit Against City Challenging Widespread Civil Rights Violations at Welfare Centers," Legal Services NYC (press release), August 11, 2009, www.legalservicesnyc.org/news-and-events/press-room/356-lsnyc-files-lawsuit -against-city-challenging-widespread-civil-rights-violations-at-welfare-centers; Joel Berg, "De Blasio Admin. Making City's Safety Net More Humane," *City Limits*, September 5, 2014, https://citylimits.org/2014/09/05/de-blasio-admin-making-citys-safety -net-more-humane/.

Chapter 7: We Control the Clocks

1. Jim Stinson, "Falcon Transport Faces Employee Lawsuit After Closure," *Transport Topics*, May 3, 2019, www.ttnews.com/articles/falcon-transport-closes-suddenly-laying -about-550-employees; Ashley, "Company: We Didn't Tell Truckers About Shutdown Because We Wanted to Get Paid," *CDL Life News*, May 8, 2019, https://cdllife.com/2019 /company-we-didnt-tell-truckers-about-shutdown-because-we-wanted-to-get-paid/.

2. LaToya Ruby Frazier and Dan Kaufman, "The End of the Line," *New York Times*, www.nytimes.com/interactive/2019/05/01/magazine/lordstown-general-motors-plant .html?action=click&module=RelatedCoverage&pgtype=Article&region=Footer.

3. Alexandra Orchard, "The 1972 Lordstown Strike," Walter P. Reuther Library (blog), Wayne State University, http://reuther.wayne.edu/node/10756.

4. Stevenson v. The Great American Dream, Civil Action File No 1:12-CV —3359-TWT (2013), https://law.justia.com/cases/federal/district-courts/georgia /gandce/1:2012cv03359/187886/81/; Alex Vandermaas-Peeler et al., "A Renewed Struggle for the American Dream: PRRI 2018 California Workers Survey," Public Religion Research Institute, www.prri.org/research/renewed_struggle_for_the _american_dream-prri_2018_california_workers_survey/.

5. Antonia Crane, "A Regulars' Guide to What Happens When Your Favorite Strip Club Unionizes," *Mel Magazine*, February 19, 2019, https://melmagazine.com/en-us /story/a-gentlemans-guide-to-supporting-your-favorite-stripper-as-she-attempts-to -unionize-her-club.

6. Uber Technologies registration statement, filed with the Securities and Exchange Commission, April 11, 2019, www.sec.gov/Archives/edgar/data/1543151/00011931251 9103850/d647752ds1.htm; State of California Department of Industrial Relations, "Worker Misclassification," www.dir.ca.gov/dlse/worker_misclassification.html.

Chapter 8: Labor's Forgotten Fight

1. Lonnie Golden, "Irregular Work Scheduling and Its Consequences," Economic Policy Institute (briefing paper no. 394), April 9, 2015, www.epi.org/publication /irregular-work-scheduling-and-its-consequences/; Peter Moore, "Poll Results: Working Hours," YouGov, July 24, 2014, https://today.yougov.com/topics/economy/articles -reports/2014/07/24/poll-results-working-hours.

2. David Rosnick, "Reduced Work Hours as a Means of Slowing Climate Change," Center for Economic and Policy Research, February 2013, http://cepr.net/document s/publications/climate-change-workshare-2013-02.pdf.

3. M. B. Schnapper, *American Labor* (Washington, DC: Public Affairs Press,, 1972), 250.

4. Fred Best, "The History and Current Relevance of Work Sharing," in *Work Sharing: Issues, Policy Options and Prospects* (Kalamazoo, MI: W. E. Upjohn Institute for Employment Research, 1981), 4, https://research.upjohn.org/cgi/viewcontent .cgi?referer=https://www.google.com/&httpsredir=1&article=1155&context=up _bookchapters.

5. Andreas Crimman, Frank Wiessner, and Lutz Bellmann, "The German Work-Sharing Scheme: An Instrument for Crisis," International Labour Organization, 2010, https://pdfs.semanticscholar.org/4d75/e849a5b5c41dd9da92c5992a95d7cc0b8e49.pdf.

6. Anna Coote, Pritika Kasliwal, and Andrew Percy, "Universal Basic Services: Theory and Practice," Institute for Global Prosperity (report), May 16, 2019, https:// ubshub.files.wordpress.com/2019/05/ubs_report_online.pdf.

7. Will Stronge and Aidan Harper, "The Shorter Working Week: A Radical and Pragmatic Proposal," *Autonomy*, February 6, 2019, https://apo.org.au/sites/default/files /resource-files/2019/02/apo-nid219086-1330926.pdf.

8. "How Do Americans Feel About Medicare for All? This Poll Tells Us," *MarketWatch*, January 23, 2019, www.marketwatch.com/story/poll-finds-medicare-for -all-support-drops-when-details-are-included-2019-01-23.

9. Kaiser Family Foundation, "Health Insurance Coverage of the Total Population," www.kff.org/other/state-indicator/total-population/?currentTimeframe=0&selected Distributions=employer&sortModel=%7B%22colId%22:%22Location%22, %22sort%22:%22asc%22%7D; Juliet Schor, *The Overworked American* (New York: Basic Books, 1991), 66; Cynthia Meyer, "How Much Are Your Benefits Really Worth?"

Forbes, September 24, 2018, www.forbes.com/sites/financialfinesse/2018/09/24/how-much-are-your-benefits-really-worth/#2d86b8847879.

10. Mark Dudzic, "Time for Unions to Step Up on Medicare for All," *Jacobin*, June 1, 2018, jacobinmag.com/2018/06/medicare-for-all-health-care-unions; Jessica Corbett, "Medicare for All Sponsor Rep. Jayapal Challenges Biden's Comments on Labor Unions and Health Insurance," *Common Dreams*, July 6, 2019, www.commondreams.org/news/2019/07/06/medicare-all-sponsor-rep-jayapal-challenges-bidens-comments-labor-unions-and-health?utm_campaign=shareaholic&utm_medium=referral&utm_source=facebook.

11. Steve Early and Rand Wilson, "How a Telephone Workers' Strike Thirty Years Ago Aided the Fight for Single Payer," *Jacobin*, July 13, 2019, jacobinmag.com/2019/07/telephone-workers-strike-single-payer.

12. Jamie K. McCallum, "Getting the Common Goods," *Jacobin*, August 8, 2018, jacobinmag.com/2018/08/north-carolina-teacher-union-strike-education-schools.

13. Valerie Strauss, "Survey: Teachers Work 53 Hours Per Week on Average," *Washington Post*, March 16, 2012, www.washingtonpost.com/blogs/answer-sheet/post/survey-teachers-work-53-hours-per-week-on-average/2012/03/16/gIQAqGxYGS_blog.html?utm_term%3D.203e55cf72a0&sa=D&ust=1564426741817000&usg=AFQjCNEo8D4Ee-ZKh82auxjYl6_AEgfaAg; Niraj Chokshi, "94 Percent of U.S. Teachers Spend Their Own Money on School Supplies, Survey Finds," *New York Times*, May 16, 2018, www.nytimes.com/2018/05/16/us/teachers-school-supplies.html.

14. This is a rough calculation that involves estimating future GDP, future population change, and future productivity rates. Invariably, it leaves out some factors that would be important to consider in a more precise measure.

15. Benjamin Kline Hunnicutt, *Free Time: The Forgotten American Dream* (Philadelphia: Temple University Press, 2013), 82.

16. Mohamed Younis, "Four in 10 Americans Embrace Some Form of Socialism," Gallup, May 20, 2019, https://news.gallup.com/poll/257639/four-americans-embrace-form-socialism.aspx.

17. Ted Callahan, "Business Owners Work Twice as Much as Employees, Survey Finds," *Inc.*, April 13, 2006, www.inc.com/news/articles/200604/overworked.html.

INDEX

MICHELLE LEFTHERIS

JAMIE K. MCCALLUM is professor of sociology at Middlebury College. His first book, *Global Unions, Local Power*, won the American Sociological Association's prize for the best book on labor. His work has appeared in scholarly journals and popular outlets such as the *Washington Post*, *Mother Jones*, *Dissent*, and *Jacobin*.